WITHDRAWN

CENTRAL
ASIA
READER

CENTRAL ASIA READER

THE REDISCOVERY OF HISTORY

EDITED BY H. B. PAKSOY

M. E. Sharpe

Armonk, New York ▪ London, England

129830

Copyright © 1994 by M.E. Sharpe., Inc.

All rights reserved. No part of this book may be reproduced in any form
without written permission from the publisher, M.E. Sharpe, Inc.,
80 Business Park Drive, Armonk, New York 10504.

Library of Congress Cataloging-in-Publication Data

Central Asia reader: the rediscovery of history / edited by H.B. Paksoy.
p.   cm.
Includes index.
ISBN 1–56324–201–X—ISBN 1–56324–202–8 (pbk.)
1. Asia, Central—History.
I. Paksoy, H.B., 1948–
DK857.C45 1993
958—dc20
93–31045
CIP

Printed in the United States of America

The paper used in this publication meets the minimum requirements of
American National Standard for Information Sciences—
Permanence of Paper for Printed Library Materials, ANSI Z 39.48–1984.

MV (c) 10 9 8 7 6 5 4 3 2 1
MV (p) 10 9 8 7 6 5 4 3 2 1

Contents

H.B. Paksoy

Introduction

Although Western news coverage and academic interest in Central Asia have increased greatly in recent years, direct contact with the region remains limited, and to date very few original Central Asian writings have been made available in Western languages. Individuals interested in the area but lacking the language facility to work with primary sources have tended to rely on Russian-language editions or even tertiary works. Thus, the thinking of Central Asians themselves has remained a "black box," even for many specialists. It is this fact that occasions publication of the present volume of translations from Central Asian sources.

There is significance in the very fact that Central Asians managed to publish some of the materials sampled here despite decades of severe censorship and intensive ideological warfare. Such writings drew the ire of Communists and Russian nationalists alike. Many an author was threatened publicly or privately, and some were forced to recant in writing. Yet they persisted, and bits of true history kept finding their way to the printers, even surfacing in fictional genres with accurate historical footnotes.[1]

These writings are manifestations of an effort by Central Asians to "rediscover" their own history as the basis for cultural survival as well as current political action.[2] Central Asia possessed a rich cultural and political history before it fell under tsarist rule in the mid-to-late nineteenth century.[3] Although tsarist Russia cloaked its motives of economic exploitation and imperial aggrandizement with an ostensible "civilizing mission,"[4] later echoed by its Soviet successors, the divide-and-conquer policies pursued by both regimes were

H.B. Paksoy earned his doctorate from Oxford University and has been a Faculty Associate of the Harvard University Center for Middle Eastern Studies. His works on Central Asia include *Alpamysh: Central Asian Identity Under Russian Rule* (1989) and *Central Asian Monuments* (1992). Dr. Paksoy is founder and past editor of the *AACAR Bulletin*, published by the Association for the Advancement of Central Asian Research.

clearly intended to undermine the civilization they aimed to subjugate. Under tsarist and Soviet rule, a confusing and shifting variety of legal statuses, borders, ethnic designations, and linguistic divisions were imposed on the subject populations of the region.[5]

The effort to recover the true history of the region, as opposed to Moscow's version of "voluntary unifications" and the like, has engaged Central Asian writers with unprecedented urgency. The selections in this volume exemplify this effort. Most of them were written within the past few years, but some date back to earlier periods of political ferment.[6]

Since this region of the world always belonged to the Central Asian peoples, whose ancient culture, monuments, written documents, and original writing systems predate by centuries the first mention of the Rus in the chronicles, no attempt was made to Russianize place or personal names. Except for proper names already established in English, all names and terms have been transliterated directly from the language or dialect in which they were first produced.

Editor's notes have been added where appropriate to clarify concepts or allusions that may be unfamiliar for Western readers and also to direct readers' attention to related works and sources. The specialists whose translations are included herein are Audrey L. Altstadt, Hisao Komatsu, Shawn T. Lyons, Joseph Nissman, H.B. Paksoy, and David S. Thomas.

Many of the documents assembled in this collection were first published in translation in the pages of the *AACAR Bulletin*, published by the Association for the Advancement of Central Asian Research, and are reproduced here with permission.

Notes

1. See H.B. Paksoy, "Central Asia's New Dastans," *Central Asian Survey*, vol. 6, no. 1 (1987).

2. As for the nature of "identity," historical or contemporary, there is ample evidence that Central Asians had their own formulas for defining, safeguarding, and, when necessary, defending their collective identities going back centuries if not millennia. These means employed by the Central Asians must be studied on their own terms, not fit into models developed to study other manifestations of "nation" and "nationalism" elsewhere.

3. Russian rulers had been eyeing the region since 1552, when they took Kazan. To accomplish the aim of conquest, a special "Asiatic Department" was created within the Russian Imperial General Staff. Central Asia was finally overrun by the Russian offensive forces between 1865 and 1884. See H.B. Paksoy, Special Editor, "Muslims in the Russian Empire: Response to Conquest," *Studies in Comparative Communism*, vol. 19, nos. 3 and 4 (Autumn/Winter 1986). For a glimpse of the operations of the "Asiatic Department," see Charles Marvin, *The Russian Advance Towards India* (London, 1882).

4. Russia's purported "civilizing mission" is articulated in Foreign Minister Gorchakov's famous Memorandum of 1864 to the tsarist diplomatic corps as the explanation to be provided all governments around the world. A copy is found in William K. Fraser-Tytler, *Afghanistan*, 2d ed. (Oxford, 1953). For another Russian functionary's frank outline of tsarist Russia's motivations of economic exploitation and recovery of

prestige, see M.A. Terentyef, *Russia and England in Central Asia*, F.C. Daukes, Tr. (Calcutta: Foreign Department Press, 1876), 2 vols. The original Russian edition of this work was published in St. Petersburg in 1875.

5. Tsarist administrations sought to fragment the Central Asians as much as possible and applied varied (and changing) ethnonyms and legal designations to these fragments. The process was repeated, with new variations, under Soviet rule. In addition, Soviet functionaries in the 1930s "discovered" and officially established "new" languages such as Uzbek, Kazakh, and others, so that Central Asians "had to have" translators to communicate with each other or, preferably, to adopt Russian as their lingua franca. And how, one asks, did Central Asians communicate before Soviet rule? How did they sustain a press? At a conference held in Ankara in 1993, scholars from all the newly independent states of Central Asia agreed on a unified Latin alphabet; a slightly varying subset was subsequently issued for Uzbek.

6. In the aftermath of Russia's defeat in the Russo-Japanese war of 1904–5 and the revolution it sparked, Emperor Nicholas II was forced to permit the creation of a State Duma, or parliamentary body. Aside from the many well-known restrictions on the Duma's power, it should be noted that the representation for Central Asians was insignificant (25 in the First Duma, which had 500 members). The Central Asian leadership, for their part, began to organize political parties in anticipation of taking part in what they hoped would become a more pluralistic political system. Both the First and Second State Dumas summoned to St. Petersburg were dismissed after a few weeks, having offered a glimmer of freedom before dashing the hopes of many. A decade later, during World War I, when ethnic Russians were mobilized for the front and wartime losses grew, Central Asians were pressed into service as laborers, to dig frontline trenches (a pattern repeated in World War II in the "penal battalions"). In 1916, efforts to conscript the formerly exempt population sparked the beginning of the Turkistan national liberation movement. It is this movement that is otherwise termed the "Basmachi" movement by the Soviets who attempted to denigrate it as banditry. See Society for Central Asian Studies, *Programmnye dokumenty musulmanskih politicheskikh partii 1917–1920 gg.*, Reprint Series No. 2 (Oxford, 1985); Richard Pipes, *The Formation of the Soviet Union* (Harvard, 1970), Second Printing; H. Seton-Watson, *The Russian Empire, 1801–1917* (Oxford, 1967); H.B. Paksoy, "Basmachi" (Turkistan National Liberation Movement, 1916–1930s), in *Modern Encyclopedia of Religions in Russia and the Soviet Union* (Academic International Press, 1991), vol. 4, pp. 5–20.

1

REDISCOVERY OF HISTORY

Ayaz Malikov

The Question of the Turk
The Way Out of the Crisis

Editor's Introduction

Ayaz Malikov, the author of this article published in the newspaper *Azerbaijan*[1] in March 1990, here suggests that promises made to the nationalities since 1917 should be kept and fulfilled by the Soviet state. Failing that, the nationalities ought not be barred from pursuing their realization. As in the past, some were quick to see in this cultural demand a political menace, the old bogeyman "pan-Turkism," which was conjured up not in the Turk domains but in Europe during the balance-of-power struggles of the nineteenth and twentieth centuries. The literature on this issue is nascent but documents the works and motives of the "creator" of this notion and the methods of its propagation into the Turk lands.[2] "The entire English-speaking world," said one Azerbaijan Turk scholar, "forms a cultural whole and is not regarded as a threat to the rest of the world merely on the basis of that cultural unity. When Turks in Azerbaijan look to *Dede Korkut* or the *Orkhon* stelae, this is no different from Americans reading Shakespeare."

Notes

1. Published since October 1989 under the editorship of Sabir Rustemhanli, the newspaper had a reported circulation of 200,000. Editorial Board: Ziya Buniatov, Bahtiyar Vahabzade, Bayram Bayramov, Kasim Kasimzade, Ahmet Elbrus (Assistant

"Tiurkskii vopros: Puti vykhoda iz krizisa" is adapted from the March 24, 1990, issue of the bilingual newspaper *Azerbaijan*. This translation by Audrey L. Altstadt was first published in the fall 1990 issue of *AACAR Bulletin* (vol. 3, no. 2). Italicization follows the original.

Ayaz Malikov (Candidate of Physics and Mathematical Sciences) is a member of the administration of the Tatar Society Center, Kazan.

Editor), Aliyar Seferli, Ismail Shihli, Yasar Aliev, Nadir Jabbarov, Rustem Behrudi, Jumsut Nuriyev, Feride Memedova, Firudin Jelilov, Firudin Abbasov, Elmira Akhundova, Sherif Kerimli. Reportedly, the members of the editorial board were replaced after the spring 1993 "reversal" that returned Haydar Aliyev to power.

2. See Edward Ingram, *The Beginnings of the Great Game in Asia 1828–1834* (Oxford, 1979); idem, *Commitment to Empire: Prophecies of the Great Game in Asia 1797–1800* (Oxford, 1981); idem, *In Defense of British India: Great Britain in the Middle East 1775–1842* (London, 1984). Although the original players in the "great game" were Britain and Russia, Germany joined later in the century and the French were not disinterested.

THE QUESTION OF THE TURK: THE WAY OUT OF THE CRISIS

We, of the more than thirty Turk nationalities of the country, at this critical juncture of our history, must all look into the past and the present in order to find a path to our future. We must, of course, understand that no one will do this for us; or if they do, it will only produce, as we have seen in the past, the results which we now reap.

We Turks traversed a long historical path, from the states of the ancient khans of the Ordos, of the Altai and Sayan, and to the present time. Behind us are more than 2,000 years of political history, full of attainments, loss, and tragedy. More than once along this path we have faced the threat of disappearance, but our forebears always found the strength and the confidence in themselves and the hope to return with renewed strength to the world arena as active members of the world community of nations—with our own face and with our own goals. We must realize that we stand at one such critical moment in our history.

In the recent historical past, at the beginning of the twentieth century, Tatars freely read books, journals, and newspapers published in Azerbaijan; and Tatar newspapers and books proliferated throughout Central Asia, Caucasia, and Siberia. And now, when the French-speaking peoples launch a satellite to guarantee TV programs for France, the French of Canada, and the rest of the world, and when in 1992 the Turkish Republic plans to launch a satellite for telecommunications in its native language for three million Turks abroad, we inexorably remain behind the rest of the world.

Designating our path to development, we must proceed from the reality of the existing world and of our position. The total number of members of Turk groups and nationalities of the country is now close to 50 million—that is, equal to the population of France—an average of 2.5 million people for each Turk nation. The smallest groups, such as the Khakass, the Nogai, and the Balkar, number about 70 thousand; among the largest, the Kazakhs, the Azerbaijanis, and the Tatars number seven to nine million each. The Uzbeks are close to 20 million. Other Turks live in China, Mongolia, Afghanistan, Iran, the Turkish Republic, Syria, and Iraq.

We must work out our own strategy of development. Our first step should be the publication in our languages of all the basic world classics. But some nations, especially those few in number who do not have the status of a union republic, do not have the means to resolve this issue, and it is necessary to recognize this. What can be done? It is necessary, in my view, to create *a single bank of translations of world literature in Turk languages.* Every translation from any language of the world into one of the Turk languages would be placed in this bank and then it would be easy to make the shift to any other Turk dialect. Besides this, it is necessary as quickly as possible to publish all ancient Turk literature in Runic and in Brahmin and in all other alphabets used at any time by all ancient Turks. Our children do not even know that before the Arabic alphabet we had our own system of writing. *All the ancient Turk legacy of our people must be published as quickly as possible.* The cultural organization for coordinating such activity could be the Oriental Institute of the Academy of Sciences of the Azerbaijan SSR. It could unite all the forces of our peoples [and] intellectuals in the fastest resolution of this issue. Publication could be cooperative. This guarantees the ability to cooperate and reduces bureaucratic red tape. The publication of the ancient Turk heritage for the small Turk peoples could be undertaken by the larger ones: the Azerbaijanis have the power to guarantee a material basis for publications in Balkar and Karachay; the Kazakhs could publish in Altaian and Khakass; the Tatars, in Nogay. The other peoples have the means themselves to publish this literature. Azerbaijan or Turkmenistan could help the Gagauz, since the language of the Gagauz is Oghuz.

Our peoples do not know their own history. The history of the Russians is taught in schools beginning with ancient Slavs, the history of the Germans, from the ancient Germans, the history of the French, from the ancient Celts and the Gauls. In the same way, our children must begin their studies with the history of the ancient Turks. The existing textbook of the History of the USSR is a variation on the History of Russia, while the history of the other peoples serves only as background decoration against which the history of Russia is played out.

The publication of a textbook The History of the Turks should also be undertaken by the Oriental Institute in Baku. This calls for the mobilization of all the intellectual forces of the country in the field of Turcology. This textbook must be published immediately and included in the curriculum of all the schools of all Turk regions of the country.

The journal *Sovetskaia Tiurkologiia* must realize that it is the sole journal in the country dedicated to the study of the Turk people and has a responsibility before all the Turk peoples. At present this journal is especially for academicians. Sometimes the impression is created that if our language were to die out, it would be better for this journal—it would not be distracted from "pure art" by waves of human life. The journal *Sovetskaia Tiurkologiia* must address problems not only of a purely academic nature but also concerning the teaching of our languages in the various regions of the country. It should publish statistical data about our children who do not know their own language and analyze the reasons for this. The journal *Sovetskaia Tiurkologiia* must recognize the difference between itself and the journal *Shumerologiia* or *Assirologiia*. It has the business of dealing with living languages of living peoples with their own problems.

Unification of the alphabet is necessary and should be undertaken immediately. This must be introduced in such a way that differences in spelling of the same word in various Turk languages are completely liquidated or, in other cases, kept to a minimum. It would be even better if we all proceeded to Latinization. This is especially important considering that many Turks live abroad. Our goal must be the achievement of understanding by Tatars and other Turk readers of books and newspapers published in Baku, Tashkent, or Kazan, as it was before the [1917] revolution. Is it not strange? At the beginning of the century the intelligentsia of our peoples actively tried to see into the life of another Turkic people and into its literature by reading its literature in the original. Nowadays you cannot find one such representative of the intelligentsia. The tradition of Alimjan Ibrahimov, Uzeyir Hajibeyov, Boraganskii, Sakin Seyfullin, and Sheyhzade Babich is completely gone.

It is necessary to expose once for all the false thesis that the knowledge of any Turk language is just the knowledge of one local language. Any Turk language opens the door to the other Turk languages; that is, every Turk language is simultaneously a local language and the language of international communication between close Turk peoples. This should be taught correctly. It is necessary to have the knowledge of this fact spread among our society in order to liquidate the traces of a policy of weakening and destruction that has been pursued for decades. As a result of this pressure we do not have sufficient numbers of Turcologists from our own people. There is not one Tatar or Bashkurt Turcologist from the younger generation. There are Turcologists from other nationalities, but not from among the Tatars or the Bashkurt. The young have been inoculated with disrespect for their own language.

It is necessary to introduce a single coordinated cultural policy and it is necessary not to be afraid of the accusation of "Pan-Turkism"! By that accusation, we will discern those who benefit and are guilty of our current deplorable condition.

When you begin to read one or another Turk literature, you will be amazed at the lack of coordination in the terminology. *It is necessary to create a terminological commission with the goal of creating new terminology in all spheres of activity.* All films issued by Turk-language studios should be dubbed promptly to guarantee their distribution in the republic. Goods in the field of culture are also goods and it is necessary that the terms of their sale guarantee the profitability of their production. While there is a market of seven million Azerbaijanis for the "Azerbaijanfilm" studios, there are in all 50 million Turks in the country. It is the same for books, whether artistic or in other fields of activity. *Every successful book should immediately be offered for sale in all the Turk areas of the country.* Why do the books of Chinggis Aytmatov and

Chinggis Huseyinov not immediately come out in our languages at the same time they come out in Russian?

Of the 50 million Turk population of the country, 12 million live in republics and oblasts which have "autonomous" status. Obviously, Azerbaijan, Uzbekistan, Kazakhstan, Turkmenistan, and Kyrgyzstan must use their authority and influence in the higher organs of power in the country in the defense of the interests of the other Turk peoples. Within the limits of the law, the constitution of the country, customs, and morals, we must demonstrate support for each other.

We must proceed from the idea that the Turk peoples of the country have the same rights in all areas of life as other peoples, and that deprivation or limitation of these rights is illegal and immoral and contrary to nature. In the final analysis, we must be represented also in the United Nations organization, but this is a problem for the distant future, when we have greater integration and when our stature in the world has grown. The main issue is to escape from provincialism in the perception of the world and its activities. It is necessary to understand, finally, that in the world there are no divinely ordained centers and damned provinces, that all this is the work of human hands. To perpetuate a feeling of provincialism is one of the means of braking the development of one or another nation, that is, a method of war against it.

According to the newspaper *Argumenty i fakty*, Soviet internal propaganda is conducted in eighty languages for 2,257 hours per week or 322 hours per day. At the same time, the Turk people of our country are deprived of the radio stations and transmission on short-wave that are allocated to them according to international and the intra-Union electronic communications agreements. These radio stations and hours are allotted for propaganda abroad. Many Turk peoples are dispersed throughout the country, but the radio stations of their republics on medium and long waves hardly reach the whole territory in the republic itself. Is this not derision? This is a waste of our peoples' means and an infringement of their rights. With our resources and our time they build radio stations and broadcast abroad in Swahili, Greek, and other languages while we Turks suffer from national and cultural underdevelopment. *It follows, obviously, that resolution of the question of ending the use of the radio stations and broadcast hours for propaganda abroad and transferring them to the Turk people, who have been deprived of the means of communication throughout the whole country, is a necessary minimum.* As for Tatars, Azerbaijanis, Bashkurts, and others who have gone out to the oil fields of Siberia and other places, it is necessary to protect their right to hear radio in their native language and not just Voice of America, Radio Liberty, and the BBC.

This is a narrow but very important question. It is necessary also to create an all-Union system of television in all the basic languages of the country for the whole territory of the USSR. This includes, of course, Turk. This is necessary for the guarantee of development of the culture of our nation. But right now, this is guaranteed only to the Russian nation.

It is necessary to adopt an all-Union law on the extra-territorial cultural autonomy of nations. Let us look at an example. Suppose tomorrow in Kazakhstan, Siberia, or Uzbekistan a huge construction project begins, for which thousands of workers arrive from Russia—Russians—but also thousands of Azerbaijanis and thousands of Uzbeks. Will there be comparable guarantees that the children of members of these nations will be educated in their native language ... ? The answer is simple! Only Russian schools will be built, not Azerbaijani or Uzbek schools. Perhaps there will be Kazakh schools, if the project is in Kazakhstan. Where is the equality of nations proclaimed in the Constitution and in our propaganda? From this emerges the necessity of adopting *an all-Union law guaranteeing to children of all nationalities of the country education in the native language, independent of the place of residence on the territory of the country.* Failing this, the government should return to the parents the money that was designated in the budget for the education of their children.

The number of Russians in Naberezhnye Chelny and the number of Tatars in Moscow is approximately equal, but can one compare the number of schools in Tatar language in Moscow to the number of Russian-language schools in Chelny? Of the native population of Cheliabinsk Oblast fifteen percent is constituted by more than a half million Tatars and Bashkurts deprived of all possibility of national development. There is not one school, not one child-care center, not one professional instructional institution in the native language. The people are deprived of radio, television, and press in the native language. There is no national theater. Yet just over a hundred years ago, Cheliabinsk was a large commercial Tatar-Bashkurt *aul.* The question is not that Russian children have excessive rights. They have natural rights, and these rights must be further developed and realized. But the children of other nationalities must have exactly the same rights.

Up to the present time, the entire effort of the Tatars and Bashkurts to realize their own rights has encountered opposition and accusations of nationalism—an experience from the 1930s, when such was necessary to excuse the terror (in this case spiritual) toward other nations. *It is necessary to adopt an all-Union law on national communities and their rights, and the rights of the Russian community on the territory of the country can be the standard, being close to international norms and the Helsinki and Vienna accords.* In striving toward all these goals we should be guided by the rights of nations, strengthened by all-Union and international legal acts, the declarations of rights of the peoples of Russia, acts on decolonization, and other documents having force on the territory of the USSR.

Everyone who suffers for his people and its future will inevitably be interested in its history in order to understand why his nation departed from the rest of the peoples of the world. Why are the rights of the Tatars, Azerbaijanis, or Uzbeks not the same as those of the Swedes, the Czechs, and the Turks [of the Turkish Republic]? Why [he asks] does his people remain "second class," a dependent subject in international life and not included among the other peoples of the planet? And then he notices that the same applies to all the other Turks! That the Turks in the USSR and China and Afghanistan and Iran have similar problems. Finding a designated path out of the crisis requires first of all a consciousness of the crisis. It is impossible to cure a disease without realizing that it exists. If we unite, then there is no doubt we will find a way out of the situation that has been created. We need unity and confidence.

We must be aware that no one but ourselves will solve this problem for us. But it requires energy and effort, a reliance on confidence and success. And this we must find in the more than two thousand years of history of the Turks. Our ancestors also fell into crisis and found a way out!

Harekette Bereket! [Activity is fruitful!]

Muhammad Ali

Let Us Learn About Our Heritage
Get to Know Yourself

Editor's Introduction

In August 1988 "Get to Know Yourself" was serialized in two consecutive issues of the newspaper *Yash Leninchi* (Young Leninist), published in Uzbekistan; it was printed under the rubric "Let Us Learn About Our Heritage." The editors of *Yash Leninchi* (renamed *Turkistan* in 1992) provided the following information about the author of "Get to Know Yourself."

> Poet Muhammad Ali, the Uzbekistan Lenin Komsomol and Karakalpak ASSR Berdak State Prize Laureate, is well known to readers. He is one of our poets who has contributed to our literature on historical topics. He has *dastans* titled *Mashrab* and *Gumbazdagi Nur*, and his books on topics of revolutionary history, *Kadimgi Koshuklar* and *Baki Dünya*, are renowned. Today you will read another of his historical essays.

"Get to Know Yourself" may be understood as an effort by Ali to facilitate the reconstruction of the history of Central Asia at a time when the Soviet leadership was pledging to fill in historical "blank spots." Although worded very carefully, the piece is a clear departure from historical accounts propagated under the auspices of the Communist Party apparatus.[1]

It should be noted that the effort to recover the history of Central Asia had begun, under various guises, in the early 1970s, long predating Mikhail S. Gorbachev's "openness" (*glasnost*) campaign.[2] What is distinctive about the piece by Ali is that it was not written in the form of a yarn, short story, or other

---

"Öz özingi anglap et." First serialized in *Yash Leninchi* (Tashkent) in August 1988. This translation by H.B. Paksoy appeared in the fall 1989 issue of the *AACAR Bulletin* (vol. 2, no. 3).

genre used in earlier works of this type—for example, by Alishir Ibadinov in his "Sun Is Also Fire," printed in another Uzbek serial publication.[3]

Notes

1. This process is extensively documented in Wayne S. Vucinich, ed., *Russia in Asia* (Stanford: Stanford University Press, 1972); Lowell Tillett, *The Great Friendship: Soviet Historians on the Non-Russian Nationalities* (Chapel Hill: University of North Carolina Press, 1969); Cyril E. Black, ed., *Rewriting Russian History: Soviet Interpretations of Russia's Past* (New York: Praeger, 1956).
2. See H.B. Paksoy, "Central Asia's New Dastans," *Central Asian Survey*, vol. 6, no. 1 (1987).
3. "Kuyash Ham Alov," *Gülistan*, 1980, no. 9; see H.B. Paksoy, ed., *Central Asian Monuments* (Istanbul: Isis Press, 1992).

GET TO KNOW YOURSELF

Recently two authors, G. Borovik and A. Mikhailov, participating in the Central television's "Position" program, discussed the proposition that old monuments of the ancient cities of Bukhara and Samarkand have no connection (!) to the Uzbek people. . . . This certainly begs the question: If they are not related to the Uzbek people, to whom are they related? Arabs? Mongols? Russians? Such questions cause one to think, and tax the imagination. Seeking justice is a difficult endeavor, but the struggle for truth is both necessary and an obligation.

The Ancient Setting

I. The land between the two great rivers of Central Asia, the Amu Darya and the Syr Darya, was known to the ancients as Turan.[a] Later, it became known as Turkistan, and, after the invasion of the Arabs, Maveraunnehr. In the ancient Turk language, the Syr Darya was known as Enchioghuz, the Amu Darya as Öküz [Ox]. There are suggestions that "Enchioghuz" is related to "Enchiöküz." It is also thought that this is a derivative of "Ikinci Öküz" [Second Ox].

Greek troops entered and occupied Central Asia under the command of Alexander in 329 B.C. At that time, Greek historians recorded in transcription that the river was named Öküz in the Turk language. Consequently, in Europe, this river became known as Oxus. The nineteenth-century Hungarian historian A. Vambery[b] wrote a book about his visit to our homeland under the title *Travels to Transoxiana* which testifies to the fact that the land in question was known as Turan.

In Firdawsi's *Shahnama*[c] there is plenty of information about ancient Turan. This world-renowned poet wrote about the Iranians and the Turanians with affection and in detail, including the fights between the Iranian king Kavus and his predecessor Keyhusrev and the Turanian king Afrasiyab; the Rustam dastan; the

Suhrab and Siyavush dastans; and the story of Afrasiyab's daughter Manija, putting down their relations on paper, from various aspects. When referring to Turan, and its inhabitants, Turks, the poet uses such terms as the "Men of Turan," "Land of Turan," "Turanian troops," "Inhabitants of Turan," "Men of the Turks," "Land of the Turan," "Turk Cavalry," "Offspring of the Turks," "Business of the Turks," "Maidens of Turan," "Heroes of Turan." These clear gleanings of that author provide us with a good picture.

II. One of the prominent personages in *Shahnama*, referred to as Afrasiyab, the ruler of Turan, is Alp Ertunga, styled Tonga Alp Er in other sources. The great scholar Mahmud Kashgari, who explained the term "Turan" in his *Diwan Lugat at-Türk* [hereafter *DLT*], writes:

> Tunga: A creature of the tiger family. It is the one that kills the elephant. This is its root meaning; however, this word has remained with the Turks and its meaning persists among them. It is often used as a title, thus: King Afrasiyab, chief of the Turks, had the title "Tunga Alp Er," meaning "A man, a warrior, as strong as a tiger." [*DLT*, 605]

Also, our great poet Yusuf Has Hajib, in his *Kutadgu Bilig*,[d] describes Afrasiyab in the following words [l. 276]:

> If you observe well you will notice that the Turkish princes are the finest in the world. And among these Turkish princes the one of outstanding fame and glory was Tonga Alp Er. He was the choicest of men, distinguished by great wisdom and virtues manifold. What a choice and manly man he was, a clever man indeed—he devoured this world entire! The Iranians call him Afrasiyab, the same who seized and pillaged their realm.

. . .[e]

III. The observations of Mahmud Kashgari require a closer look. Explaining the word "Kent" (city), he wrote:

> Among the Oghuz and those who associate with them, it means town among the Turks. The chief city of Ferghana is called Öz Kent, meaning "city of our souls." Samiz Kent, meaning "fat city," is called thus because of its great size; in Persian it is Samarkand. [*DLT*, p. 173]

Interesting information is provided in an explanation of Afrasiyab's daughter Koz:

> Name of the daughter of Afrasiyab. She is the one who built the city of Kazvin. The root form of this is "kaz oyni," meaning "Kaz's playground," since she used to live and play there. For this reason some of the Turks reckon

Kazvin within the borders of the Turk lands. Also the city of Qum, since, in Turkic, Qum is "sand," and this daughter of Afrasiyab used to hunt there and frequent it. Others of them reckon (the borders) from Marv as-Shahijan since her father, Tonga Alp Er, who is Afrasiyab, built the city of Marv three hundred years after Tamhurat built the citadel. Some of them reckon all of Transoxiana as part of the Turk lands, and first of all Yarkand (Baykand). This used to be called Dizruin, meaning (in Persian) "city or castle of brass" because of its strength. It is near the city of Bukhara. [*DLT*, p. 509]

Specifically about the ruler of Turan, Afrasiyab, there is interesting information in *Samariya* by the nineteenth-century Samarkand historian Abu Tahirhoja. This historian explains the origin of the name Samar: "the name of a Turk Khan. He established this *kishlak* [winter quarters]." The Russian orientalist V. Bartold, in his *Turkistanin Madani Hayati Tarihi* [History of Civilization in Turkistan],[f] wrote: "The region between the nomadic Turk empire and the Sasanid dynasty's state is termed Amu Darya. For the Iranians, the land beyond Amu Darya was known as Turkistan, meaning the land of the Turks."

The lesson to be derived from these examples: When referring to Turks living in Turan, or Turkistan, the Turks thus referenced are not only Uzbeks. Also included are the Kirghiz, Kazakh, and Turkmen. The great tribes of the Turks have been domiciled in this region, and called their own lands "Turkistan." In various eras, numerous Turk tribes—there are 92 (!) such tribes in the composition of the Uzbeks—arrived from the northeast, augmented, influenced, and elevated the population.[g] This historical current continued for many centuries.[h]

Here it is necessary to reflect on one point. To the land between the two rivers, the ancient Turan or Turkistan, without regard to the historical evidence, the contemporary historians refer with its Arab designation, "Maveraunnehr." First of all, this does not designate any country; it is also contrary to historical evidence. In his collected scholarly works, the great historian Bartold regards this land as "Turkistan" and considers all the events there, from the ancient to the contemporary, with that designation.

Two Maidens Wearing Satin Waistcoats

I. A look at the history of the Uzbeks tells us that it is closely related to that of the sister Tajik peoples. Their lives and histories are intertwined with each other, and have contributed enormously to world civilization. The friendship of the Uzbeks and the Tajiks is an amazing event, the like of which is not observed elsewhere. Uzbek is one of the Turk languages, whereas Tajik belongs to the Indo-European. Although their languages have different origins, in every other quarter [the Uzbeks and the Tajiks] share similarities. Their way of life, traditional ceremonies, hospitalities, and culinary arts are the same. They intermarry; they wear the same clothes; their tastes are complementary. It is not so easy to determine which of two maidens wearing satin waistcoats is Uzbek or Tajik, until she speaks in her own tongue, nor does it occur to anyone to try. Likewise, it is noteworthy that their arts and music are in common, especially their "shashmakam."[i] The melodies of the Tajiks and the Uzbeks are very much intermingled, and as difficult to distinguish as the maidens. While on the topic, the great Abdurrahman Jami,[j] in his treatise dedicated to music, classifies the Turk rhythmic patterns into four: "Turki asli jedid, Turki asli kadim, Turki hafif, Turki sarilar." If the Persian-Tajik poet studied the Uzbek music, the Uzbek poet Alishir Navai wrote the *Furs Salotini*.[k] These examples display how the two people's histories, lives, and cultures are so entirely combined. Though their languages are different, their similarities are truly amazing.

In the days old, it was said that the Persian mind was suited to the pen, and the mind of the Turk possessed sword-sharp intelligence. The nature of the Persians exhibited a passion for knowledge; they wrote the history of their home-land, created discourses. Today we read those treatises, become more familiar with world history, and appreciate them. They applied themselves to the affairs of state in the palaces, served as the scribes, artists. They distinguished them-selves by producing books of advice (*Kabusnama, Chahar Makala,* and the like),[l] which is naturally related to the secrets of their involvements. The factor in keeping language in demand is invention, the constant activity of the enlight-ened pen in all fields of knowledge and literature. *Hudaynamak* and *Shahristanhoy Iran* (unfortunately, these two rare books did not come down to us, but we know them from the writings of Firdawsi and Tabari), *Shahnama, Siyasatnama, Gulistan,* and many other books were born to this world by the endeavors of the men of the pen.[m]

The sword-sharp-minded Turks were not usually found in the cities, but mainly preferred to reside in the kishlaks, summer pastures, and steppes. Thus they were in the vanguard in battle, and the duty and the primacy of the sword fell to them. Thus the renown of the Turk troops. They were at the head of the state, and Turkistan was ruled by Turk dynasties from the fifth century. The majority of the Iranian rulers—Seljuks, Safavids, Halokuiy, Nadirshah Afshar, and Kajars[n]—are members of the Turk families. For these reasons, in contrast to the Iranians, Turks did not become well acquainted with the pen but followed the path of the sword.

"The political primacy of the Turks in present Turkistan was established in the sixth century," writes Bartold.[o] The invading Arabs arrived in this land, and in the first place, fought against the Turks, because they constituted the major power. The Sogdians in the Zarafshan valley and the Khorazmians along the Amu Darya did not pose a serious threat to the invaders. The sizable influence of Turk Hakans[p] and their troops confronted Iran and Byzantium in the west and the Chinese in the east. Naturally, without the Turks losing their power, it was not possible for the Arabs to subdue Turkistan. Arabs defeated the Turks in a battle along the Syr Darya during the third decade of the seventh century. After this loss, the Turk lands were broken into pieces. Arabs established rule, and the

Arabic language gained influence. In this language the affairs of state were conducted, volumes were penned, representatives of civilized peoples produced poetry and universal works in Arabic.

II. Thus, prior to our present era, Arabic should have gained primacy, but it did not, and instead Persian began gaining influence. The Badawis [Arabs] accepted this language and began to contribute more to its development than did the Persians. During this period, there were large migrations from Iran into Turkistan. This is why, as noted above, Mahmud Kashgari wrote that "after the arrival of Persians, these cities became more Iranized," which indicates that this scholar was aware of the settlement policies. As a result, madrasas of the Persian style began to be built in Turkistan, and the Persian language and literary traditions became important. With the rise of the Samanids, this development reached its zenith, and Persian was elevated to the status of the language of state. Bartold wrote: "During the tenth century the refined language of the educated strata was differentiated from Iranian; we know this from poets of Turkistan origin such as Rudaki who held a highly esteemed position among the Persians." Thus it became necessary for the population to know Persian well, as the affairs of state and education in the madrasas were conducted in it. Naturally, scholarship, history, and literature were produced in that language. The knowledge of this language became a necessity of life for the Turks; thus they not only learned it, but also began to produce works in it. At the time, it was difficult to encounter a Turk who did not know Persian-Tajik. Many Turks fell under the influence of this state language, aspired to secure pecuniary interest through state-sponsored positions, and went about speaking Persian. They even were afflicted with the malady of forgetting their mother tongue.

That current continued at length. We learn this from the writings of Alishir Navai, recorded five centuries prior to our present time: "witty and elegant Turk youths busied themselves with making poetic pronouncements, in Persian. . . . This passion, born among the people, did not manifest itself wisely or intelligently in their native language."

"Turk ulus" [the Turk nation], the poet states, "should express their passions in their own language." And he gave the reason: "[Otherwise] comprehension may be channeled into this course, and in time, may be found inclined to stay, and perhaps [become] powerless to leave that domain." Of course, time and practice are capable of deeply influencing the mind, and render reversal difficult. The mind comes under the influence of time and practice; in other words, the power and force of tradition constitute an enduring set of values. Customs remain alive and their rules do not change. Accordingly, these practices were not altered, and the influence of Persian-Tajik language in twentieth-century Turkistan still continues. Among all Turk and Uzbek peoples, the language of state was Persian-Tajik, even within the political entities of Timur, Ulugbek, and Babür.[q] Affairs of state were conducted in that language; historical treatises and literature were created and became popular. Thus the "witty and elegant" youths of the Turk nation, its poets, scholars, and historians, in addition to their own language, were capable of creating works in the Persian-Tajik language.

As alluded to above, the works of those poets and scholars who did not write in the influential language did not gain a following. That, in turn, cast doubt on ability and talent. It is possible to provide many examples on the influence of tradition. Historical works, names of dastans (here also related to the Persian-Tajik literature), and poetry in the genre of *hamse* were produced in Arabic: *Hamse, Lujjat-ul asrar, Mantik-ut tayr, Hazayin-ul maani, Mahbub-ul kulub*, and so forth. The name of the work devoted to the sum total of Turk language, *Diwan Lugat at-Türk*, is itself Arabic! *Muhakamat ul-Lugateyn*[r]—Arabic! A principal of the Golden Horde in the Syr Darya region, Muhammadhoja (fourteenth century), wrote to the poet Khwarazmi: "In the depths of your heart, you possess many pearls / on earth, you wrote Persian dastans / I wish you would utilize our language / to produce a monument in my court this winter."

Khwarazmi later wrote his famous *Muhabbatnama* dastan. The poet was not able to break out of the mold, and despite the invitation to "create a work in our language" [i.e., Chaghatay-Turki], he composed portions of it in Persian-Tajik. Yusuf Amiri (fifteenth century) named the chapters of his dastan *Dahnama* in Persian-Tajik. About the *Bang va chagir munazarasi*, the poet said: "I constructed it using Turk vocabulary and Persian style." In the work, poems in Turk and Persian are mixed. We also observe this in Yakini's *Ok ve yay munazarasi*. Ulugbek wrote the introduction to *Zijji Kuragani* in Persian and translated it into Arabic. Alisher Navai wrote *diwans* in Persian. *Baburnama* contains many Persian poems and *rubai*. Muhammad Yakub Chingi (seventeenth century) compiled an Uzbek–Persian/Tajik dictionary, with an introduction in Persian. Nadira wrote a *diwan* in Persian-Tajik.

If we were to continue in this vein, we would have to mention all the representatives of the Uzbek literature. Pahlavan Mahmud. Husrav Dehlavi.[*] Jelaleddin Rumi,[s] Mirza Abulkadir Bedil, Zebunnisa, and Gulbeden are among the "witty and elegant Turk youths" who composed works in Persian-Tajik. In doing so, they were largely adhering to the aforementioned traditions. Abu Nasr Farabi[t] wrote poems in Persian, two of which are extant. His utilization of Persian ought to be considered an "expediency of the times."

To derive a lesson: When considering the poets and scholars who have produced works utilizing Arabic and Persian-Tajik, before labeling them as belonging to this or that people, we must of course consider the effects of the tradition. Passing judgment on their pedigree based on their choice of language will not be

---

*In his Urdu-language *diwan Gurrat-ul kamal*, the poet writes: "I am of the Turks of India," indicating that he is a Turk. In his book *Hindustanin keshf edilishi*, J. Nehru wrote: "The most famous work on India in this era is by a Turk who lived in the fourteenth century, Amir Husrev."

correct; if we look closer, they turn out to be the representatives of other nations. There is fairness. . . .

The Headwaters

I. Recently the renowned film director Latif Fayziev spoke on television regarding movies connected to our history. Discussion turned to the slavery of the [Brezhnev] years of stagnation. The situation was thus. The director was working with Indian firms on a movie about Babur.* However, we were not permitted to produce that film. The same director intended to make a movie about Chinggis. Again, no permission. . . .

Recently, one of the Moscow newspapers announced that the Kirghiz film-director T. Okeav was to make the movie *Chingiz Khan* in collaboration with a U.S. firm. For two years, the movie was scheduled for production, both for television (in eight parts) and for the screen (four parts). . . . "We were not permitted." Our aforementioned film director wished to make the movie *Samarkandnama*. Scenes involving Mukanna, Timur, and Spitomin were to be included, but . . . once again, no permission! The project about Omar Khayyam died. . . .

One must wonder. Should not even the smallest word be allowed about the reasons? The framework of these movies embraces the distant past of the peoples of Central Asia. Whether the permissions were denied because [the films] pertain to the historical past of the people, or whether there were other reasons, the film director did not indicate.

It is regrettable. There are also those who look at our history with sophistry. One example. Professor M. Vakhabov, in his article "O pravde—tolko pravdu" [About the Truth, Only the Truth] (*Pravda Vostoka*, June 21, 1988), wrote that Timur is being idealized, but he did not support his argument with a serious fact. Whatever facts he cited are devoid of substance. An earnest and truthful reconstruction of the activities of a historical person is not idealization, but a necessity. Not fully detailing the narration would be a falsification of history. . . . And never mind idealization; [Timur] is to be disgraced! It is a humanistic duty to write history. But the professor is correct in one aspect. It is not essential to idealize Timur; that is unnecessary. Timur was a world conqueror who established an empire by the power of the sword, an oppressive ruler, a typical medieval sovereign. . . . But, describing Timur only in those terms would of

---

*In this regard, it is helpful to remember the words of Rajiv Gandhi, the Prime Minister of the Indian Republic. In his book *Hindistanin Keshfedilishi* [Discovery of India] (Moscow: Khudozhestvennaia literatura, 1987) Gandhi published "Sovet kitabhanlariga maktub" [A Letter to Soviet Booklovers] in which he said: "Ulugbek, a descendant of Timur, astronomer and ruler of Samarkand, utilized the works of Indian mathematicians. Babur, young *jigit* of Ferghana, the fearless commander and cultured author, founded our Moghul Empire in the Ganges valley, and began referring to himself as an Indian."

course be a subjective historical treatment. Samarkand, known as one of the magnificent cities of the world. The Ulugbek observatory. *Zijji Kuragani*, the works of Alisher Navai, and *Baburnama*, have elevated the classical Uzbek literature to exalted heights. . . . Whether we like it or not, these are connected to the Timurid period, and we cannot deny these historical facts. Consequently, the Timurid period is an inseparable part of the history of our homeland and of the world.[u] Timur and his period must be weighed on the scales of justice by our historians and written about accordingly, and the resulting revelations taught to our youngsters openly. Otherwise, if a blind spot is created, his name erased from books and the press, does not that create a distorted, counterproductive and alluring attraction? The truth must be addressed by its own name; idealization is not being defended here. White is white, black is black. Time has come to write them by their names. As Bartold said, if past experts are proved correct, then it is easier to see the truth.[v]

Karl Marx spoke of Timur's activities, stating that Timur strengthened the role of the ruler and updated the laws then in force, and that these precautions appear in direct contrast to the harshness of his military campaigns. "While pondering those specialist accounts detailing the historical services rendered by individuals," said V.I. Lenin, "the fact that they may provide more truthful views than those demanded by the present is not always considered, despite their closeness to the events; and even the possibility that they may bring fresher views on the issue than their predecessors might be overlooked." When evaluating our history and the known personages in it, especially with reference to the matter of Timur, it is necessary for us to keep in mind the Marxist-Leninist precepts.

II. Naturally, open works on the most profound periods of our history are rather scarce. The reason for this is that, under various excuses, those who produce works on the topic censor [themselves] and hold back information. Recall the novels *Navai* and *Yuldizli tunlar*. Our historians, who have to show activity, ought to write research on those periods according to tested concepts. And, since we write so little about our own history, it is necessary to translate into our language those works that already exist. As we did not perform our own work, we should gratefully recall the names of a group of renowned Russian orientalists. Their services to the history of our people are priceless. These scholars certainly are in no need of our praises, but for our own information we need to be acquainted with them. . . .

Vasilii Vladimirovich Bartol'd (1869–1930).[w] Of the 685 works of this Great Russian orientalist, 320 are devoted to the history of Central Asia. He participated in the establishment of the Central Asian State University. His writing of history, grounded on voluminous [historical] manuscripts, was an important contribution. Consider a sampling of his works dedicated to the history of Uzbekistan: *Turkistan at the Time of the Mongol Invasion*; *Sources on the Previous Channels and Beds of the Aral Sea from the Early Times to the Seventeenth*

Century; *Irrigation History of Turkistan*; *Ulugbek and His Times*; *Cotton Plant-ing in Central Asia from the Earliest Times to the Arrival of the Russians*; *Twelve Lectures on the History of the Turkic People in Central Asia*; *Mir Alisher and Political Life*; *The Burial of Timur*; *History of the Turk-Mongol Peoples*; *History of the Central Asian Civilization*; *History of Turkistan*; and *The People's Move-ment in Samarkand in 1365*—every one of these works details our past and history. Reading and learning them is as necessary as water and air. Unfortu-nately, at this time, the majority of these works are not available in Uzbek! This is the importance we have attached to our beloved history and to that great scholar! On the other hand, these same works have been translated into other languages; for example, *Ulugbek* into Turkish (1930), German (1936), English (1958), and Persian (1958); *Mir Alisher* into German (1933), Turkish (1937), and English (1962). This ought to be a lesson to us.

If *Mir Alisher and Political Life* were to be issued in Uzbek to mark the five hundred fiftieth anniversary of the great poet's [Navai's] birth, it would be an opportunity to comply with the wishes of the great scholar [Bartold], for he desired his works to be translated into Uzbek. Similarly, *Ulugbek and His Times* ought to be translated and published by 1994, in honor of the six hundredth anniversary of the great astronomer's birth. To name a street in Tashkent to honor Bartold's services to our history and people would also speak of our regard for this Russian scholar and the Russian people.

Vasilii Lavrentievich Viatkin (1869–1932), renowned archeologist, professor. In 1913 he excavated the "fresco of the Afrasiyab wall." During 1908–9, he unearthed and identified the outstanding historical monument of our people, the Ulugbek observatory, which had been buried. He proposed, in the newspaper *Turkestanskie vedemosti*,[x] that a statue of Ulugbek should be erected in Samarkand. We should not forget that this proposal was made in a colonized country of Tsarist Russia. *Mirza Ulugbek and His Observatory in Samarkand*; *Old Monuments of Samarkand*; *Afrasiyab—the Ancient Samarkand Setting*; and *Ancient Samarkand Architecture* occupy an important place in the understanding of the history of Samarkand. He also arranged for the publication of an *Uzbek Language Textbook for Russian Schools* (1923) and a *Persian Language Text-book*. It is necessary to know the works of Viatkin in Uzbek, for it is not sufficient to have them only in Russian.

Alexandr Iurevich Iakubovskii (1886–1953), famous Soviet orientalist. This scholar has many works on the history of Uzbekistan. The opportunity to collect and publish them both in Uzbek and in Russian presents itself. His works such as *About the Ethnogenesis of the Uzbek People*; *Mukanna Kuzgoloni*; *Timur—An Experiment in Characterization*; and *Central Asian Feudal Society and Commer-cial Relations with Eastern Europe in the Tenth–Fifteenth Centuries* provide us with contemporary and relevant information. It is essential that E.E. Bertels's[y] *Navai and Attar* as well as his monograph on Navai, and A.A. Semenov's arti-cles devoted to our history be translated and published in Uzbek. Azerbaijan scholar Ziya Buniatov's[z] historical monograph on the Kwarazm Shah ought to be appreciated.

Alas, the works cited are only a sampling on our history and literature penned by world-renowned scholars. Another point. We could ask why historical-scholarly works are printed so scarcely in Uzbek, and the works of Uzbek scholars are generally not published (Y. Gulamov's *Kwarazm History* and M. Yoldashev's *Khiva State Archives* are exceptions). Indeed, we may wonder what our students and those among us who believe themselves to be educated—who are familiar with the histories of Jan Hus and Ivan Bolotnikov—know. We are astonished to discover that they are not acquainted with Mahmud Tabari.[a'] V.O. Kliuchevskii stated that general history cannot be known without a knowledge of local history.

III. We do not know our own history well. This is almost an axiomatic statement. The most deplorable aspect is that we are not being encouraged to learn and know our history. Sufficient effort is not being expended to train specialists in various eras of our history, nor is proper use made of the specialists we have. Training of talented textualists, capable of analyzing old manuscripts, is neglected. These trends must be reversed. Recently a Society of Historians was established in our republic. We hope that this organization will work to evaluate the facts and disseminate the results, rather than falling into atrophy once again. While we thirst to be acquainted with our beloved history, to solve its many mysteries by utilizing historiographical methods, we primarily view the dereliction of the Uzbek SSR Academy of Sciences and scholars therein with contrition. In the past, the name of Uzbek SSR Academy of Sciences vice president E. Yusupov has been abundantly visible in the press, and he also repeatedly appeared on televison and radio. His sincere statements on questions concerning the life of our republic—on economy, philosophy, ecology, and sometimes on history and problems of preservation of heritage and civilization—are an example. He speaks especially about turning the economy in the new direction, and also on the success of preparing national workers and cadres. In order to produce more cotton, the main endeavor ought to be in learning cotton cultivation; generally, the new national labor cadres should be channeled in that direction. Groups of laborers are brought from the central regions to work in the industrial plants and factories; the scholar believes that serious steps must be taken to prepare national laborers and cadres.

These are the views of an established scholar of the social sciences in our Academy. We are entitled to demand solutions to the problems of our republic from those sciences. At present, the results are nothing to be proud of.

Restructuring efforts are passing and, lamentably, we are not benefiting from this auspicious current to strengthen our scientific-scholarly endeavors in a timely manner. At this point it occurs to me there is a question that ought to be addressed by our academy and history scholars—the question of the Uzbek people's ethnogenesis and the the the creation of their history.

It requires collective labor to document the ethnogenesis (meaning the formation) of a people. To understand this synthesized movement, it is necessary to invoke the aid of branches of knowledge such as archeology, ethnography, linguistics, and history. Investigations of eras and social forces are made with inevitable accompanying assumptions, instead of sound learning of ethnic history and study of the history of peoples. Knowledge of the arrival of the people, their identity, the streams from which they flowed to form rivers, the whereabouts of those mountain ranges giving birth to those cascading streams, is the main objective, rather than sitting on the shore of the river and pinning your hopes on it. Ethnogenesis and people's ethnic history is the beginning of history. Currently, it is precisely this history that is not studied. . . . It is necessary to state, for the purposes of comparison, that the history of ethnogenesis is being researched among the sister Tajik, Tatar, and Bashkurt peoples.

Considering the importance of the topic, the presidium of the Uzbek Academy of Sciences, at the beginning of the 1980s, passed a resolution for the study of the Uzbek people's ethnogenesis. Those who heard it wondered with amazement. An unoffical consultative group was established, and Ahmadali Askarov,[b'] a corresponding member of the Uzbek SSR Academy of Sciences (now he is a full Academician), was appointed as the supervisor to this group. More than twenty historians were summoned. But nothing went beyond the words: the decision remained on paper. It is now clear that the effort was not taken up with a serious hand. However, in 1986, a book entitled *Materials Pertaining to the Ethnic History of the Peoples of Central Asia* was published, containing scholarly reports by eleven authors. The curious thing is that, despite the Academy presidium's decision to create an ethnic history, it was not undertaken in a scholarly manner. Moreover, no practical aid was rendered to the group; the attendant needs of the summoned scholars were not taken into consideration, and in truth they were not even gathered in one place. . . . The leadership of the Academy, who, in keeping with the inclination of the years of stagnation, think the human factor is dry words, ought to take the matter seriously. We do have capable scholars who can undertake the task—A. Askarov, R. Mukiminova, B. Ahmedov, K. Shaniyazov, and others—but the lethargy may be perpetuated. It is necessary speedily to undertake the study of the ethnogenesis of the Uzbek people, their dawn! So far, no words have appeared about the history of our people. If we know our history well, we can respond to those claims that the ancient treasures of Bukhara and Samarkand have no relation to the Uzbek people, and show how illogical they are.

Summary

"Granted, each individual may be proud of being the offspring of a particular people, praising that fact to the heavens, and experience the accompanying pride, it is no harm"—so wrote Valentin Rasputin in his article "Knowing Oneself as a

Citizen" (*Pravda*, July 24, 1988):

All may be proud of their origins . . . the Armenian of being an Armenian, the Estonian of being an Estonian, the Jew of being Jewish, the Buriat of being a Buriat. Now permit the Russians to become members of this "free, friendly family." They too have contributed something to world culture and civilization.

With pleasure, I wished to convey these sincere words of the Russian author to the esteem of my Uzbek people.

Editor's Notes

a. See W. Barthold, *Turkestan Down to the Mongol Invasion*, 4th ed. (London: E.J.W. Gibb Memorial Trust, 1977) (original 1900), p. 64.

b. Vambery, a Jewish-Hungarian professor of Oriental languages, was the original articulator of the "Pan-Turanian" notion developed among the European players in the "Great Game in Asia." Documents located in the Public Records Office in London indicate that he was in the British service. Vambery wrote a series of books (the first of which is cited by Bartold). See A. Vambery, *Travels in Central Asia* (London, 1865); idem, *Sketches of Central Asia* (London, 1868); and idem, *Das Türkenvolk* (Leipzig, 1885). For archival references, see M. Kemal Öke, "Arminius Vambery and Anglo-Ottoman Relations 1889–1907," *Bulletin of the Turkish Studies Association*, vol. 9, no. 2 (1985).

c. *Shahnama* was written in the eleventh century, on the basis of an older oral tradition, under the Turkish Ghaznavid rule. See C.E. Bosworth, *The Ghaznavids*, 2d ed. (Beirut, 1973). An English translation of *Shahnama* by Theodor Nöldeke was published in Bombay in 1930.

d. *Kutadgu Bilig* was written in the eleventh century by Balasagunlu Yusuf. Yusuf was the "Khass Hajib" (Grand Chamberlain) to the Karakhanid court of Tavgach Bugra Khan. See Bosworth, *The Ghaznavids*. For an English translation by R. Dankoff, see *Wisdom of Royal Glory* (Chicago: University of Chicago Press, 1983).

e. Here Ali provides quotations referring to Turkistan from Alishir Navai's *Tarih-i Mülk-i Ajam*, written after 1485. Reportedly of Uyghur descent, Navai (1441–1501) was one of the premier literati and statesmen of his time. He wrote voluminously and with apparent ease in Chaghatay, a Turk dialect, and Persian, and long served as "prime minister" of the Timurid Huseyin Baykara (r. 1469–1506) of Herat and Khorasan. Much of his work remains untranslated. For collected works, see A.S. Levend, *Ali Sir Nevai* (Ankara, 1965–68), 4 vols.

f. The Russian original was published in 1918. The same argument is also made by Bartold in *Turkestan Down to the Mongol Invasion*, p. 64.

g. See Z.V. Togan, *Türkili Türkistan*, 2d ed. (Istanbul, 1981). Originally written during the 1920s, this work provides lists of the tribes composing various confederations, including the Uzbeks. See the section of this collection devoted to Togan's "The Origins of the Kazaks and the Özbeks."

h. The author seems to agree with Frye and Sayili. See R.N. Frye and A.M. Sayili, "The Turks in Khurasan and Transoxania at the Time of the Arab Conquest," *The Moslem World*, 35 (1945).

i. This is a style of melodic tonality, contour, and pattern. Traditionally, each such "key" and pattern, which number in the dozens, is given a name.

j. Jami (d. 1492), a Persian, was Navai's friend and fellow man of letters.

k. No reference to this title is found in the available Navaiana.

l. *Kabusnama* is by Iskandar Kai Ka'us; *Chahar Makala* by Nizami Arudi Samarkandi. For English translations, see Iskandar Kai Ka'us, *A Mirror for Princes*, tr. R. Levy (London, 1951); and E.G. Browne, *Literary History of Persia* (London, 1902).

m. *Siyasatnama* was written by Nizam al-Mulk (d. 1092), "prime minister" to Al-parslan (r. 1063–1072), and his son Malik Shah (r. 1072–1092) of the Seljuks (dynasty r. 1040–1156). For an English translation, see Nizam al-Mulk, *Siyasatnama: The Book of Government or Rules for Kings*, tr. H. Darke (London, 1960). As for "Gulistan," so many books are so titled that the reference is not readily identifiable.

n. The Seljuks were preceded by the Ghaznavids (994–1186) and followed by the Khwarazm-Shahs (1156–1230). Safavids: 1501–1736. Halokuiy (*sic*): Kara—or Akkoyunlu? The latter ruled 1449–78; both are tribal confederations related to the Oghuz/Seljuk. Nadirshah Afshar: major period of rule generally considered to have been 1730s–1747. Kajars: ruled 1794–1925.

o. *Turkestan Down to the Mongol Invasion*, p. 186.

p. Khans of the Turk Empire before the eighth century.

q. Timur (properly, Temür; corrupted in Western languages as Tamerlane, Tambur-lane, and so forth): a Barlas Turk and founder of the Timurid empire (r. 1369–1405). See *Tüzükat-i Timuri*, tr. Major Davy (Oxford, 1783). Ulugbek (d. 1449), Temür's grandson, ruled Samarkand and environs and was the author of important astronomical and mathe-matical works that, beginning in the seventeenth century, were translated into Latin and printed in Oxford, and influenced European studies. See Kevin Krisciunas, "The Legacy of Ulugh Beg," in *Central Asian Monuments*, ed. H.B. Paksoy (Istanbul: Isis Press, 1992). Bartold utilized a French translation by Sédillot, *Prolégomènes des tables astronomiques d'Oloug-beg* (Paris, 1847–53). See Barthold's *Four Studies on the History of Central Asia*, Vol. II: Ulugh-Beg (Leiden, 1958). Babür (1483–1530), another direct descendant of Temür, was the founder of the Moghul empire in India. He was also an accomplished author in Chaghatay. For his memoir, *Baburnama*, see *The Babur-Nama in English*, tr. Anette S. Beveridge (London, 1922).

r. Despite its title, this influential treatise by Navai on the comparison of Turk and Persian languages (in which Navai staunchly defends "Turki") was written in Turki, also termed Chaghatay in that era. For an English translation, see Ali Shir Navai, *Muhakemat al-lughateyn*, tr. Robert Devereux (Leiden, 1966).

s. "Rumi" was born in Balkh 1207, lived in Asia Minor, died 1273 in Konya; then in the domains of the Seljuks and their successor principalities, now in the central plains of the Turkish Republic.

t. Abu Nasr Farabi: Turk philosopher (d. 950?). See Muhsin Mahdi, tr., *Alfarabi's Philosophy of Plato and Aristotle*, tr. Muhsin Mahdi (New York: Free Press/Macmillan, 1962).

u. Ali's "rehabilitation" of Timur appears to follow the arguments made by Iakubovskii in "Timur (opyt kratkoi kharakteristiki)" [Timur—An Experiment in Charac-terization], *Voprosy istorii*, 1946, nos. 8–9.

v. Bartol'd vehemently advocated a critical approach to sources. This argument is constantly used, in various forms, by Central Asian authors. Concerning the reference to Marx, immediately following: Bartol'd often took exception to the writings of Marx. Reportedly, on one public occasion, when queried as to what Marx would have said about the topic on which he was lecturing, Bartol'd replied: "I know of no Orientalist named Marx."

w. V.V. Bartol'd (Wilhelm Barthold) descended from a German family settled in the Russian Empire. His persistent opposition to Bolshevik historiography landed Bartol'd for a time in a quiet internal exile in Baku. He died in 1930 at the age of 61. His collected works (*sochnineniia*) were published in Moscow in a ten-volume set in the 1960s.

x. On this newspaper, see H.B. Paksoy, *Alpamysh: Central Asian Identity under Russian Rule* (Hartford, 1989), p. 19.

y. E.E. Bertels, a high-level functionary in the Oriental Institute in Moscow during the 1930s–50s, was charged with "managing" the history of the "Soviet East." See ibid.

z. Ziya Buniatov (Bunyat oglu): director of the Oriental Institute of the Azerbaijan SSR Academy of Sciences; later, vice president of the Azerbaijan SSR Academy of Sciences.

a'. Muhammad bin Jarir at-Tabari, d. 923. His works were translated into Western languages beginning 1879, and published from 1901 on.

b'. Academician Ahmadali Askarov: a deputy chairman of the Uzbek SSR Academy of Sciences. An archeologist by training, Askarov oversees most of the social science departments, including history. According to recent oral reports, he may have been promoted to a ministerial post in Uzbekistan.

Zeki Velidi Togan

The Origins of the
Kazaks and the Özbeks

Editor's Introduction

A professor of history for over half a century, Zeki Velidi Togan (1890–1970), a Bashkurt Turk, studied and taught in institutions of higher learning on three continents, including the United States.[1] His first book, *Türk ve Tatar Tarihi* (Turk and Tatar History), was published in Kazan in 1911. The renowned scholars N. Ashmarin and N. Katanov (1862–1922),[2] both of Kazan University, and V.V. Bartold (1869–1930) of St. Petersburg University, invited Togan to study with them.

In 1913, Togan was asked by the Archeology and Ethnography Society of Kazan University to undertake a research trip to Turkistan. After successful completion of that endeavor, the Imperial Russian Academy of Sciences,[3] jointly with International Central Asia Research Society, sponsored Togan for a more extensive expedition. Portions of Togan's findings began to be published in scholarly journals prior to the First World War. His lifetime output approaches four hundred individual items in at least five languages. He also had facility in several others.

Like the Ukrainian scholar Mikhail Hrushevsky (1866–1934) and the Czech Thomas Masaryk (1850–1937), Togan was not only a scholar devoted to writing about the history of his nation, but also worked to secure its intellectual, cultural, civil, and political independence. He became a leader of the Turkistan National

Excerpted from *Bugünkü Türkili Türkistan ve Yakin Tarihi*, 2d ed. (Istanbul, 1981), p. 31ff. The first edition was published in Istanbul in 1947. It should be noted that there was an original edition in the Arabic alphabet, but it was not widely circulated due to the Second World War. This translation by H.B. Paksoy appeared in *Central Asian Survey*, vol. 11, no. 3 (1992).

Liberation Movement in Central Asia (1916–1930s), called the Basmachi Movement by the Russians. A revealing anecdote is offered by A. Inan, a close colleague of Togan both as a historian and as a leading member of the Turkistan National Liberation movement. The event takes place in June 1922 in the vicinity of Samarkand:

> When a Bolshevik military unit, detailed to liquidate us, opened fire, we took refuge in a nearby cemetery. As we began defending ourselves, I noticed that Togan had taken out his ever-present notebook and was busily scribbling. The circumstances were so critical that some of those among our ranks even thought that he was hurriedly recording his last will and testament. He kept writing, seemingly oblivious to the flying bullets aimed at him, and the accompanying sounds of war. I shouted at him from behind the tombstone that was protecting me, and asked why he was not fighting. Without looking up, continuing to write, he shouted back: "You continue firing. The inscriptions on these headstones are very interesting."[4]

Togan's investigation of the origin of the Kazaks and the Özbeks is adapted from his *Türkili Türkistan*, a project he worked on during the 1920s, a period when he was establishing extensive contacts with the Central Asian population from Ferghana to the shores of the Caspian on behalf of the Turkistan National Liberation Movement. After he left Central Asia, and earned his doctorate in Europe, he continued his research using published sources. Though completed in 1928, the work was not published until 1947, in Istanbul.

Togan's analysis and documentation in the excerpt printed here may contribute to the clarification of the issues involved in efforts to rediscover the "ethnogenesis" of the "Uzbeks," "Kazakhs,"[5] and other Central Asians. It should be recalled that these designations are primarily geographical, tribal, or confederation names, not ethnonyms. Often they were taken from geographic reference points by travelers and then were mistakenly or deliberately turned into ethnic or political classifications. Early in the eighth century, Central Asians themselves provided an account of their identity, history, and political order.[6] Later efforts to identify and disseminate information concerning the genealogy of Central Asians can be traced to a wave of native Central Asian leadership that was suppressed in the Stalinist liquidations. Examples from the period survive in abundance, in Central Asian dialects, published in three alphabets in various Central Asian cities.

Notes

1. In addition to Togan's *Hatiralar* (Memoirs) (Istanbul, 1969), this account makes use of bibliographic material appearing in *Fen-Edebiyat Fakültesi Arastirma Dergisi*, Atatürk Üniversitesi, Erzurum (Sayi 13, 1985) and information provided by Togan's colleagues, students, and family friends.

2. Despite their names, neither was Russian, but both had been baptized. Togan calls

Katanov a Sagay-Turk from the Altai region, and Ashmarin a Chuvash-Turk.

3. For a description of the formation of the Academy, see R.N. Frye, "Oriental Studies in Russia," in *Russia and Asia: Essays on the Influence of Russia on the Asian Peoples*, ed. Wayne Vucinich (Stanford: Stanford University Press, 1972).

4. Over the years I have been told of this incident independently by several students and friends of both Inan and Togan. Later in life it seems to have occasioned numerous droll exchanges between Inan and Togan; every time Inan mentioned the incident, Togan relished recounting the story of Inan's having been "wounded" in the same battle. The two men endured arduous times together, both in Asia and in Europe, and later in their careers became colleagues at Istanbul University, where, reportedly, each sent his students to the seminars of the other. On one occasion toward the end of their lives, when Inan became seriously ill, Togan asked his doctoral students to visit Inan at the hospital and read him passages from Togan's *Hatiralar* (which was still in manuscript), especially the portion about "Inan's wounding." Indeed, Togan records the fighting in his memoirs, including Inan's "wounding," but not his own "note-taking." He simply states that he "read the headstones written in the Kufi script" (*Hatiralar*, p. 414). Togan identifies the location of the cemetery as Qala-i Ziyaeddin.

5. Note that Togan and other historians spell these words Özbek and Kazak, respectively. "Özbek" is the only form encountered in the material published in Tashkent during the 1928–39 period, when a subset of the Latin alphabet was used. The term "Cossack" (Russian: *Kazak*), incidentally, is a corruption of "Kazak" (Russian: *Kazakh*), though there is little, if any, ethnic relation between them. Similarly, the term "Tatar," as found in the *Kültigin* (of the *Orkhon* group) stelea of the eighth century A.D., is a correct rendition. During the Mongol irruption of the thirteenth century, Western authors inaccurately used "Tartarus" (which actually refers to "the infernal regions of Roman and Greek mythology," hence, hell), yielding the form "Tartar." By that time "Tartarus" had already been assimilated into Christian theology in Europe. Possibly St. Louis of France was the first, in 1270, to apply this unrelated term and spelling to the Chinggisid troops of Jochi.

6. These were recorded on scores of stelea, written in their unique alphabet and language, and erected in the region of Orkhon-Yenisey. See Talat Tekin, *A Grammar of Orkhon Turkic*. Indiana University Uralic and Altaic Series, vol. 69 (Bloomington/The Hague: Mouton, 1968) (contents dating from the eighth century).

THE ORIGINS OF THE KAZAKS AND THE ÖZBEKS

The Concepts of Tatar, Kipchak, Togmak, and Özbek

Tatar, Kipchak, Togmak, and Özbek: The nomadic populace of the entire *Desht-i Kipchak* [Kipchak steppe], from the Tarbagatay mountains to the Syr Darya River, and from Khorezm to the Idil [Volga] basin and Crimea, were termed "Togmak" during the era of the Mongols, prior to the spread of Islam. Among the Khiva Özbeks, the term (in Ebülgazi)[a] known as "Togma"; Baskurts "Tuvma;" Nogay (according to the Cevdet Pasha history),[b] "Tokma" designated individuals without a known lineage, or fugitives to be sold as slaves, being offenders of the law. The negative connotation ascribed to this term, generally referencing the Kipchaks and Altin Orda (Golden Horde) Tatars, must have occurred after the spread of Islam. It is not known that the Jochi Ulus utilized that appellation. It appears that this tribe, known as "Togmak," had been designated as "Özbek" after "Özbek Khan" (1312–1340). According to Bartold, the terms "Özbek" and "Özbek Ulus" have been utilized in Central Asia to distinguish this tribe and its entire military population from the "Chaghatay"; until the dissolution of the Altin Orda during the fifteenth century, and the dissemination of its urukᶜ as Özbek, Kazak, and Nogay Ulus. Their identifying battle cryᵈ was the word *alach*.

It is necessary to define some of the ethnic terms in use in the Jochi Ulus: The Özbeks of today, living in Transoxiana and Khorezm, comprise the dominant group known under the general rubric "tatar" in the Jochi Ulus. However, it is possible that the term "tatar" was used in a wider context, applying not only to the dominant group but perhaps also to the dominated. The term Kipchak also has dual connotations, applying narrowly and specifically to the Kipchak lineage as well as generally and broadly to the entire populace of the Kipchak steppe, including the Özbeks. According to our findings, the term "tatar" earlier applied within the Jochi Ulus only to the Turk and Mongol elements issuing from the east, to the dominant component, and "kipchak" to the subject nomadic tribes of the steppe. The term "Togmak" became the general term of reference to all. After the Özbek Khan, the word "Özbek" applied to all "Tatar" and "Kipchak" in their totality, replacing "Togmak." However, the Kipchak and the "Tatar," arriving from the east during the age of the Mongols, mixed with the elements of the older civilization of the land, as opposed to the nomadic tribes, and started forming, let us say, the "Yataq Tatar" or "Yataq Kipchak."* Then, "Tatar" began to assume a wider meaning than "Özbek," and the term "Özbek" became the appellation of the nomadic aristocraciesᵉ of the Özbek, Nogay, Kazak, and Baskurt [confederations] that separated from the Tatar and the Kipchak societies. Nevertheless, although the word "Tatar" had lost its previous meaning, in the vernacular of the people it continued to be utilized as "Elin Tatari," meaning the "Aristocracy of the Land." Moreover, since the trade was in the hands of the Tatar "Ortaq"ᶠ firms during the Mongol period (especially Mongol and Uyghur), "Tatar" also meant "merchant." During the fourteenth and fifteenth centuries, when the dominant military-nomadic Tatar and Kipchak amalgamation of the Jochi Ulus emerged as the Özbeks, those not belonging to the ruling tribes formed other strata as follows:

1. "As," of the old civilization of the Kipchak steppe, in the vicinity of Astrakhan and Saray; "Bulgar-Kazan" Turksᵍ of the Middle Idil; Burtas and Mokshi (in Islamic and Mongolian sources, "Möks"); in the Crimea region, "Tat" and the remnants of the old Khazars; Istek and Ibir-Sibir tribes in western Siberia;

2. Kipchak and Bashkurt, who were settled. Those among them in the region of the Urals are also known as "Tepter" (*defter*), having been so recorded in registers;

---

*"Yataq" or "C[J]ataq" is used to designate settled, or semisettled, peaceful populations.

3. Some portions of today's Kazak and Baskurt, who stayed away from political life, living from earlier times as neighbors of the Siberian tribes of "Istek."

Even today, it is possible to distinguish the dominant and subject Turks within the Jochi Ulus: the dominant uruks remember the dastans of historical personages and the traditions of the steppe aristocracy, while the subject uruks remember only the dastans of the shamanistic mythology and traditions of "charva"* and are unaware of the political and historical dastans.

The Language, Customs, and Traditions
of the Old Kipchak-Özbek

The fourteenth- and fifteenth-century Arab authors (Ibn Battuta, Ibn Fadl allah al-Umari, and Ibn Arabshah) have described well the life, mores, and character of the Özbeks and the Kipchaks of the Kipchak steppe. According to Ibn Arabshah, the Özbek Turks of the Kipchak steppe are regarded as possessing the most lucid language, their men and women are the most handsome, generally displaying aristocratic bearing, not deigning to trickery or lies, being the gentle-folk of all the Turks.[h] The language of these Özbeks, living from Yedisu to Crimea, can be observed in the poetry fragments and other monuments coming down to us, is generally the same; and its Kipchak characteristics have been partially preserved in the speech of today's Özbek, Kazak, and Mangit-Nogay.[t] Their way of life and customs, parallel to "Türk-Chigil" and "Türkmen-Oguz" group,[i] is the same. Their written histories,[‡] folk literature, and especially heroic epics of the Kipchak steppe such as *Chinggis, Jochi and his Sons, Edige, Toktamis, Nureddin, Chora Batir*,[j] and *Koblandi*, their verse stories, *Cirenche Chechen* recitations, and others, are the same everywhere. The melodies of the Baskurt and nomadic Özbeks are today recited among the Crimean and Constanza Nogays. The Nogay dastans are recited word for word among the Karakalpak and the Kazak of Khorezm. The old and the new Kipchak Turks did not engage in "black service"[§] occupations and considered themselves as the master; they have not made the transition to farming except under extreme necessity, regarding it an occupation contrary to the spirit of the steppe aristoc-

---

*From the Persian "chaharpa," referring to keeping four-legged animals.

†These characteristics are as follows: (1) "ch" of other Turkish dialects becomes "s" or "sh"; (2) in the particles ending with letters "l" and "n," those letters become "d" in the concatenation process; (3) "gh" and "g" in the middle or at the end of a word become "v" or "y" if they are preceded by a vowel; (4) if the "gh" or "g" occurs before a vowel, it will extend that vowel; (5) instead of "ä," a long "e" is used.

‡*Tarikh-i Dost Sultan*; *Tarikhi Kitay* of Baba Ali; *Secere-i Türk* of Ebülgazi Bahadir Han; *Camiüttevarih* of Ali Calayir.

§*Kara Hizmet* (Black Service) refers to manual labor.

racy; and even under severe economic crisis they did not allow their daughters to marry sedentary grooms. In this regard, the Nogays had shown the greatest exaggeration, and were cut down in their tens of thousands and even hundreds of thousands during the Kalmak [Mongol] and Russian occupations. Among them, the historical personae and epic heroes such as Chinggis, Toktamis, Edige, Er Tagin, Urak Mamay, and Adil Sultan personify the spirit and the ideals of the steppe aristocracy. In the collective and unified *dastan* literature of the Özbek of the old Jochi Ulus, comprising the current Özbek, Kazak, Mangit-Nogay, and Baskurt, the following elements of ethics, moral qualities, and characteristics are discernible: exaltation of endeavor; readiness to die in defense of honor; the principle of espousing society and state above all; enduring difficulties with ease; belief that efforts expended in overcoming obstacles facilitate progress; willingness to undertake long and arduous journeys; women's desire only for men in possession of these qualities; and the elevated position of noble women and mothers in the society. These are all proclaimed in the literature of the old Tatar and Kipchak aristocratic strata, meaning Özbek literature. Generally, the good and the bad customs and habits of the old Turks are evident even more overtly among the Özbek-Kipchak: imperturbability (levelheadedness); dislike of confusion; moderation; courage; an affinity for being in charge; harshness in battle but extreme calmness in peace; not killing but selling of prisoners; purity of heart and honesty; their extreme sincerity taken advantage of by the enemy; amplifying small conflicts between individuals and uruks, causing them to drag out over years and even generations; becoming materialistic under severe economic conditions, which culminates in the selling of family members or stealing and selling of others. All these are the attributes of the Özbek and the Kipchak, recorded by the Arab travelers beginning with Ibn Battuta, since the time of the Özbek Han.*

Division of the "Özbek" Society into Özbek, Kazak, and Mangit-Nogay

The division of the Özbeks into "Özbek," "Kazak," and "Mangit-Nogay" took place not in the Idil basin but while they were living in the Syr Darya basin. Sons of Jochi "Batu" and "Berke" Han had influence over the Chagatay Ulus; most of Transoxiana was subject to the Altin Orda. Khorezm and the lower Syr Darya, beginning from the Otrar region, belonged to the Jochi Ulus according to the division of the Mongols. In the military organization of the Jochi Ulus, this area constituted the "Sol Kol" tribes; in the administrative division, it formed the "Gök Orda." During 1358–61, when the affairs of the Altin Orda (also known as Ak Orda) became muddled, the "Kiyat" beys, commanding all the troops of the "Sag Kol" [Right Flank] tribes, brought them to Crimea, and the "Sol Kol" [Left

---

*Such records are found in ibn al-Faqih, Idrisi, ibn Fadl allah al-Umari, Bedreddin al-Ayni, and the English Jenkinson.

Flank] tribes to Syr Darya. At the time, since the lineage of Batu had come to an end, according to the *yasa* [Mongol customary law][k] and the law of inheritance, the ultimate rule was passed on to the descendants of Shiban Han,[*] Jochi's fifth son. Many Özbek uruks in today's Turgay province, in the vicinity of "Ak Göl" [White Lake], raised to the throne as Han Hizir, who was a descendant of the Shiban. Nayman, Karluk, Uyghur, Kongrat, and Böyrek uruks were in favor. However, the rule of this descendant of Shiban was confined to a portion of the "Sol Kol" confederations and the "Tura" stronghold of the Tobol basin in western Siberia. The uruks of the Syr Darya of the Sol Kol raised "Kara Nogay Han," a son of Sü Bas, descendant of "Tokay Temür," who had not until that day been involved in the affairs of government. It appears that the "Sol" uruks of this region comprised Shirin, Barin Kipchak, Argun, Alchin, Katay, Mangit, and Kürlevüt, collectively known as "Yedi San."[l] The bases of these Sol Han were in the cities of Yenikend, Cend, Barchinlig Kent, Sabran, Otrar, and the core, Siginak. Evidently, some of those uruks were even then involved in the affairs of the Transoxiana. Among the soldiery of Temür,[m] the Kipchak and the Nayman played important roles. During the era of Temür's sons, Özbeks became rather powerful (1427), under the leadership of "Barak Han," a descendant of Tokay Temür. When Barak was killed in 1429, descendants of Shiban Han occupied Syr Darya basin. Accordingly, the real center of the Jochi Ulus (Ak Orda) moved next to Transoxiana. At the same time, Mangit, who were backing the descendants of Tokay Temür, acquired great influence under the rule of "Edige Beg," which means "Temür Bek of the Altin Orda." Other uruk joined them, and all together became known as "Mangit," because of the appellation of the dominant uruk, and on the other hand as "Nogay" (probably because they raised Kara Nogay Han).[†] Hence I have used the appellation Mangit-Nogay throughout this work. At the beginning of the sixteenth century, "Shiban-Özbek" Han and the uruks subject to them arrive and settle in Transoxiana and Khorezm. At that time, the western regions of today's Kazakistan, as well as Baskurt and Tura lands, became subjected to Mangit-Nogay in their entirety. In this manner, a strong Mangit-Nogay society is constituted as opposed to the Özbeks.

The aforementioned rulers, Kirey and Canibek, sons of Barak Han, were subject to the famous Ebulkhayir of Shiban descent. In 1466 they left this Han

---

[*]It is incorrect to read this name as "sheyban," which is an Arab tribal name. The reading Shiban is based upon their genealogy as written in the Uyghur alphabet and in some manuscripts. . . .

[†]The name "Nogay" may have been propagated due to Price Nogay (or "Nokay"; d. 1299), ancestor of Edüge Bey, who had lived on the Byzantium frontier and ruled the Ön Kol uruk. But no records to that effect were encountered. Later, the term "Nogay" was ascribed to the tribes carrying this appellation by other uruks living to the west and north of them. Mangit rulers, in their letters addressing the Russians, referred to themselves as "Nogay Ruler." The tribes living to the east and south, in Transoxiana and Khorezm, called them "Mangit."

and became "kazak," sought asylum from the descendants of Chagatay to their east (the Hans ruling in the environs of Kashgar and Yedisu), acquired the obedience of some uruks to themselves, and with that aid once again obtained the allegiance of uruks that owed fealty to them but were living in the domains of the descendants of Shiban. Accordingly, next to the "Shiban Özbek," a "Kazak Özbek" society was established. Thus, the Özbek society comprised three powerful groups during the second half of the fifteenth century. What earlier belonged to the Gök Orda Han and the descendants of Tokay Temür became the domains of Shiban Han. The possessions of the Shiban are taken over by the Nogay princes. Kazaks, on the other hand, demanded shares in both as well as in the Chagatay domains. During the mid-sixteenth century, the "Mangit-Nogay" princes were situated in "Arka" and "Ulu Tav," which constitutes the center of today's Kazakistan; began meddling in the affairs of lands west of Idil, even the shores of Azak; and slowly shifted westward. The lands in contention, the lower Syr Darya basin and Arka regions, became depopulated. As a result, these regions came under the rule of Kazak Hans, who previously had lived in Talas and Chu. During the second half of the seventeenth century, first the "Nogay" and later, during the first half of the eighteenth century, "Kalmak" matters became upset, and Kazak Hans became the sole ruler of all steppes east of the Yayik [Ural] river. Nogay withdrew toward Crimea and the northern Caucasus.

Kazak Hans, after separation from the Shiban Özbeks, began referring to their neighboring Kazaks as "Kazak Özbekleri." In Haydar Mirza Douglat's history, they are also so termed.[n]

Kazaklar

The Word "Kazak" and the Concept of Being a "Kazak"

The name "Kazak" was at first reserved for the rulers; later, it also applied to tribes owing fealty to them and to the states they wished to establish. Prior to that time the name "Kazak" did not even apply to a tribal confederation, let alone to the state. Generally, the term "Kazak" was employed to designate those who were left without a family (*boydak*) due to a rebellion of political nature; sometimes those who withdrew from society, to the mountains and wildernesses, to await more favorable times before taking over governmental matters, without the benefit and protection of the tribe; to adolescent boys who had been separated to help them become accustomed to life; and to those who left their lands to become ordinary brigands. Under the influence of the Turk, the tradition of sending the sons out with a weapon also became accepted among the Russians and recorded in Islamic sources, and is referenced as "Kazak" in Turkish even today as well as in the past. A political person becoming Kazak leaves that designation after settling down in a land following conquest, or joining another political personage to legitimize himself. He remembers his "Kazak" past as days of his youth when he learned to endeavor and endure difficulties (like Temür, and among his sons Ebu Sait Mirza, Hüseyin Baykara, Babür Mirza, and, from among the Özbeks, Shiban Han and his followers). Of course, a man can be a Kazak only for a few years in his lifetime. In that context, the concept of "Kazak" is in opposition to statehood. Kasim Han and his son Hak Nazar, descendants of Canibek and Giray, who had become kazak toward the end of the fifteenth century, tended to view their own states in that way, as temporary.

At the end of the sixteenth century (1599), the Kazak rulers left the "Chu" region under pressure from the northeastern Kalmaks, and took refuge in the strongholds of Tashkent and environs. Until 1723 and another Kalmak rout, they settled in those regions and attempted to have the steppe tribes convert to sedentary agriculture. In pursuit of that policy, "Tug Baglayip," which means announcing the official flag of the state, established some sort of administrative apparatus and attempted to establish a state "devlet tüzümek" by grouping the troops into "Yüz" [hundred] and "Bin" [thousand]. The Orda (headquarters) of the Han was divided into three, namely "Uluyüz," "Ortayüz," and "Kichiyüz." Among the Özbek, the terms "Han" and "Kalgay" were used to designate the ruler, the first heir, and the second heir; among the Nogay, "Bek," "Nuradin," "Keykubad" signified the same ranks. It is thought that the act of dividing the Han Orda into three (names alternately used were "Ulugorda," "Ortaorda," and "Kichikorda") was inherited from a time when an experiment in pursuit of establishing a governmental structure was conducted. However, the pressure of the Kalmaks, and later, the Russians (from Siberia), did not allow them to establish a permanent government and live under that structure, encompassing the elements of all the tribes. The tribes living in the territories northeast of the steppes, having termed themselves "Kazak," adopted the Özbek and Nogay aristocracy's equivalent of an "animal husbandry, tent-dwelling" way of life. The weakness of the Kazak statehood was of course affected by that.

The Growth of Kazaks

The portion of the steppe inhabited by the Özbeks became the domains of the Nogay, who became subject to the Kazak Hans. During the sixteenth century (at the time of the Saydak and Yusuf Mirza), the Mangit-Nogay on the eastern side of the Idil alone numbered about two million. The formation of the Temür state in the east and conquest of Istanbul and the annexation of Crimea in the west forced the tribes of the Idil to choose between "Bukhara" (Transoxiana) and "Rum" [Asia Minor]; I shall return to [this matter] in the history section below. This did not allow the retention of the tribes in the lower Idil and Yayik in order to structure a powerful state. When in 1558 the Russians intruded into these domains, depriving the tribes of their herds and forcing them to live under individuals such as Alchi Ismail, who worked with the Russians, the tribes were dispersed. Continued attacks of the Kalmak, and finally their settling between Idil and Yayik during 1643, forced an important portion of the Nogay, with the political and aristocratic strata at their head, to move to Crimea, and from there to the Caucasus and further west. But the overwhelming majority of the two million Nogay living to the east of Idil remained there. A portion of them migrated to Khorezm and the Syr Darya basin. In that regard, new tribes arrived in Transoxiana from the Kipchak steppe at the time of the Abdülaziz (1645–1680) and Süphan Kulu (1680–1702), the descendants of Astrakhan Hans now ruling in Bukhara, strengthening the Kazak Hans. Likewise, the "Kazak" tribes living in Turgay and Ural consist of those tribes earlier included under Nogay. During the second half of the sixteenth and the seventeenth century the evacuation by the Turk tribes of the Idil basin was so serious, especially after the Kalmak migrations to the west of Idil and to Jungaria, that the Idil-Yayik region was virtually empty until the nineteenth century. The "Kazak" tribes arriving here in 1801 under the rule of Bükey Han of the Kichiyüz consisted entirely of "Nogay" tribes who had lived there earlier.

During the third quarter of the eighteenth century, the Kazak Hans were in control of the region from "Idil" and "Yayik" to Jungaria, receiving patents from the Russian (St. Petersburg) and Chinese (Beijing) governments, regarding the patents as those governments' special praises of the Kazak Hans. The tribes, living over such a wide territory and apart from each other on the steppes, did not distance themselves from each other in language and customs. On the contrary, they have preserved the unity of their dialect, customs, and traditions, despite their illiteracy, because of their intermixing at the time of the Kalmaks, and later during the competition of the Hans, migrating from one region to the next, from east to west, and then again from west to east. The emergence of their common heroic personae—through their struggles with the Kalmak on the steppes, through large gatherings (for example, the wedding celebrations of the Hans and the Beys, and "as" feasts, or "Yog" ceremonies),° through the participation of representatives of all "Kazak" tribes in the poetic contests held at such occasions, and through the recited poems which propagated the styles and common traits throughout the tribes—preserved the traditions and customs. Today, from Jungaria to the Idil basin, the dialect of the Kazaks is altogether the same. However, their long life away from the influence of a central Han; their nonparticipation in large political events, resulting in isolation from international political life; and their preoccupation with tribal politics in addition to living with the spirit of "Kazaklik" have not failed to influence these Turks. Generally, in political and intellectual life the old "Kazaklik" is still regarded as a virtue. They are also wary of other, neighboring Turks. This, of course, is the negative aspect of Kazaklik. On the other hand, since the Kazaks are not under the strong influence of an old culture, they are better and speedily able to grasp the contemporary scientific methods and ideas faster than the neighboring cultivated Turk tribes.

Kazak tribes and their divisions: "Uluyüz" included eleven uruks:* Duvlat (its *oymak* are: Buptay, Cimir, Siyqim, Canis), Adban, Suvan, Chaprasti, Esti, Ochakti, Sari Uysun, Calayir, Qangli, Chanchkili, and Sirgeli. According to old reckoning, "Uluyüz" population totals 460,000. They live in the Yedisu and Syr Darya provinces.

"Ortayüz" has five uruks: Girey, Nayman, Argin, Qipchaq, and Qongrat. Girey has two oymaks: "Uvak Girey" (aris: Cantiqay, Cadik, Chiruchi, Iteli, Qaraqas, Mülgü, Chobar-Aygir, Merket, It-Imgen, Cas-Taban, Sarbas, Chi-Moyun) and "Qara-Girey" (aris: Morun [soy: Bayis {tire: Morun, Siban, Qurdcay, Tuma} and Baysiyiq {tire: Semiz Nayman, Bulatchi, Toqpaq}] and Bay-Ciket [soy: Cumuq and Tugas]). Girey live in the Kara Irtis, Irtis, Obagan, Kisma Isim, and Oy river basins. "Nayman" tribe has twelve oymaks: Aqbora, Bulatchi, Ters Tamgali, Törtovul, Kökcarli, Ergenekti, Semiz Baganali, Sadir, Matay, Sari Cumart, Qazay, Baltali. Nayman were living in the direction of Ulutav, Balkas, and Tarbagatay. According to old reckoning, they number 500,000. Of their lineage, Baganali has three aris: Toqbulat (soy: Ciriq, Ibiske, Qizil Taz, Qara Bala, Sari Sargaldaq); Sustan (soy: Boydali, Bes Bala); Aq Taz (soy: Teney, Baliqchi, Qarmaqchi, Seyid [tire: Bay Emet, Churtay {ara: Ataliq, Mamay, Babas, Bulatchi Nayman}, Cumuq, Calman, Badana]). "Argin" tribe is divided into three large oymak: Mumin (aris: Bigendik, Chigendik [soy: Atigay, Bagis, Qancagali, Tobuqti, Qaravul, Sari, Chaqchaq {tire: Tuman, Amancul, Küchey, Baqay, Cüzey, Aq Nazar, Tenet, Qarabas, Qalqaman, Bay Emet, Qochkar}, Cetim], Madyar, Tölek); Quvandiq (aris: Altay, Qarpiq, Temes, Agis, Qalqaman, Aydabul); Söyündük (aris: Qurucas, Quzgan, Qusqal, Töki); in addition, there is an independent "Qara Qisek" aris (containing the soy: Törtovul, Taraqti). According to old reckoning, Argin number 89,000. They are living in the Irtish, Isim, Tobol basin. "Qongrat" tribe is subdivided into two large oymak: Köktin Ogli and Kütenci (aris: Cemtimler, Mangitay, Qara Köse, Quyusqansiz, Teney, Toqbulat, Baylar-Cancar, Busman). Qongrats are living in the Syr Darya basin. "Qipchaq" has four large oymak: Kök Mürün, Küldenen, Buchay, Qara Baliq. Qipchaq possess numerous aris, soy, and tire. They principally live in the "Oy," "Tobol," and "Turgay" basins.

"Kichi Yüz" is composed of three tribes: Alimoglu (in the Kazak pronunciation, "Elimolu"), Bayoglu (Kazak pronunciation, "Bayoli"), Yedi Urug (Kazak pronunciation "Ceti-ru"). The aris of "Alimoglu" are Qarasaqal (soy: Chunqara [tire: Qangildi, Kütkülech, Sekerbay, Batan, Car Boldi], Saribas [tire: Baqti-Berdi, Bavbek, Nazim], Busurman [tire: Nogay, Gasikür, Cekey], Törtqara [tire: Turum {ara: Chavdar, Aviqman, Qachan, Toguz Seksen}, Toqman {ara: Saqal, Can-Keldi, Sekerbay, Kütkülech, Khan Geldi}, Qasim {ara: Ayit, Seksek, Madi, Baqcan}, Appaq {ara: Qara-Kese, Ak-Bes, Batan}]), Qara-Kisek, Kite, Tört-Qara, Chümekey, Chekli, Qara-Kisek, Qazan-Taban, Istek, Bayis, Esen Geldi, Cakev. Aris of "Bayoglu" are Aday (soy: Baliqchi, Aqman, Tübüs [tire: Zarubay, Chunqay, Bavbek, Tabunay, Chikem, Bebkey], Mugal [tire: Chavlay, Cheküy], Chibeney [tire: Cumart, Chelim], Qonaq [tire: Urus, Toq-Sara], Qosay, Tüküchey); Cappas (soy: Kineki, Kirman, Sumruq, Andarchay, Qoldiqay, Qara-Köz, Qalqaman), Alacha, Baybaqti (soy: Qanq [tire: Küli Sunduq, Bavbek, Aliz], El-Teke, Bataq [tire: Chabachi, Qolchiq, Sagay, Cavgati, Tuqabay, Buganay, Köchmen, Itemke]), Masqar (soy: Qutluch-Atam, Babanazar, Masaq), Beris (soy: Sibaq, Nogay, Qayli-Qach, Can-Mirza [tire: Toqman, Bes-Qasqay], Isiq), Tazlar, Isen-Temir, Chirkes (soy: Küsün [tire: Samay, Umurzaq, Ütegen, Ulcabay], Cavqachiq, Qis-Kistek, Küyüs, Ilmen), Tana, Qizil-Kurt (soy: El-Chula, Subi), Seyikhlar, Altun (soy: Calabaq, Aydurgay, Sagay). The aris of "Yedi Uruk" are: Tabin, Tama, Kirderi (soy: Yabagu), Cagalbayli, Kireyit, Tilev, Ramazan.

---

*Uruk→Oymak→Aris→Soy→Tire→Ara.

Of these tribes, "Elimolu" is living in the Ural province, along the lower reaches of the Syr Darya, southeast of Aral Lake, on the eastern side of Khorezm and in eastern Bukhara; "Bayolu" tribe is in Bökey Orda, in Ural province, Mangislak, and all of Üst Yurt. "Yedi Uruklar," on the other hand, are living in Ural and Turgay provinces. According to old reckoning, the population of "Kichi Yüz" is shown to be 800,000.

Özbekler

The Özbek Tribes Arriving in Transoxiana

The Özbek of the present day arrived with all the organizations and institutions existing among the Shiban Özbeks and Transoxiana and Khorezm Jochi Ulus. In fact, the hierarchy ("orun") occupied in government by the tribes was the same. Özbeks, while succeeding the descendants of the Temür, replaced the existing establishments with their own.

Also arriving were the elements close to the palace circles of the "Ich Eli" of the Altin Orda, meaning quite civilized components. Moreover, according to the terminology of chronicler Ötemis Haci,* the descendants of Shiban arriving in Transoxiana comprised the ruling elements of the old "Özbek Eli" (meaning Golden Horde), "famed Tura named Mangit Villages," meaning western Siberian "Tura" province where the settled Mangit ulus lived.P Turgay province, with its center in today's "Ak-Göl," "Chalkar-Göl," belonged to the descendants of Shiban. Previously, Abulhayir Han, who took away the "Tura and Baskurt" regions from the other branch of the Shiban descendants from west Siberian Han Mahmudek, was governing these territories. Abulhayir later obtained the lower reaches of Syr Darya and, in 1431, Khorezm. Abulhayir pursued the policy of basing the governance of the state upon the southern and northern agricultural and settled regions of the Jochi Ulus. Hüseyin Khorezmi, the great scholar of the time, wrote a Turkish poem praising this ruler, entitled "Kaside-i Burde," appended to one of his works.† Another scholar, named Mesut Kohistani, wrote a Persian language history book depicting the life of this ruler.‡ During the sixteenth century a large portion of the Özbeks made the transition to village and agricultural life in the Zarafshan basin and in Khorezm. They perhaps belong to the elements arriving from the Syr Darya and "Tura" regions where they were already making the transformation. Shiban Han was a ruler accustomed to tra-

---

*The only manuscript of the history of Golden Horde and the Özbeks, written circa 1550 by Ötemis Haci of Khorezm, called *Tarikh-i Dost Sultan*, is in my private library. Only an early fragment of it is in the Tashkent Library. The referenced portion is from page 72b in my manuscript.

†Previously, the existence of this work was known only from the quotations made of it in other works (see E. Blochet, Paris manuscript catalog, II, 122), but in 1924 I found a copy of it in the Berlin State Library (Hartmann manuscript catalog, no. 69).

‡See *Encyclopedia of Islam*, I, pp. 102–4, entry "Abul-Khayir." A copy of this manuscript, under the title "Tarikh-i Abul-Khayir Khani," is in the British Museum.

versing the area between Syr Darya and Astrakhan. Shibanli Mehdi and Hamza Sultan, who had arrived in Transoxiana before Shiban, were the sons of Bahtiyar Sultan, the ruler of the settled regions, strongholds, and castles of the "Tura" province. It is thought that the Özbek arriving with them did so at the time of later Temürids.

Turning to the tribal organization: "Özbek" are referred to everywhere as "doksan iki boy Özbek" [Ninety-two Tribe Özbek]. Here *boy* means tribe. For the Baskurt, the term "Twelve Tribe Baskurt" is used. Among the Özbek, there is a "genealogy" naming their ninety two-tribes.

There are slight discrepancies between the new and the sixteenth-seventeenth–century manuscript copies of the genealogy (for example, the "Akhund Kurbanali," "Khanikov," and "Sheykh Süleyman" published versions). Undoubtedly, this genealogy lists those tribes at the time of the Altin Orda, meaning prior to the separation of the Mangit-Nogay and the Kazak. They are as follows: Min, Yüz, Qirq, Üngechit, Calayir, Saray, On, Qonrat, Alchin, Nayman, Argin, Qipchaq, Chichak, Qalmaq, Uyrat, Qarliq, Turgavut, Burlas, Buslaq, Chemerchin, Qatagan, Kilechi, Kineges, Böyrek, Qiyat, Bozay, Qatay (Khitay), Qanli, Özce Buluci (?), Topchi (?), Upulachi, Culun, Cit, Cuyut, Salcavut, Bayavut, Otarchi, Arlat, Kireyit, Unqut, Mangit, Qangit, Oymavut, Qachat, Merkit, Borqut, Quralas, Qarlap, Ilaci, Gülegen (?), Qisliq, Oglan, Küdey, Türkmen, Dürmen, Tabin, Tama, Mechet, Kirderi, Ramadan, Mumun, Aday, Tuqsaba, Qirgiz, Uyruci, Coyrat, Bozaci, Oysun, Corga, Batas, Qoysun, Suldiz, Tumay, Tatar, Tilev, Qayan, Sirin, Kürlevüt, Chilkes, Uygur, Yabu(=Yabaqu), Agir(=Agiran), Buzan, Buzaq, Müyten, Macar, Qocaliq, Choran, Chürchüt, Barin(=Behrin), Mogul, Nöküs [Nukus].

Thirty-three of these tribal names belong to the Mongol, others to the renowned Türk tribes of the Jochi Ulus, the remainder to those unknown to us today. The tribes such as Barlas and Kavchin, who were living in Transoxiana prior to the arrival of the Özbeks, but joined them, are not named here. Of the stated ninety-two tribes, approximately forty-five are part of the Özbek today. The aforementioned Mongol tribes are of course those constituting the Mongol units sent to the Jochi Ulus. The majority of those tribes carrying Mongolian names are now found in the Transoxiana and Khorezm. It appears that the genealogy, which has been handed down traditionally, indicates the belief of its owners, the Özbeks of Transoxiana and Khorezm, that they are descendants of these tribes, and therefore represent the entire forces constituting the foundations of the Altin Orda, and its transmission of the related organization to Transoxiana. Today, the subdivisions of the tribes are as follows:

(1) Qongrat tribe: They have five oymak. The first is Qancagali, consisting of following aris: Orus, Qara-Qursak, Chölik, Quyan, Quldavli, Miltek, Kür-Tugi, Gele, Top-Qara, Qara-Boz, Nogay, Bilgelik, Döstelik. The second oymak, of nine aris: Aq-Tana, Qara, Churan, Türkmen, Qavuk, Bes-Bala, Qarakalpaq, Qacay, Khoca-Bece. Third oymak, Qostamgali, again nine aris: Kül-Abi, Barmaq, Küce-Khur, Köl-Chuburgan, Qarakalpaq, Qostamgali, Seferbiz, Dilberi, Cachaqli. Fourth, Qostamgali oymak, seven aris: Tartugli, Agamayli, Isigali, Qazancili, Üyükli, Bükechli, Qaygali. Fifth, Qir oymak, five aris: Güzili, Küsevli, Ters, Baliqli, Quba. All of these branches of the Qongrat uruk are found in the Amu Darya delta, in the provinces of Khuzar (Ghuzar) of Bukhara, Sirabad, Qurgan-Tepe. They have, to a large extent, retained the nomadic ways in Bukhara. Those in Khorezm are settled;

(2) Nayman tribe. Three oymak: Qostamgali, Uvaqtamgali, Sadir. They live in Khorezm and Samarkand;

(3) Kineges, made up of five oymak: Qayrasali, Taraqli, Achamayli, Chikhut, Abaqli. They live in Shehrisebz and Khiva;

(4) Mangit, made up of three oymak: Toq-Mangit, Aq-Mangit, Qara-Mangit. They live in Khiva and Qarsi;

(5) Tuyaqli, living in Samarkand and Kette-Qurgan;
(6) Müyten, living in Samarkand and Kette-Qurgan;
(7) Saray, living on the borders of Shehrisebz-Yekke-Bag;
(8) Barin, living in Ferghana province and Kette-Kurgan tümen;
(9) Khitay and (10) Qipchak: They constitute the most important segments of Samarkand and Kette-Kurgan. They are very numerous in Khiva and Ferghana;
(11) Min, living in Samarkand, Penchkent, Jizzakh, and in Ferghana;
(12) Üch Uruk: Misit, Tama, Yabu. They live in the vicinity of Ziyaeddin of Bukhara;
(13) Burqut, living along the borders of Chilek and Kermine;
(14) Arlat, living in Qara-Köl;
(15) Qangli, living at the border of Jizzakh tümen;
(16) Qirk, Yüz, Min: living in Jizzakh tümen;
(17) Batas, living in the vicinity of Qarsi, Ghuzar;
(18) Qaraqalpak, made up of five oymak: Qara-Qoylu, Qara-Singir, Oymavut, Istek, Achamayli, and living in the Amu Darya delta and north of Samarkand, at "Ak-Tepe."

Those Özbek who have best preserved the old dialects and traditions are especially those living in the "Jizzakh" tümen (Qirq, Qangli, Saliq, Türk, Türkmen, Nayman, Mangit, Qitay-Yüz, Solaqli, Tuyaqli, Alacha, Burqut, Sirkeli, Baymaqli, Calayir, Qirgiz, Yüz, Quyan-Tuyaqli, Parcha-Yüz, Qarapcha, Quschi, Oraqli, Toqcari, Qostamgali, Saray, Qancagali). However, these tribes are numerically small. In eastern Bukhara, those tribes maintaining nomadic life, in the vicinity of Dushanbe, are "Laqay," "Marqa Kichi Yüz," and, around Feyzabad, "Qarliq."

Concerning the Özbek tribes in Afghanistan Turkistan, we are only in possession of a table prepared by the Indian Mir Izzetullah at the beginning of the nineteenth century.* Accordingly, the Özbek tribes there are as follows: At "Serpül" near "Sibirgan," "Achamayli" oymak of the "Min" tribe; next to them, at "Sayyad," "Achamayli" and "Qazayagi" of the "Min"; at Sencayrek, the "Qipchak" uruk; at Kunduz, all "Qatagan"; in the vicinity of "Balkh," "Saray" and "Möyten" uruks. At "Eskemis" of Badakshan, "Bürge" and "Timis" oymak of Qatagan. In "Narin," Chagatay" uruk. Mir Izzetullah also provides information on the oymak of Möyten and Qatagan uruk: Möyten is made up of seven oymak: Tilikhane, Germsili, Qazayaqli, Chagar, Sum, Aqsayiq, Chüchen. Qatagan uruk has three oymak: Bes-Qaban, Salcavut, Tört-Ata. "Bes-Qaban" has five aris: Laqqa (=Laqay), Yangi-Qatagan, Kesmever, Qayan, Manas. Kesmever has four tire: Aq-Taglik, Endicani, Qalasi, Bomin. "Manas" has three tire: Temis, Sar-Bagis, Bürge. "Tört-Ata" has four aris: Sariq-Qatagan, Churaq, Bassiz, Mardad. "Churaq" has two tire: Qiz Atizi, Sölen. Mardad has three tire: Üchata, Bozan, Cutuduq.

Among the Özbek tribes, there are those adopting the nickname of "Bekzad." In the past, those had played an active role in the governance of the land and the army, and performed the enthroning ceremony of the hans. Among them, in Khiva especially Qiyat-Qongrat, Uygur-Nayman, Qangli-Qipchak, Nüküs-Mangit tribes; in Bukhara, at the time of descendants of Shiban, "QusChu," "Nayman," "Qarluq," and "Böyrek" tribes; at the time of the Mangit (according to Radloff) Min, Arlat, Barin, Batas uruks were well known. The "Qatagan" are also regarded "Bekzad." Among the uruks: Tuyaqli, Möyten, Khitay (Qatay), Mangit; and the majority of Qongrats in Bukhara are among the last arriving from Desht-i Kipchak. These were earlier members of the "Mangit-Nogay" confederation, as well as the "Kazak," arriving later in Transoxiana.

---

*A manuscript of Mir Izzetullah's Persian-language work *Ahval-i Sefer-i Bukhara* is in the French National Library (Suppl. Pers. 1346). We are utilizing that copy. The translation of that work by Wilson in the *Calcutta Quarterly Magazine and Review* (III-IV, 1820) is incomplete and very defective. About the journey of Mir Izzetullah and his work, see *Yeni Türkistan*, 1928, no. 14, pp. 41–44.

Editor's Notes

a. Abulghazi Bahadir Khan (1603–1663), *Secere-i Terakime* (The Lineage of the Turks), completed in 1659. The French translation by Desmaisons is no longer satisfactory, for it lacks critical apparatus; an English translation is long overdue.

b. Cevdet Pasha (1822–1895) was an Ottoman historian, administrator, and educational and judicial reformer. See Stanford J. and E.K. Shaw, *History of the Ottoman Empire and Modern Turkey* (Cambridge: Cambridge University Press, 1977), vol. II.

c. In a footnote, below, Togan provides the nomenclature applied to subdivisions from the tribal confederation down to the smallest unit. An *uruk* is comprised of *oymaks*, which are made up of *aris*, a composition of *soy*.

d. *Uran:* the word shouted in the heat of the battle, to allow combatants to identify and gauge the whereabouts of their fellows without taking their eyes off the common adversary. It is an integral part of identity in Central Asia, forming a triad, along with *tamga* and *dastan*. The term *tamga*, originally referring to the "seal" of a given group, was later borrowed by Russians to designate customs levies (Russian: *tamozhnia*). The tamga was embroidered on tents, incorporated into rugs, filigreed into jewelry, and used as a cattle brand. A list of early tamgas is found in Kashgarli Mahmut's *Diwan Lugat at Türk* (twelfth century; hereafter *DLT*). A *dastan* is an "oral history" of the origins, customs, practices, and exploits of ancestors. See the discussion of the *Dede Korkut* dastan in this collection.

e. According to a popular etymology of the designation Özbek, it is derived from "Özüm Bek," meaning "My Essence is Princely."

f. *Ortaq*: "partner." Among the Mongols, the khan provided capital to his "partners" so that they could take caravans from one end of the Mongol domains to other, to trade with neighbors. Elizabeth Endicott-West and Thomas Allsen have been jointly exploring this topic.

g. On the Bulgar Turks see O. Pritsak, "Kultur und Sprache der Hunnen," *Festschrift für Dmytro Cyzev'ky* (Berlin, 1954); and R.N. Frye, "City Chronicles of Central Asia: Kitab-e Mullazade," *Avicenna Commemoration Volume* (Calcutta, 1956).

h. Here Togan provides the Arabic quotation in a footnote.

i. The lineages, inter alia, of the Chigil and the Oguz Turks are outlined in *DLT*.

j. See H.B. Paksoy, "Chora Batir: A Tatar Admonition to Future Generations," *Studies in Comparative Communism*, vol. 19, nos. 3 and 4 (Autumn/Winter 1986).

k. The original compilation of Mongol customary law was designated *Altan Tobchi*. See *The Secret History of the Mongols*, translated, inter alia, by F. Cleaves. For a later survival of the *yasa*, see V.A. Riasanovsky, *Customary Law of the Nomadic Tribes of Siberia*. Indiana University Uralic Altaic Series, vol. 48 (Bloomington, 1965).

l. *Yedi San:* Seven Reputations. The term "san" may also signify surname, or even the manner with which those tribes may have presented themselves in a gathering or in battle.

m. Togan uses this spelling. The name of Temür (Timur) (d. 1405) was corrupted in Western languages as Tamerlane, Tamburlane, and so forth.

n. See N. Elias and E. Denison Ross, eds., *The Tarikh-i Rashidi of Mirza Muhammad Haidar Dughlat* (London, 1898), pp. 119, 122, 272–74.

o. For the significance of the "as" and "Yog" ceremonies, see A.T. Hatto, *The Memorial Feast for Kökötöy Han* (Oxford, 1977).

p. Another relevant history on the region, compiled from several manuscript sources and edited by Y. Bregel, was published as *Firdaws al-ikbal: History of Khorezm* (Leiden, 1988).

2

REDISCOVERY OF
CULTURAL MONUMENTS

Naim Karimov

Exposing the Murderer of *Alpamysh*

Editor's Introduction

Naim Karimov is a noted Uzbek literary scholar, critic, and editor of the journal *Ozbek Tili va Adabiyati* (Uzbek Language and Literature). His articles have appeared in such Uzbek-language publications as *Sharq Yulduzi*, *Yashlik*, and *Fan va Turmush*. Among his most recent works is a biography of Cholpan, the Uzbek poet and dramatist Abdülhamid Süleyman (*Cholpan* [Tashkent: Fan, 1991]).

EXPOSING THE MURDERER OF *ALPAMYSH*

> *Alpamysh* is but one of the epic poems devoted to heroes. The subject of this extraordinary epic poem is the heroism of Alpamysh, which emanates from the most ancient heroic traditions.
> —Aybek[a]

Introduction

The longing for a society based upon truth and justice has existed since the appearance of humankind. Lenin and Stalin sought to convince humanity that the state that they constructed was indeed such a democratic structure.

In the mid-1930s Sulayman Stalskii, an ordinary minstrel singer, was called "the twentieth-century Homer."[b] Jambul Jaboev began to be considered the best representative of the Eastern people's oral tradition.[c] Throughout the national republics the people's oral works were studied with great fervor. In 1935 the

---

" 'Alpamish'ning katly om etilishi," *Sharq Yulduzi* (Eastern Star), 1992, no. 12. This annotated translation by Shawn T. Lyons first appeared in the *AACAR Bulletin*, vol. 6, no. 2 (Fall 1993).

hundredth anniversary of the first abridged publication of the Karelo-Finnish epic *Kalevala* was widely celebrated. Having been inspired by this, Stalin's countrymen, despite the violent suppression in Georgia, established as a holiday in December 1937 the seven-hundred-fiftieth anniversary of the Shota Rustaveli epic, *The Hero Who Wore Tiger's Fur.* Less than six months later, the leading nation of a country that had been united through coercion celebrated the seven-hundred-fiftieth anniversary of the creation of *The Lay of the Warfare Waged by Igor.* The Armenians in September 1939 trumpeted to the entire world the epic *David of Sasyn*, created a thousand years earlier. At last, after a year had passed and on the eve of the world war, the five hundredth anniversary of the Kalmuk people's epic *Jangar* was the cause for great celebration in Elista (capital of the Kalmuk republic).

Notwithstanding the absence of evidence to confirm that these various epics were created 500, 750, and especially 1000 years before, the attention at the all-state and public levels that was directed toward the people's creative works was a demonstration of the socialist state's true democracy and enlightenment. It was precisely this that was as necessary as air and water for the Soviet government and the Communist Party.

The Uzbeks, without question, are among those who possess one of the most ancient cultures of the world and thus have ample reason for their pride. *Koroglu* is a brilliant example that confirms the antiquity and richness of the Uzbek people's oral works of the fifteenth and sixteenth centuries and the affinity of the forty epics that comprise this group. It would be correct to designate *Alpamysh*, from among the epics not included in this group, as the most ancient epic, equal in terms of age to *David of Sasyn*.[d]

In those years the Uzbek Communist Party, led by Osman Yusupov, was galvanized by measures being employed in the Soviet states in the field of propagandizing the people's works.[e] Suddenly the party began to prepare celebratory activities for Alisher Navai's five hundredth birthday and the thousandth anniversary of *Alpamysh*. Hamid Alimjan,[f] after studying two or three available manuscript copies of *Alpamysh* in 1938, published an annotated and abridged version that was transcribed from Fazil Yoldash Oghli.[g] Since that time, *Alpamysh* has been presented in the elementary-school textbooks as an authentic oral monument of the Uzbek people. L. Penkovskii attempted to translate this work into Russian; later, in order to accelerate preparations for the all-union celebration of *Alpamysh*, V. Derzhavin and A. Kochetkov were assigned to this important task.

Hamid Alimjan, who studied *Alpamysh* with great love, was perhaps the first to appreciate that the purpose of these celebrations was not simply the epic's publication, but rather the beneficial effects of these celebrations upon the future development and brilliance of our language and literature. In his preface he states as follows:

With regard to language, *Alpamysh* reflects the Uzbek language's full richness and color. The complexity and ornateness of the epic reveal the language's eloquence. One encounters the most ordinary words as well as the most obscure, such as military terms that require study. Various terms pertaining to animal husbandry are even common. Because we were ignorant of this, we spread false traditions about the poverty of the Uzbek language. Within *Alpamysh* are numerous words and expressions that have particular significance for the contemporary literary language.

At last *Alpamysh* has achieved great importance for our writers. . . .

Alpamysh demonstrates the absolute necessity of our writers' having a firm knowledge of folklore. In general, folklore has an important role in enhancing Uzbek literature, infusing popular forms into the literary language, and simplifying, yet ultimately making more profound, Uzbek Soviet literature.

The hopes of loyal Uzbek intellectuals, like Hamid Alimjan, were very high on the thousandth anniversary of *Alpamysh*.

The State's Internal "Cold War"

The former Soviet state emerged victorious from the Fatherland War [World War II]. But because of Stalin's personal mistakes in what was history's worst war, nearly forty million citizens perished. Nevertheless, the tyrannical king's military "genius" was acclaimed as the central reason for the great triumph. Stalin began to be recognized by the countries abroad. Within the state the name of Stalin was sanctified. These events fostered a profound change in the outlook of this "people's hero." Although a person of average intellect and education, Stalin, always welcomed by the thunderous applause of toadies, considered himself the world's most intelligent, learned leader and a master of the highest aesthetic judgment. Those artistic and literary works that did not conform to his "high taste" were deemed instruments of bourgeois ideology, harmful, aimless, and substandard. Consequently, a merciless struggle against such works and their authors was initiated.

The All-Union Communist Party Central Committee decision "About the Journals *Zvezda* and *Leningrad*," adopted August 16, 1946, launched a struggle within the country against the literary and artistic community. This decision was a presage of the "cold war," which would claim countless victims. Stalin lived in an age when the "katiusha" had been invented.[h] Hence, he refined the art of mowing down in a single breath of fire a row of his victims. In the fall of that year successive decisions were fired out—"About the Dramatic Theater Repertoire and Measures for Improving It" and "About the Film *Big Life*." One of the measures in 1948 which proved very harmful to Soviet culture was entitled "Concerning V. Muradel's Opera *Great Friendship*." The unrelenting fire at the shore of literature and art was not Stalin's own but rather that of his "small artillery." *Pravda*, allied with the journal *Bolshevik* and the official decisions of the All-Union Communist Party Central Committee, ruined numerous talented and creative people.

The difference from the documents that were adopted in the Khrushchev and Brezhnev eras was that [under Stalin] the Communist Party always monitored the degree of their implementation and created each opportunity for the executioners. For this reason, the Cold War's winds, howling across the land, were much harsher in 1948–49.

On February 20, 1947, A. Fadeev, secretary of the USSR Writers' Union, lectured on the conditions and tasks of Soviet criticism during a meeting in the Gorky Institute of World Literature. Several facts that were advanced in this lecture were first published in the writers' journals *Oktiabr* and *Bolshevik*; subsequently, at the eleventh presidium of the USSR Writers' Union, these lectures were further developed.

In his lectures Fadeev was obligated to take the view of A. Zhdanov[i] regarding the postwar literary situation and to adopt in his speech the party's policies on literature as enunciated in the Central Committee decision "About the Journals *Zvezda* and *Leningrad*." In Fadeev's speech, a number of literary documents, including V. Shishmarev's pamphlet titled "Aleksandr Veselovskii and Russian Literature," which was published by Leningrad University in 1946, were severely criticized.

Veselovskii possessed an encyclopedic knowledge of West European literature. Out of the depth of that knowledge, he produced a comparative method of study of West European literature. But Stalin's clear animosity toward such great scholars, already evident in 1937, meant that in 1946 the creation of scientific and academic works about Veselovskii was a sacrilegious act. Having exposed that error, Fadeev drew attention to Veselovskii's rejection of the Russian revolutionary democratic literary tradition of the past in favor of the Roman-German school. Fadeev's views gained importance through articles published in *Literaturnaia gazeta*, *Sovetskaia kultura*, and *Pravda* in the June 30 and July 1, 1947, issues. The All-Union Central Committee directed public attention to the later article, which warned of the impending danger to postwar Soviet society from abject subservience to Western culture. For this reason a disgraceful ideological struggle was begun under the slogan of "anticosmopolitanism" in Soviet literature and art. The writers, critics, and art specialists who were active in this wing of the party shamelessly took advantage of these conditions, which enabled them to undermine their more famous colleagues. The Communist Party exploited this struggle in order to persecute intellectuals who were either proud of their own culture or intoxicated by Western culture.

L. Klimovich,[j] in a *Pravda* article of January 11, 1949, titled "Against Cosmopolitanism in Literary Study," observed that V. Zhirmunskii and H. Zarifov's *The Uzbek People's Heroic Epic* (Moscow, 1947) was guilty of remaining under the harmful feudal views of Veselovskii.[k] He wrote:

> Zhirmunskii and Zarifov are guilty according to our science and blindly follow the "historical-comparative" method inherited from the bourgeois literary spe-

cialists. Furthermore, they believe that collections of international topics can casually be transferred from one national literature to another.

According to the custom that was established in the totalitarian state, it was essential that authors discuss the above-mentioned book within their offices and have their own self-recriminations announced to the public. This, in fact, occurred. On February 8, 1949, in a meeting at the [Uzbek] Language and Literature Institute titled "The Uzbek People's Heroic Epic," local writers were thoroughly criticized. The speech of the institute director, Izzat Sultan, was published in the second issue of *Sharq Yulduzi* with a Klimovichian title.[l]

While the famous literary specialist in his speech pointed the blade of criticism toward Zhirmunskii and Zarifov with the hope of forestalling the calamity that was approaching *Alpamysh*, other speakers kicked the epic's fallen hero, seizing the opportunity to deal with their folklore colleagues.

In March 1949 a meeting of the Tashkent literature and art specialists was held. Although the primary task of this meeting was the complete exposure of "nationless cosmopolitanism" in literature and art, and although Uzbek dramaturgy was basically connected with theater criticism, some participants were satisfied that one of the era's most militant hatchetman, namely H. Yaqubov,[m] directed further public attention toward Zhirmunskii and Zarifov.

In Moscow and Leningrad scholarly circles, the main author of *The Uzbek People's Heroic Epic* was discussed and his research and conclusions were condemned as poisonous.

The struggle against the book written by Zhirmunskii and Zarifov gained momentum, and other literary and artistic genres began to be sucked into the fire. The journal *Druzhba narodov* [Friendship of Peoples] (1949, no. 4) published an official article titled "For a Marxist-Leninist Illumination of Central Asia's and Azerbaijan's Literature, Art, and History." L. Klimovich's "Concerning One Article" was featured in the fourth issue for 1951. This article, although apparently concerned with Zhirmunskii's work that was published in *Turkologik Mejmua* [Turcology Journal] (Moscow, 1951), mentioned the Azerbaijan epic *Dede Korkut Kitabi*. The author conceded that this epic, which was included in the *Azerbaijan Poetic Anthology*, was "Azerbaijan literature's most ancient monument," but resented its comparison with ancient European heroic epics such as *The Lay of the Warfare Waged by Igor* and *The Song of Roland*.

The purpose of these performances, staged by Central Committee directors, was not only to remove the comparative-historical method from literary specialists' science, but perhaps to compare the national epic *Alpamysh* with world culture monuments. After a postwar respite, they again tore at the cultural roots of the people. S.I. Lipkin, a staunch advocate and untiring translator of Soviet Eastern people's literature, was able to understand this situation.[n]

In a 1944 decision adopted by the All-Union Communist Party concerning ideological work in Tatarstan, the popularizing of the "feudal-khan epic" *Idigey* among the Tatar people was condemned as a serious error. Fearing that the epic *Idigey* would be forbidden under the guise of a struggle against cosmopolitanism, S.I. Lipkin produced a major article defending this work in the pages of *Literaturnaia gazeta*. But the tyrannical sultan's wheel was already set in motion. Semën Lipkin and other truth-loving people were not allowed to stay it. As soon as the opportunity arose, the Central Committee adopted a disgraceful measure condemning the *Idigey* epic as harmful to the people and nationalistic in spirit.

Lipkin later wrote:

> Stalin was aware of the danger posed by bourgeois nationalists who were still active throughout the East. By praising their national epics, ancient classics, kings, and armies, they were allowed to spread the seeds of pan-Islamism and act, in effect, as agents of foreign Muslim states. It was necessary to destroy them.

With that purpose in mind, Stalin unleashed an attack in 1950–52 upon the Soviet East's ancient epics. In April 1951 the newspaper *Pravda* announced that the Azerbaijan epic *Dede Korkut Kitabi* was an inimical work. A general meeting of Azerbaijan writers had already placed a cursed seal on this ancient people's epic. In June of that year, during the Eighteenth Congress of the Azerbaijan [Communist] Party, M. Baghirov displayed his own particular adeptness in exposing the epic's "poisonous character."° D. Gajiev and M. Qulzada, in their article "Concerning a Book Directed Against the People" (*Literaturnaia gazeta*, July 7, 1951), castigated those scholars who were studying the epic. L. Klimovich, then secretary of the USSR writers' organization, called for an immediate commission on the USSR people's literature, which proved that the Azerbaijan epic was "directed against the people" and that its publication had been an error.

The malevolent *Pravda* articles and the decisions chaired by Klimovich were intended as instructions for all the national republics of the totalitarian state. Thus, the Turkmen subjected their *Korkut Ata* epic to merciless criticism. On August 14 the Kazakhstan [Communist] Party adopted measures on the serious ideological errors that pervaded Kazakh literature. At a writers' meeting in Alma-Ata, Kazakh writers were criticized for "lifting to the sky" Kenesari Qasimov, a nineteenth-century "leader of a feudal-khan movement."

The turn had finally come for the works that were the pride of the Uzbek oral tradition.

The Lasso That Was Thrown at *Alpamysh*

In one of the works written by V.M. Zhirmunskii, the similarities between *Alpamysh* and "Bamsi Beyrek," which is a part of the *Dede Korkut Kitabi*, were mentioned. Despite the critical tone of his analysis of "Bamsi Beyrek" in a *Druzhba narodov* article, L. Klimovich sought to distance the *Alpamysh* epic therefrom and defended it. Although sometimes misdirected, this scholar's efforts were intended to protect the Eastern people's cultural gems—like the epic *Alpamysh*—from the whirlwind of the 1950s. People involved in the inner circles of Uzbek folklore and literary studies understood this very well. Regardless of the slander against *The Uzbek People's Heroic Epic*, the epic itself would not fade away.

But, of course, five fingers are not all the same. While one person wishes to display his heroism by flagellating himself in a secluded place, another sets fire to a mosque in order to be favorably regarded by the "big leader."

A. Abdunabiev, who was a graduate student of the Uzbekistan Department of the Marx–Engels–Lenin Institute, recognized the fortuitous [timing] of his appearance, albeit brief, on the historical stage.[p] Aware of the ideological struggle that was then reaching its height in the nation, he noticed in Klimovich's effort to defend *Alpamysh* that here was one issue that was squelching the voice of Uzbek scholars. If they restrained themselves from throwing *Alpamysh* into the fire of the cosmopolitan-feudal past, they sensed the propitiousness of their own opportunity as they awaited the fire of that peculiar conflagration. When Abdunabiev compared *Alpamysh* with "Bamsi Beyrek," he became convinced of Zhirmunskii's truth. Since the essence of "Bamsi Beyrek" was against the people, he came to the conclusion that *Alpamysh* was, in fact, a reactionary work. Fortunately, Aybek compared *Alpamysh* with the *Dede Korkut Kitabi* in his article which appeared in the *Anthology of Uzbek Poetry*. However, he did not think about mentioning both epics as the most ancient heroic works. In his view, Aybek's comparison of the relations between these two epics was sufficient reason to state: "the copies of *Alpamysh* and the 'Bamsi Beyrek' of the *Dede Korkut Kitabi* which have reached us are not the most ancient copies."

Elated by this, Abdunabiev wrote an article smashing *Alpamysh*. Subsequently A. Stepanov, who served at the *Pravda Vostoka* newspaper, became a partner to this article, which was sent to an authoritative Moscow publisher ("Revolutionary Advocate") in the Soviet East's literary life.[q] But the hope of this "young Nero" went unrealized. The Moscow newspapers were not receptive to this dubious work. Later, with the help of the Central Committee, these brothers who found each other in the dictatorial darkness of the 1950s were able to publish their articles in *Pravda Vostoka*, January 29, 1952.

During this period in which the totalitarian system reached its apogee, an accusation against a scholar or writer of ignorance of Marxist-Leninist methodology was sufficient proof of guilt. Anyone who sought to examine earlier cultural works could be accused of subservience to the past. Abdunabiev and Stepanov benefited skillfully from this reliable technique. After writing in that particular spirit in their preface, they moved to their genuine purpose. They wrote as follows:

What are the contents of *Alpamysh*? In terms of its ideological tendencies, there is much commonality between the reactionary *Dede Korkut* and *Alpamysh*. In both works, aims and intentions that are alien to the working people are propagandized.

The *Alpamysh* epic portrays as positive heroes the governing classes of the sixteen Kungrat tribes and subtribes that gathered with their flocks around Lake Baysun. Slaves served both the flocks and the rulers. The central figures of the epic consist of the following: Baybora, khan of the Kungrat tribe; Hakimbek Alpamysh, his son; the younger brother of the khan; Baysari, one of the tribal chiefs; and Barchin, Baysari's daughter."

After an analysis of exactly that caliber, the authors reach these conclusions:

The copy of the *Alpamysh* epic attributed to Fazil Yoldash is not the people's epic; rather it belongs to the khans. The Uzbek people's heroic struggle with external and internal enemies, their devotion to their motherland, and their great confidence in the future and efforts to be at peace with other people are not reflected in this work. Moreover, the khans and beks, the bloody campaigns they instigated against neighboring peoples, and their religious intolerance and absolutely uncompromising position toward opponents are all glorified and propagandized.

Such descriptions were contrary to the earlier views of scholars such Hamid Alimjan who had studied *Alpamysh* using such words as "bravery, love and friendship epic." But others welcomed the words of M. Baghirov, the Azerbaijan people's executioner. "The *Dede Korkut* is not an epic of the people," M. Baghirov declared at a congress of the Azerbaijan Communist Party:

From its beginning to its end, this epic is devoted to praising the nomadic Oghuz tribes' ruling classes, who came only as conquerors and plunderers of the Azerbaijan land. This book, infected with the poison of nationalism, is directed against those who were not Muslims—other religious communities and the fraternal Georgian and Armenian people.

While Hamid Alimjan was preparing *Alpamysh* for publication in 1938, he wrote that "the inveterate enemies of the Uzbek people seek to obstruct publication of *Alpamysh* and similar valuable works." He could not have imagined that such baseness would be repeated fourteen years later. One lesson of history, however, is that mistakes are repeated. The birds of truth and justice had fled that brutal age. Only crows, preying upon the weak, prevailed.

One of the articles by Abdunabiev and Stepanov that had been rejected by the Moscow newspapers was published nevertheless in two issues of *Zvezda Vostoka* with the title "Under the Banner of Democracy." These militant writers, although confining themselves to praising *Alpamysh* in their first article, later, inspired by the detestable M. Milchakov's kindness toward them, in their second article slandered *Avazkhan, Zulfizar* (the authors being so ignorant that they did not even know that the two titles belonged to a single work), *Ravshankhan*, *Rustamkhan*, and other epics as "serious errors."

According to an established custom, the toady organizations had to greet party publications with joyful trumpets. The first article published in the newspaper *Pravda Vostoka* was discussed at an expanded meeting of Uzbekistan State University literary specialists. All of the academic community unanimously approved the party organ's criticism of *Alpamysh* as "directed against the people." The meeting's participants furthermore adopted a measure that removed the theme of *Alpamysh* from textbooks and investigated the entire epic genre of *Koroglu* and other folkloric works.

On this matter the Central Asia State University professors did not lag far behind their Samarkand colleagues.

The tenth plenum of the Uzbekistan Communist Party Central Committee took place on March 21–22. Being an experienced leader, First Secretary A.E. Niyazov, in his speech "On Steps for Improving the Ideological Conditions of Work in the Republic," exposed with typical Marxist-Leninist ferocity every manifestation of idealizing the past in the fields of history, language, literature, and art, and then left it for other speakers to punish thoroughly the *Alpamysh* epic. The decisions of this disgraceful plenum were the basis for greater problems within Uzbek science and culture.[r]

In March of that year there was a general party meeting of the Uzbek Academy of Sciences. Central Committee secretary H. Tursunov delivered a major speech on the necessity of studying and investigating the tenth plenum's decisions.[s] He also severely criticized scholars engaged in the social sciences. During that meeting the tasks of generating wide public animosity toward the *Alpamysh* epic were assigned.

The Murder of *Alpamysh*

On March 28 and 31, 1952, a discussion of the epic *Alpamysh* was conducted by the Uzbekistan Writers' Union at the Hamid Alimjan Literary Center. Although the epic was written in Uzbek and nearly all the participating speakers were themselves Uzbek, the discussion, in accordance with the totalitarian system's law, was conducted in Russian.

People who remember the era of Stalin's rule are not astounded by this since even now they recall the bitter taste of that dictatorial system. It is clear that only two or three representatives of the Russian "great elder brother" were present in that hall. Nevertheless, the vigilant eyes of Moscow through its Tashkent spies observed every moment of the meeting. Some hero stood there ready to silence any voice of truth. The speakers, of course, noticed this also and, fearing a summons to the familiar basement because of a careless word, criticized *Alpamysh* and the poets and scholars who had familiarized the people with this epic.

Yusuf Sultanav, the new director of the Pushkin Language and Literature Institute, delivered a speech.[t] In the folklore faculty's records located at the literature institute, which is now named after Alisher Navai, is a manuscript copy of the meeting's discussions. According to the accounts in the *Qizil Ozbekistan* newspaper:

> Yusuf Sultanav analyzed several variations of the *Alpamysh* epic and demonstrated with numerous examples that in it the interests of the feudal-khan are protected. The epic was essentially directed against the people. In the epic, khans and beks are lauded. Aggression and conquest are propagandized. Relations with non-Muslims are very hostile. The epic's main hero, Alpamysh, does not express in himself the working people's noble character and aspirations; on the contrary, he behaves in a typically tyrannical and bloodthirsty manner. The epic distorts the characters of ordinary people, but praises the representatives of the ruling classes. Thus, the very nature of the *Alpamysh* epic, as demonstrated above, is directed against the people.

The speaker was undermining not only the people's epic, but also, as confirmed by the journal *Sharq Yulduzi*, those who wrote a preface to *Alpamysh* and arranged for its publication many times. He bitterly criticized literary specialists who had staged the epic and introduced it into the middle-school programs and standard anthologies. He criticized V. Zhirmunskii and H. Zarifov's idealization of this epic in their ideologically poisonous work *The Uzbek People's Heroic Epic*. Their preface to Aybek's *Anthology of Uzbek Poetry* and their introduction to M. Shayzada's 1949 Russian-language edition of *Alpamysh* were also censured.[u]

These words may seem ordinary, perhaps even harmless, within the ideological climate of the 1950s. But if we recall that in this era the ill-fated Zhirmunskii and Zarifov were crushed by unrelenting criticism, Aybek lay sick in his bed, and Shayzada, who was excluded from the divided Writers' Union, stood on the threshold of prison, such words cannot be regarded as innocuous.

Undoubtedly, the most difficult task in the discussion fell upon the shoulders of the father of Uzbek folklore studies, Hadi Zarifov. Although the events that were taking place were a crime against the people and culture, he was not able to arouse the intellectual community's sense of truth and reason. He was warned twice to come closer to the approach of Stanishevskii, the first speaker after Yu. Sultanov, but Hadi Zarifov was too bewildered by the dogmas of N.Ia. Marr and A.N. Veselovskii.[v] At last, after an official rebuke by the secretary of the meeting, he asked for an additional fifteen minutes and returned to the problem of Uzbek folklore. Then, while discussing the harmful effects upon the people of such epics as *Yusuf va Ahmad, Alibek va Balibek*, and *Shaybaniykhan*, he engaged in criticisms of Zhirmunskii, Aybek, and especially M. Afzalov, who had all expressed a positive attitude toward these works. In the end, he had no alternative but to approve the pseudoscientific views of Abdunabiev and Stepanov.

In his speech, however, there was the subtle implication that perhaps only the copy of *Alpamysh* that was being discussed expressed an antipopular spirit; that no such animus was evident in the original *Alpamysh* epic. The Orientalist-Chekist Stanishevskii sensed that he could now deliver a timely blow to Hadi Zarifov, who was in a very depressed state, and put him out of the game. The experienced and shrewd representative of the totalitarian system had correctly determined that one could toss *Alpamysh* into the wastebasket of history by destroying Hadi Zarifov. Neither in the Institute of Language and Literature nor in the Writers' Union was there anyone brave enough to protect *Alpamysh* or to combat Abdunabiev. Already by 1937 the totalitarian system had finished off all brave people and ruined or brainwashed other, surviving scholars. Some scholars simply continued to dance to Stanishevskii's music.

The speaker continued:

> Comrade Zarifov wishes to say that because we did not find another variation of the epic, such discussions are irrelevant, and so forth. Comrade Zarifov did not mention his having recommended this epic for the sixth-to-eighth–grade anthologies. He also did not adequately discuss the inclusion of portions of this poisoned work in textbooks used by schoolteachers.
>
> Let us look at the *Alpamysh* epic from a moral perspective and consider its depiction of the people. In fact, this epic slanders the Uzbek people. In truth, it rubs dirt in the face of the Uzbek people. Only enemies could plot out such a slanderous depiction of the Uzbeks.

After this speech, Stanishevskii sought to support his conclusions with examples from the epic. Unfortunately, the artistic word does not possess the power to burn the tongue of the slanderer. If it had, might the fire in his mouth not have turned Stanishevskii into a burning torch?

But expressions like "poisoned work" and "slanderous depiction" repeated by intellectuals who translated and studied *Alpamysh* were sweet compared to Abdunabiev's description. With his nose raised into the sky, he felt himself a national hero of the 1950s. He was a semiliterate graduate student who did not value anything except that which he extracted from the talmud of Marxism-Leninism and regarded those devoted to folklore, science, and the people with contempt. He accused them of major political errors.

He said the following:

> For many years, the *Alpamysh* epic has been published, defended with tooth and nail, and its heroes proven innocent in every respect by these comrades. Only in this context can we explain the epic's having been repeatedly published in Russian and Uzbek. If you describe, without lauding, these persons [here the speaker means the epic's heroes—N.K.], the epic will not achieve any prestige among the people. And you, Comrade Zarifov, are guilty of this!

Just notice how this problem has unfolded. Now the reason for the militants' restraining of those who propagandized *Alpamysh* is clear. According to Abdunabiev, *Alpamysh* would not gain prestige among the people without the service of its propagandists.

The interrogating speaker continued:

> So, we blame the praisers of the *Alpamysh* epic for their propagandizing of a work that was against the people and alien to the Uzbek people's ideological orientation. We place the political guilt on Zhirmunskii, professors Bertels[w] and Klimovich, the cosmopolitan Zarifov, writers Maqsud Shaykhzada and Sabir Abdulla, folklore specialist Bogdanov, assistant professor Afzalov, and the poet Penkovskii!
>
> They attribute to the Uzbek working people such customs as violence, murder, thievery, aggression, and conquest, which were alien to all working people and more typical of those who were merciless barbarians. These people slandered my Uzbek people, a loyal and vital part of the great and heroic Soviet people.

Dear readers! As you read this text, you will recall the speeches of the despised Vyshinskii[x] in his 1937 court proceedings and the slander and abuse that was spread. The speeches of the totalitarian regime's saints all completely reinforce each other. All purport to speak on behalf of the people. "My Uzbek people," Abdunabiev would declare without an ounce of shame, simultaneously crushing beneath his foot the original sons of the people. If Abdunabiev had possessed the authority, would he have ordered the execution of all those mentioned above, like his master Vyshinskii?

Excuse me, dear readers! I translated this hysterical speaker's word "vandal" as "barbarian." Although in Europe this term was applied to those who destroyed cultural monuments, it was only at this particular time that such devils appeared in our Uzbekistan, so there was no such expression in the Uzbek language. Yet how are we to describe a person (for example, Abdunabiev) who destroys *Alpamysh*, a cultural monument?

Let us now return to the discussion hall after this lyric digression.

The speaker, enjoying his accusatory role, continued:

> Let them fully explain why they propagandized the above-mentioned reactionary epic! Let them openly confess their political ignorance and political blindness in their assessment of *Alpamysh*. Or let them admit the deliberateness of their propagandizing of *Alpamysh* . . .
>
> Zarifov (from the hall): I already said that!
>
> Abdunabiev: No, you have not said anything at all!

Amazing! Consider this half-literate graduate student's treatment of a respectable man who was older than the student's father! Has there ever been such a pessimist in the East? Did the dear ones of the princes and beks speak in this manner with the sultan's elites? In my opinion, no.

Our speaker, continuing in the same shameless spirit, said:

> I ask Maqsud Shayzada and Sabir Abdulla: What is the reason for your ingrati-
> tude toward our Party and beloved government's goodness? Are you not at all
> ashamed to slander the Uzbek people?
>
> Why did Sabir Abdulla produce the harmful *Alpamysh* epic as a musical
> drama and then devote it to the twenty-fifth anniversary of the Uzbekistan
> SSR? Or perhaps this thing was Sabir Abdulla's gift to the Uzbek people's
> extraordinary dramatic stage?
>
> This is not the first time that we have seen Shayzada's nationalistically
> inspired mistakes and deviations. He has allowed very serious errors to enter
> his previous works.
>
> Shayzada! I ask and demand of you: What purpose did you have in mind
> when you translated V.V. Mayakovsky's epic *Vladimir Ilich Lenin* from Rus-
> sian into the Uzbek language? How did you determine the nationalistic bound-
> aries of this work? Why did you translate this epic about the great Lenin in
> such a distorted manner? If your skills were not adequate for an exact transla-
> tion, then why did you undertake this task?
>
> Shayzada! I ask and demand of you: Why did you distort in your epic
> *Aksakal* the image of the late Yoldash Okhunbabaev, who was a great states-
> man of Soviet Uzbekistan, a true son of Lenin-Stalin's Party, and who re-
> mained among the Uzbek people and served all Soviet people?[y] What purpose
> was there in portraying Yoldash Okhunbabaev—this passionate Bolshevik and
> builder of communism—as weak and conservative? With what sort of purpose
> did you introduce into Uzbek literature the main hero of the Caucasus people's
> bloody drama *Jalaleddin*? With what, what sort of purpose, did you praise and
> tirelessly propagandize the feudal epic *Alpamysh*? Why did you intend to raise
> our young generation using this bloody example of *Alpamysh*?

It was not an investigating officer lurking inside a KGB cellar who said these
poisonous words to Shayzada and Sabir Abdulla; rather it was an ordinary graduate student, a half-literate mullah who had no relation to the world of folklore,
literature, science, and culture. But standing behind this mullah were not V.
Milchakov's followers, but perhaps a power far stronger than they. This power
was the hope for Abdunabiev's future. In him was seen not merely a potential
first secretary of the Uzbekistan Komsomol but a leader in far more important
positions. When a year had passed, Stalin died, but Stalinism did not waste away.
Stalin, of course, would have continued to sit atop his throne and inflict innumer-
able and painful sufferings upon our people.

If you pay attention, you will note that the speaker primarily refers not to
Alpamysh itself but to the beloved figures who engaged in assiduous study of this
work and contributed to its popularization among Uzbek and Russian readers.
The reason for this was that the discussion of the *Alpamysh* epic was a drama
designed by the obvious political circles. With the help of traitors like
Abdunabiev, these circles sought to isolate this generation of Uzbek intellectuals
and creators who had matured after Cholpan, and to turn those who remained

into the living dead. Abdunabiev was a person, discovered and raised by those political circles, who was absolutely obedient in his service. He was a faithful soldier who, when told to bring someone's *doppi* [hat], would bring the entire head. This was a drama that was fundamentally connected with Shayzada, Shukhrat, Said Akhmad, Shukrulla, Mirzakalan Ismaili, Hamid Sulayman, Enghin Mirza, and A. and N. Alimukhamedov as well as many other intellectuals of the prison period.[z] This drama was connected with those who were on the verge of imprisonment and the entire prison process. In this sense, the discussion at the meeting was not typical at all. It was inextricably bound to the movements of the totalitarian regime.

In addition to the speeches and lectures cited above, the speeches of Salikh Qasimov, who was one of the leaders of the institute during the 1950s, were not among the materials used. The reasons for this exclusion are not mentioned by the recorders. It would not be astounding if his speeches were, in fact, omitted. Nevertheless, Qasimov did exhibit throughout his work the spirit of the 1950s in order to retain his position.

The remaining speeches can be divided into three categories. The historian Berestnev, literary specialist Ghlam Karimov,[a'] and folklorist Mansur Afzalov, although they did not distance themselves from the denunciation of *Alpamysh*, sought to betray neither science nor friends. A second group (Mikhail Sale and Mahmydali Yunusov) introduced the notion of criticizing the *Koroglu* epic and other types of Uzbek folklore. In order to support his preconceived view, Akhunjan Sabirav "analyzed" and hacked at the epic *Zulfizar va Avazkhan* and arrived at the conclusion that it was as poisonous a work as *Alpamysh*. "Comrades," he stated, "in my opinion, it may not be necessary here to demonstrate the harmfulness of the epic, which was published at the Language and Literature Institute under the leadership of Comrade Zarifov. . . ." If we examine the speech of Akhunjan Sabirav, one senses that the intended victim, selected by some external force, was Hadi Zarifov, the main advocate of publishing the epic, and not the epic itself. The effort to topple Shayzada and Hadi Zarifov in the same insidious manner is amply clear in Hamil Equbav's speech.

After this discussion, which occurred on March 28 and 31, 1952, *Alpamysh*, one of the great oral monuments of the Uzbek people, was pronounced an epic "directed against the people." The book was collected from bookstores and library shelves. No sooner were Shayzada and Hadi Zarifov engaged with this work then it seems to have shifted to the shoulders of the respective organizations.

Conclusion

This year marks forty years since this cursed seal was stamped on *Alpamysh*. What a peculiar sort of "anniversary"! Most of those who participated in this horrible process have already died. Some might consider the revival of these old issues unnecessary. But their life may perhaps be described with [poet] Abdulla

Aripav's lines: The caravans pass and the dogs lie in their circle.[b'] We must not forget the shining memories of scholars like Shayzada and Hadi Zarifov, our cultural resiliency during that oppression, and our bakhshis [epic singers] who have recited *Alpamysh* throughout the centuries and preserved it from one generation to another. Finally, we must not forget this terrible page from our respectful people's history.

Some readers may consider the mentioning of the past by contemporary youth as a denigration of creative and scholarly people. Our purpose is not to denigrate anyone. Our purpose is to inform the present and future generations of the horror the dictatorial regime inflicted on artists and scholars. Let it be known how people were turned against each other as enemies. It is necessary that the suffering imposed upon our people and culture by the totalitarian regime not be forgotten. Let such horrors never be repeated! And, most important, let life be free of dances to the tyrannical system's stick, free of the sickness of strangling our own great leaders and cultural monuments.

Before us stand the gates of the twenty-first century. Let us pass through these sacred gates free of such weaknesses and sicknesses. Let us join the great caravan of humanity as a people.

Editor's Notes

a. Aybek (1905–1968), Uzbek author, poet. See N. Karimov's biography, *Aybek* (Tashkent: Yash Gvardiya, 1985).

b. Sulayman Stalskii (1869–1937), Daghestan people's poet. Composed works praising establishment of Soviet government.

c. Jambul Jaboev (1869–1945), Kazakh epic singer and poet.

d. For a discussion of the classification of epics see M. Mirzaev, *Ozbek Khalq Dastanlarida Turkumlik* (Tashkent: Fan, 1985).

e. Osman Yusupov (1900–1966), succeeded Akmal Ikramov as First Secretary in Uzbekistan, 1937. See M. Vakhabov, "Usman Iusupov," in *Revoliutsionery, vozhaki mass* (Uzbekistan: Tashkent, 1967), pp. 419–36.

f. Hamid Alimjan (1909–1944), Uzbek poet and literary specialist. See his essays on oral literature in *Mukammal Asarlar Toplami*, vol. 5 (Tashkent: Uzbekistan, 1982).

g. Fazil Yoldash Oghli (1872–1955), Uzbek epic singer and poet, closely associated with the *Alpamysh* epic. See Hadi Zarifov, *Fazil Yoldash Oghli—Mashhur Dastanchi* (Tashkent, 1973).

h. Katiusha—multi-rocket artillery developed during World War II.

i. A. Zhdanov defines the principles of Soviet socialist realism in *Literature, Philosophy and Music* (New York: International Publishers, 1950).

j. L. Klimovich (1908–), Soviet orientalist and antireligious expert. See his *Islam v Tsarskoi Rossii* (Moscow, 1936).

k. V. Zhirmunskii (1891–1971), Soviet orientalist, linguist, folklorist. H. Zarifov (1905–1972), founder of Uzbek folklore studies.

l. Izzat Sultan (1910–?), Uzbek literary specialist and critic.

m. H. Yaqubov (1907–?), Uzbek writer, critic. See N. Karimov, "Sakhiy Istedod Sohibi," in *Ozbek Adabiyatida Janrlar Tipologiyasi va Uslublar Rang-Barangligi* (Tashkent: Fan, 1983), pp. 3–8.

n. S.I. Lipkin (1911–?), Soviet Russian poet and translator. Completed Russian translation of the Kirgiz epic *Manas*.

o. M. Baghirov (1890–1961), Azerbaijan singer, composer, and people's artist.

p. A. Abdunabiev's career is discussed in H.B. Paksoy, *Alpamysh: Central Asian Identity Under Russian Rule* (Hartford: AACAR, 1989).

q. A. Stepanov's career is discussed in ibid.

r. A.E. Niyazov (1903–1973), Communist Party Central Committee First Secretary, 1950–55.

s. H. Tursunov (1912–?), Uzbek historian. Communist Party Central Committee Secretary, 1951–52.

t. Yu. Sultanav (1911–?), Uzbek literature specialist. Director of the Pushkin Language and Literature Institute, 1950–52.

u. M. Shayzada (1908–1967), Uzbek author, poet, and scholar.

v. N. Marr (1865–1934), Soviet orientalist and linguist who sought to reject earlier linguistic theories as inconsistent with Marxism. N. Veselovskii (1838–1906), Russian literary specialist, expert on West European, Slavic, and Byzantine literature and folklore.

w. E. Bertel's (1890–1957), Soviet orientalist. Specialized in Persian, Tajik, and Turkic literatures. Sabir Abdulla (1905–1972), Uzbek writer, poet, and dramatist. M. Afzalav, *Ozbek Khalq Ertaklari Haqida* (Tashkent: Fan, 1964).

x. A. Vyshinskii (1883–1955), chief prosecutor in the political show trials of the 1930s.

y. Y. Okhunbabaev (1885–1945), Uzbek Soviet government official. From 1938 he served as Secretary of the Uzbek Supreme Soviet.

z. The fate of some of these Uzbek intellectuals is described in the poet Shukrulla's memoirs, *Kafansiz Komilganlar* (Tashkent: Mehnat, 1991).

a'. Gh. Karimov (1909–?), Uzbek literature specialist. From 1951 he was a Tashkent University professor.

b'. A. Aripav (1941–), Uzbek poet. In 1989 he served as a deputy in the Uzbek government.

Memmed Dadashzade

Ethnographic Information
Concerning Azerbaijan Contained
in the *Dede Korkut* Dastan

Editor's Introduction

Dede Korkut, one of the historical treasures of a large portion of Central Asia, is a *dastan*, "the principal repository of ethnic identity, history, customs and the value systems of its owners and composers. . . . It commemorates . . . struggles for freedom."[1] *Dede Korkut* has been rendered into a number of languages over the last two centuries, since it caught the attention of H.F. Von Diez, who published a partial German translation in 1815, based on a manuscript found in the Royal Library of Dresden. The only other manuscript of *Dede Korkut* was discovered in 1950 by Ettore Rossi in the Vatican library. Until *Dede Korkut* was transcribed on paper, the events depicted therein survived in the oral tradition, at least from the ninth and tenth centuries.[2] The "Bamsi Beyrek" chapter of *Dede Korkut* preserves almost verbatim the immensely popular Central Asian dastan *Alpamysh*, dating from even an earlier time.[3]

Editio princeps of *Dede Korkut* was made by Kilisli Rifat [Bilge] in 1916 in Istanbul, which was followed by that of Orhan Saik Gökyay (Istanbul, 1938). The first full-text, "Baku Edition" of *Dede Korkut* was made by H. Arasli in 1939 (reprinted in 1962 with an annotated introduction and again in 1977). V.V. Bartold's *Kniga moego dede Korkuta*, on which he probably began work in the 1890s, was posthumously issued in 1950.[4] M. Fahrettin Kirzioglu's *Dede Korkut*

" 'Dede Gorgud' dastanlarynda Azerbajchan etnografijasyna dair bézi mélumatlar," *Azerbajchanyn etnografik mechmuesi* (Azerbaijan Journal of Ethnography), 1977, no. 3 (Baku: "Elm"), pp. 182–94. A publication of the Institute of History, Azerbaijan SSR Academy of Sciences. This translation by H.B. Paksoy first appeared in *Soviet Anthropology and Archeology*, vol. 29, no. 1 (summer 1990).

Oguznameleri appeared in Istanbul in 1952; Ettore Rossi's *Kitab-i Dede Qorqut* was published in Italian in the same year, followed by Joachim Hein's 1958 German edition. After Muharrem Ergin's *Dede Korkut Kitabi*,[5] there came two English versions, the first of which was a collaborative effort among three well-known scholars,[6] and the second, a highly readable *Book of Dede Korkut* by Geoffrey L. Lewis.[7] In 1978 a Persian edition became available in Tabriz.[8] A Serbo-Croatian rendition, *Knijka Dede Korkuta*, was published in 1983 by Slavoljub Djindjich, who also reported the ongoing work on a Czech translation.[9] A Lithuanian edition was evidently issued in Vilnius in 1978 under the title *Dede Korkudo sakmes*.[10]

Dede Korkut is shared by a large assortment of Turkic groups, including, but not limited to, the Oghuz/Türkmen[11] confederations, whose origins are easily traceable to pre-Islamic times, and their numerous current-day descendants, also encompassing the Azerbaijan population. Oghuz literati of the middle ages also composed numerous genealogies, many of which were edited by a seventeenth-century ruler of the Türkmen who collected them into two separate volumes. Since the early eighteenth century, these have been translated into French, English, and Russian.[12] These genealogies are quite apart from the dastan genre, and constitute yet another series of reference markers on the identity map. Moreover, there is another dastan connected with the Oghuz, named for the eponymous Oghuz Khan.[13]

Memmed Dadashzade is an ethnographer-folklorist at the Institute of History, Academy of Sciences, Baku, whose work on the significance of *dastans* is pathbreaking. His "Ethnographic Information Concerning Azerbaijan Contained in the *Dede Korkut* Dastan," originally written in Azerbaijan Turk, is a fine sample of the ongoing efforts by Azerbaijan authors to reclaim their historical and cultural heritage. The latest round of those efforts commenced almost ten years before the "openness" and "restructuring" campaigns of Gorbachev.[14] Many a topic is broached here for the first time since the previous generation of Turk scholars and literati (who raised the same issues) were lost to the Stalinist "liquidations"[15] or to the "ideological assault" waged on all dastans in 1950–52.[16] After the publication of Dadashzade's article in 1977, a series of similar works appeared in various periodicals and volumes that were clearly intended for the Azerbaijan audience.[17] The tentativeness, careful wording, and particular formulation of some arguments found in the Dadashzade paper are directly attributable to the constraints that were prevailing at the time[18] and made this study a work of courage.

Despite the interest of the Azerbaijan intellectual community, *Dede Korkut* was not widely available to the population of Azerbaijan. As Professor Zemfira Verdiyava observed in 1988: "*Beowulf* is always waiting for its purchasers in the shops of England. And in which shops have we seen our own *Dede Korkut*?"[19] That year, a full version of *Kitabi Dede Korkut* was reissued in Azerbaijan Turk,[20] with an up-to-date bibliography and the following prehistory: "Sent for publication on July 11, 1985. Permission for printing received February 2, 1988."

Notes

1. See H. B. Paksoy, *Alpamysh: Central Asian Identity Under Russian Rule* (Hartford, CT: Association for the Advancement of Central Asian Research, Monograph Series, 1989), p. 1.
2. These manuscripts were evidently copied during the sixteenth century from separate originals, for they exhibit variations. See the introduction by Geoffrey L. Lewis to his translation of *The Book of Dede Korkut* (London, 1974, 1982).
3. See H.B. Paksoy, "Alpamysh zhene Bamsi Beyrek: Eki At, Bir Dastan" [Alpamysh and Bamsi Beyrek: Two Names, One Dastan], *Kazak Edebiyati* (Alma-Ata), no. 41, 10 October 1986 (rendered into Kazak by Fadli Aliev from *Türk Dili*, no. 403, 1985). The discussion pertaining to the dating of dastan *Alpamysh* boiled over during the "Trial of Alpamysh" of 1952–56, when all dastans of Central Asia were officially condemned by the Soviet state apparatus. According to Borovkov, Hadi Zarif, and Zhirmunskii, as well as earlier writings by Bartold, the dastan *Alpamysh* "existed probably in the foothills of the Altai as early as the sixth–eighth centuries at the time of the Türk Kaghanate." For details, see H.B. Paksoy, *Alpamysh*, p. 53.
4. Published by the USSR Academy of Sciences (1950, 1962). Descendant of a German family settled in the Russian empire, the celebrated historian Bartold (1869–1930) reportedly worked on this translation from the 1890s, completing the work in the late 1920s. Since Bartold had run afoul of the Bolshevik notions of history and was banished, publication had to await his "rehabilitation" by the Soviet authorities.
5. Published in two volumes (Ankara, 1958, 1963).
6. *Dede Korkut*, tr. Faruk Sümer, Ahmet Edip Uysal, and Warren S. Walker (Austin, 1972).
7. See the introduction by Geoffrey L. Lewis to his translation of *The Book of Dede Korkut*.
8. See E. Seferli and H. Yusifov, *Gadim ve Orta Asirlar Azerbaijan Edebiyati* [Ancient and Middle Ages Azerbaijan Literature] (Baku, 1982). Introduction. This is a "textbook for university students."
9. Djindjich's translation was published in Belgrade in 1981. On the Czech translation see Hamdi Hasan, "Kitaplar," *Türk Dili*, Mayis, 1983.
10. Cited in the bibliography in *Kitabi Dede Korkut* (Baku, 1988).
11. On the Oghuz, see Faruk Sümer, *Oguzlar (Türkmenler)*, Expanded Third Edition, 688 pp. (Istanbul, 1980); O. Pritsak, "The Decline of the Empire of the Oghuz Yabgu," *The Annals of the Ukrainian Academy of Arts and Sciences in the US*, II (1952); Z.V. Togan, *Türkili Türkistan*, 2d ed. (Istanbul, 1981); V.V. Barthold, *Four Studies on the History of Central Asia: A History of the Turkman People*, Vol. III (Leiden, 1962); Kashgarli Mahmut's *DLT* contains contemporary information on the Oghuz, also making the identification that the Oghuz and the Türkmen are one and the same group. Moreover, C.E. Bosworth, in his *The Ghaznavids*, 2d ed. (Beirut, 1973), provides details of the Oghuz/Türkmen activity in the tenth–eleventh centuries. Additional information on the Oghuz are found in the works cited by Sümer and Bosworth.
12. Abul-Ghazi Bahadur Khan (1603–1663), ruler of Khiva, was asked by his Türkmen subjects to compile the authoritative genealogy of their common lineage from many extant variants at the time. He prepared two, under the titles *Secere-i Terakime* (probably completed in 1659) and *Secere-i Türk*. According to Y. Bregel, in his introduc-

tion to the facsimile of Munis and Agahi's *Firdaws al-Ikbal: History of Khorezm* (Leiden, 1988), the latter was completed c. 1665 by another person. *Secere-i Türk* is rather difficult to locate, making a determination of the sources for the translated works tenuous. This is especially true with respect to the early French and English translations: [Bentinck], *Histoire Généalogique des Tatars*, 2 vols. (Leiden, 1726); and Abu Al Ghazi Bahadur, *A History of the Turks, Moguls, and Tatars, Vulgarly called Tartars, Together with a Description of the Countries They Inhabit*, 2 vols. (London, 1730); [Miles], *Genealogical Tree of the Turks and Tatars* (London, 1838). The Imperial Russian Academy at St. Petersburg published a facsimile of *Terakime* in 1871, edited by Desmaisons, who later prepared a French translation. A modern-day translation is long overdue. See H.F. Hofman, *Turkish Literature: A Bio-Bibliographical Survey* (Utrecht, 1969), for additional comments. See also *Türk Seceresi*, ed. R. Nur (Istanbul, 1343/1925). One of the earlier Russian translations prepared is *Rodoslovnoe drevo tiurkov* (Kazan, 1906), with an afterword by N. Katanov (1862–1922). Apparently this 1906 version was not published until 1914, minus Katanov's name from the title page and his afterword from the body of the book. See A.N. Kononov, *Rodoslovnaia Turkmen* (Moscow-Leningrad, 1958), p. 181. In order to understand the reason, one must turn to Z.V. Togan's memoirs, *Hatiralar* (Istanbul, 1969), where Togan relates an incident (which took place prior to 1917) when Katanov poured his heart out to Togan.

13. Z.V. Togan compiled his version, *Oguz Destani: Residettin Oguznamesi, Tercüme ve Tahlili* (Istanbul, 1972) (published posthumously), from twelve manuscripts. Though originally composed and later put down on paper in a Turk dialect prior to the thirteenth century, it was widely rendered into Persian. Known translations include *Oughouz-name, epopee turque*, tr. Riza Nur (Alexandria: Société des publications Égyptienne, 1928); *Die Legende von Oghuz Qaghan*, eds. W. Bang and R. Arat (Berlin: Phil.-Histr. K1. XXV, Sitzb. d. Preuss. Akad. D. Wiss., 1932). To my knowledge, there is no English rendition as yet. See also Denis Sinor, "Oguz Kagan Destani Üzerine Bazi Mülahazalar," *Türk Dili ve Edebiyati Dergisi* (tr. from French by A. Ates, 1952); Faruk Sümer's book-length article, "Oguzlar'a Ait Destani Mahiyetde Eserler," *Ankara Üniversitesi DTC Fakültesi Dergisi* (1959); and the introduction by Geoffrey L. Lewis to his translation of *The Book of Dede Korkut*.

14. See examples cited by Audrey L. Altstadt, "Issues in National Identity in Soviet Azerbaijan" (The New Hampshire International Seminar, Center for International Perspectives, University of New Hampshire, April 7, 1989); idem, *The Azerbaijani Turks: Power and Identity under Russian Rule* (Stanford: Hoover Institution Press, 1992), Studies of Nationalities series, pp. 188–91, 208–10.

15. See Altstadt, *The Azerbaijani Turks*, especially pp. 112, 122–25, 131–50, for a listing of the scholars and literati liquidated during the "great terror" and the particular methods used for the purpose.

16. See Alexandre Bennigsen, "The Crisis of the Turkic National Epics, 1951–1952: Local Nationalism or Internationalism?" *Canadian Slavonic Papers*, vol. 17 (1975).

17. The following constitutes a partial list: T.I. Hajiyev and K.N. Veliyev, *Azärbaijan dili tarikhi: Ocherklär va materiallar* [History of the Azerbaijan Language] (Baku: Maarif, 1983). Fully 130 of the 180 pages in this college-level textbook are devoted to the discussion of oral literature and the literature of the thirteenth–seventeenth centuries, including *Dede Korkut*; *Azärbaijan filologiya mäsäläläri* [Matters of Azerbaijan Philology], II (Baku: Institute of Philology, Azerbaijan Academy of Sciences, 1984), contains papers dedicated to *Dede Korkut*. Periodic journals began providing space to the debate as well: Azamat Rustamov, "*Dädä Gorkut*'la bagli yer adlari" [Place Names Connected with *Dede Korkut*], *Älm vä Häyat*, 1987, no. 9; Mirali Sayidov, "*Dädä Gorgut* gahramanlaryning kökünü düsünürken" [Thinking About the Origins of the *Dede Korkut* Heroes], *Älm vä*

Häyat, 1987, no. 10; Penah Halilov, "*Kitabi Dede Gorgud*'un jografiyasi" [Geography of *Dede Korkut*], *Älm vä Häyat*, 1988, no. 8; Kemal Veliyev, "Bir daha *Dädä Gorgut* Seirlari hakkinda" [Once Again on the Poems of the *Dede Korkut*], *Azärbaijan*, 1981, no. 11; Bakir Nabiyev, "Epik zhanr vä muäsir häyat" [Epic Genre and Contemporary Life], *Azärbaijan*, 1986, no. 7; Akif Hüseyinov, "Näsrimiz vä kechmishimiz" [Our Prose and Our Past], *Azärbaijan*, 1982, no. 10; [Round Table], "Mevzumuz: Tarihimiz, abidälärimiz, därsliklerimiz" [Our Topic: Our History, Monuments, and Textbooks], *Azärbaijan*, 1988–89; this series included discussion of *Dede Korkut* by contributors including Zemfira Verdiyeva (Doctor of Philology, Professor) and Arif Hajiyev (Doctor of Philology and Professor).

18. See L. Branson, "How Kremlin Keeps Editors in Line," *The Times* (London), January 5, 1986, p. 1; Martin Dewhurst and Robert Farrell, *The Soviet Censorship* (Metuchen, NJ, 1973). Further, see Mariana Tax Choldin, *A Fence Around the Empire: Censorship of Western Ideas under the Tsars* (Durham: Duke University Press, 1985).

19. *Azerbaijan*, 1988, no. 6. Cf. Altstadt, "Issues in National Identity in Soviet Azerbaijan," p. 28. A Russian version appeared the same year, approved for publication in a record-breaking seven days: *Dede Korkut* (Baku, 1988). It was translated by Anar, a well-known Azerbaijan author and poet who does not sign his family name: Resul Oglu Rizaev. A significant work that appeared not long afterward is Kamal Abdullayev, *Gizli Dede Korkut* [The Secret *Dede Korkut*] (Baku: Yazici, 1991).

20. *Kitabi Dede Korkut* (Baku, 1988).

ETHNOGRAPHIC INFORMATION CONCERNING AZERBAIJAN CONTAINED IN THE *DEDE KORKUT* DASTAN

The *Dede Korkut* dastan, orally recited since the ninth–eleventh centuries, is the most precious written document of our mother tongue. It is a wealth of sources reflecting the true spiritual world, way of life, traditions, and customs of our people. From this perspective, the information contained in the *Dede Korkut* dastan is important to our learning about Azerbaijan's ethnography during the Middle Ages.

The *Dede Korkut* epos is connected with the Oghuz tribes arriving in Azerbaijan. From the dastan we learn that the Oghuz reached Azerbaijan long before it was set down on paper. Turkish-speaking tribes, Khazars,[a] Kipchaks,[b] and Oghuz, beginning with the sixth–seventh centuries, settled within Azerbaijan, mixing and merging with the populations there.[1] Despite the Khaliphate's exempting the tribes from taxes and other tolls in the vicinity of Derbend,[c] and other efforts[2] to stem the Turkish-speaking tribes, they continued to arrive in Azerbaijan. Especially during the ninth to eleventh centuries, large numbers of Oghuz reached Azerbaijan.[3] Speaking of these Oghuz, the great poet of the eleventh century, Getran Tebrizi Emir Shamsaddin [1012–1088][d] wrote:[e]

These Turks arriving from Turkistan
Accepted you as their ruler
Separated from their relatives and relations
Began living under your rule
Now they are everywhere
Prepared to serve you[4]

It is an accepted fact that the Oghuz arriving in Azerbaijan in both the sixth–seventh and the ninth–eleventh centuries settled there and merged with the Azerbaijan populations.

Academician V.V. Bartol′d (W.W. Barthold), in his last work on *Dede Korkut*, stated: "it is not possible to surmise that this dastan could have been written anywhere but in the Caucasus"[5]—the latest researcher confirming this commentary on the dastan *Dede Korkut*.

Although it could be said that the dastan *Dede Korkut* reflects the history of the Turkmen, Azerbaijan, and Turkish peoples in literary form, and this work's language is close to that of other Turkish-speaking people, its vocabulary, phraseologic expressions, and grammatical structure is closer to Azerbaijan [Turkish] than the others.[6]

In addition to the milieu and the language[7] in which the dastans were created, expression characteristics, composition of vocabulary, and grammatic structure, this dastan reflects today's Azerbaijan people's lifestyle, customs, and traditions. These customs and traditions are connected with the name of the Oghuz who have arrived and settled in Azerbaijan over the centuries, intermixing with the existing tribes there.

It is well known that, especially in the past, when different groups of people came into contact, they regarded each others' lifestyles, politics, and customs as worthy of emulation. Accordingly, each group, and later, tribes and neighboring peoples gradually learned each others' way of life. When neighboring tribes live in the same area over a prolonged period, mixing and merging with each other, they acquire an affinity for each others' customs. Consequently it is always the local [first-arrived] tribe that has superiority in the process of the resulting amalgamation. The arriving Oghuz, who melded with the Azerbaijan tribes, thus joined the existing way of life.

The *Book of Dede Korkut* comprises twelve sections, or dastans, which reflect the details of tribal life. Because a person named Dede Korkut participates in the events of all twelve dastans, some critics regard him as the author of these dastans. However, since they are not the product of a single era[8] they could not have been authored by one individual, but are the works of different *ozans-ashiks* [poet-bards][f] of various eras.[9]

In the dastans, Dede Korkut appears as the *aksakal*,[g] the advisor or sage, solving the difficulties faced by tribal members. Within the tribe, "Let Dede Korkut name this boy. Dede Korkut arrived; 'the name of your son ought to be Bogach. I hereby name him . . . ,' he said."[10] In Azerbaijan dastans and recitations, there is a prominent tradition of aksakals, the elders, naming young men. Gurban, who gained fame as a sixteenth-century *ashik* poet, says: "Then they wished to name the boy. A wise old man said: 'I named the boy Gurbani, because I found this through a sacrifice.' "[11] Among the population, respected aksakals are wise and know how to solve problems; among ashiks they are generally called *dede* [grandfather]. In the past, this term designated respected tribal elders, and now is used within families; in many localities of Azerbaijan, it replaces *ata* [ancestor or father].

The dastans reflect the life of the tribes occupied with animal husbandry, living in the northwest regions of Azerbaijan from Derbend to Tumanisi, around the mountain foothills; "even in the summer, the snow and ice does not melt on the Kazilik mountain."[12] Among these tribes were also those who settled and engaged in farming. In the dastans we find:

> The buds of our mountains are large
> On those mountains, we have vineyards
> Those vineyards bear bunches of dark grapes
> When crushed, those grapes become scarlet wine
> Whoever partakes of that wine becomes intoxicated[13]
> . . . . [14]
> I caused the dry rivers to be filled with water[15]
> The ornament of the vineyard and the orchard is water.[16]

Although there are references to farming, viticulture, and orchards, identified with settled life, in the dastans, they occupy a small place; what is primarily reflected is the life connected with nomadic animal husbandry.

These tribes live in *kishlak* [winter quarters] and *yaylak* [summer pastures]. The summer pastures were in the vicinity of Derbend.[17] There the heroes receive as a reward "The yaylaks on the opposite mountains."[18] Rewards of this sort were requested on behalf of those demonstrating their bravery: "Give him a long-necked white horse[19] to ride—he is talented. Let this boy have plenty[20] of sheep from your white sheepfold, so he may grow up intelligent—he is virtuous. Give this boy a red camel from your herds,[21] so he may transport loads—he is able."[22]

The principal wealth of these nomadic tribes comprised sheep, cattle, horses, and camels, which are discussed at length in the dastans:

> Ey mother, in a place where there are horses,
> Ought there not be a colt?[23]
> Where there are white sheep,
> Should there not be a single lamb?
> At a place where there are red camels,
> Would not a baby camel[24] be found?[25]

As noted above, there is much discussion pertaining to horses, cattle, and red camels in the dastan *Dede Korkut*. It is sometimes surmised that, given the natural setting, they have not widely utilized camels for transportation in Azerbaijan. This may be incorrect, since from the sixth–fifth centuries B.C. until the first half of the twentieth century, camels were extensively used for transportation. The red camels encountered in *Dede Korkut* are also referenced in many written documents,[26] recitations, and *dastans*. Ashik Abbas includes camels among the most desirable items to give his beloved:

> Almighty God, this is my wish
> Let me see my beloved live to be a hundred
> With increased wealth and success
> Sixty camels forming a train.[27]

The primary means of transportation for the nomadic tribes depicted in *Dede Korkut* was the camel. Just as "stables of horses" were important for riding, "trains of camels" were necessary for "loading," to transport goods. These tribes also utilized other means of conveyance, such as carts, to a lesser extent.[28]

The heroes of the dastans lived in *chadir* [tents] made from fine cloth, and in the alachik and chardak.[h] There is information regarding some of these dwellings in "How Salur Kazan's House Was Pillaged":

> How did the enemy rend you, my beautiful home
> There where the white pavilions stood the traces stay
> The field remains where the Oghuz nobles galloped
> The hearth remains where the dark kitchen stood.[29]

or:

> Son, pillar of my great tent with its golden smoke-hole,
> Whom I swaddled in the gold-framed cradle.[30]

In these works, the barren campsite is depicted. From these verses it can be gathered that these tribes also possessed and lived in structures other than tents. The white, gold, and yellow pavilions mentioned in the dastan constituted the partitions inside a home.[i] In addition, the dastans speak of roofed and trellis-type dwellings; these were not universally utilized by all members of the tribe. Bayindir, Salur, and the Beys[j] lived in graceful pavilions with embroidered silk decorations and carpets, while the ordinary members of the tribe occupied light-roofed and trellis structures.

Concerning the food consumed by protagonists in the dastans, mention is made of meat, *kimiz*,[k] yoghurt,[31] *kavurma*,[l] *komech*,[m] etc. Their clothing—woven by girls and women—comprised the *kaftan*, *cubbe* [robe?], *cuha* [broadcloth], *chirgab* [underwear?], fur and leather hats, *capug* [coarse cloth], *shalvar* [loose trousers] and *tulbend* [muslin, gauze]. All these articles of clothing, with the exception of the iron armor[32] worn in battle, were produced from the crops grown by the tribes. The cubbe was sleeveless and put on over the head. The kaftan, as depicted in the dastan, was long-sleeved and long-skirted, worn under the cubbe; it was made by an engaged girl for her fiancé. As it was embroidered, it was regarded as a precious gift. In the section "When the Inner Oghuz Rebelled Against the Outer Oghuz and Beyrek Died" many a bey confronted Kazan Khan and attempted to persuade Beyrek to join them. Beyrek declined, citing Kazan's munificence to him. He listed the presents he received: "Many a time I wore magnificent kaftans,"[32] given him by Kazan.[33]

The *Dede Korkut* mentions implements used in working and farming, principally related to animal husbandry. Some are in common use today: *cilav-yuyen* [reins, bridle], *yeher* [saddle], *uzengi* [stirrup], *nal* [horseshoe], *kendir* [hemp], *sicim* [cord], *bichak-chahmak* [knife], *dagarcik* [pouch], *kamchi* [whip], *badja* [milkpail]. Many terms for weapons are also found in the dastans, because the population of Azerbaijan had to defend themselves against invaders during the ninth–eleventh centuries. The heros of *Dede Korkut* dastans make use of various weapons. In "How Salur Kazan's House Was Pillaged," shepherd Karaja, depicted as a people's hero,[n] recites them in the following verses:

> Don't talk rubbish, there's a good infidel dog!
> Rabid infidel, who shares with my dog
>   a dog dish of my slops,[34]
> Why boast of the dappled horse you ride?
> I wouldn't swap my goat with the spotted head for it.
> Why boast of the helmet[35] you wear?
> I wouldn't swap my cap for it.
> Why boast of your sixty-span lance?
> I wouldn't swap my dogwood[36] stick for it.
> Why boast of your quiver with your ninety arrows?
> I wouldn't swap my colored-handled sling for it.
> Come over here from far and near,
> See the beating your men will get; and then be off.[37]

and:

> Give me your chestnut horse,
> Give me your shield of many colors,
> Give me your pure sword of black steel,
> Give me the eighty arrows in your quiver,
> Give me your strong bow with its white grip.[38]

In addition to the *tugulga* [*tolga*—iron helmet], *altmis tutam gonder* [sixty-span lance], *ok* [arrow], *yay* [bow], and *kalkan* [shield] in these verses are weapons such as the *gurz* [iron-mace], *chomak* [wood-mace], and *sungu* [short-lance]. In addition to weapons of iron the shepherd's *sapan* [slingshot] is mentioned. In "How Salur Kazan's House Was Pillaged," how the shepherd Karaja joined the fighting with the sapan he carried in his belt is related as follows: "the pouch[39] of the shepherd's slingshot was made of a three-year-old calf-hide. The rope of his slingshot was made of hair from three goats. Every time he swung, he released a twelve-batman° stone.[40] The first time he released a projectile, he downed two [adversaries]. The second time he swung, three and four fell."[41]

The sapan is still used, as the "weapon" carried by most shepherds in their belts for self-defense. It is usually woven from goat-hair,[42] although a sapan made of wool is also encountered in some places. The width at the widest part is 15–20 centimeters, and the length of each arm, depending on the user's height, is 40–50 centimeters, woven in a single piece. The center piece is the palm or pouch (now called *tas yeri*—place for the stone), sometimes made of leather.

In the dastans, there is also mention of making *taragga*.[43] From the context it is clear that this weapon was utilized to produce a powerful noise. The word taragga is in use today, for a folded-paper toy made by children, which when moved quickly produces a noise reminiscent of a pistol report.

In *Dede Korkut* dastan, issues pertaining to family and way of life occupy a special place. As is known, the ninth–eleventh centuries in Azerbaijan constituted a complex era. From a political point of view, this complexity was not confined to the unending struggles for sovereignty, battles, and turmoil, but extended to social relations. Islam attempted to influence the way of life of these mobile tribes by every means.

In the dastans, relations among family members are principally based on tribal customs and traditions. Women, just like men, participate in the social and agricultural life of the tribe. In addition to running the home, they manage an important part of livestock raising, the primary tribal activity. Men are occupied with planting and hunting. At first it seems as if women are excluded from farming.ᵖ On closer reading, the women are portrayed to be as brave as the warrior men. They hunt and enter battles with weapons in hand. This bravery of the women is reflected in the first dastans. In "Bogach Khan Son of Dirse Khan," Dirse Khan's wife goes after her son who has not returned from the hunt. It says: "Dirse Khan's lady turned away. She could not bear it; she called her forty slender maidens to her side, she mounted her white horse and went in quest of her dear son."[44] In the section "Bamsi Beyrek Son of Baybora," one of the heroines, Lady Chichek, enters into a contest of skill with Baybora, equalling him in archery, wrestling, and horse racing.[45] In the fight against an adversary, Kazan's wife wields her sword alongside him.[46] Kanturali's fiancée contests with him. Among these tribes, when describing girls and women, it is stated: "They could draw [their bows] to their right and left, the arrows they discharged would not fall on the ground."[47] There was great respect for women.

> Come here, luck of my head, throne of my house,
> Like a cypress when you go out walking.
> Your black hair entwines itself round your heels,

Your meeting eyebrows are like a drawn bow,
Your red cheeks are like autumn apples,
My woman, my support, my dignity.[48]

Thus women were described within the tribe. There are no references to bigamy in the dastan. In "Bogach Son of Dirse Khan," despite Dirse Khan being goaded: "Him who has no son or daughter God most High humiliated, and we shall humiliate him too,"[49] and though Dirse Khan is angered and blames his wife, he does not consider taking a second wife.

We do not encounter in the dastans instances of girls or young men being forced to marry. Both parties had to agree; if they saw and did not like each other, "if the heart was not filled with love," they did not marry. In one of the dastans, when a young man wished to marry, his father said:

" 'Son, finding the girl is up to you; I'll see that you're fed and provided for.'

Thereupon, Kanturali, that dragon of heroes, rose from his place and took his forty young men with him. He searched the Inner Oghuz, but could not find a girl; he turned around and came home again. His father said:

'Have you found a girl, son?'

Kanturali replied:

'May the Oghuz lands be devastated; I could not find a girl to suit me, father.' "[50]

It can be seen from this exchange that men did not marry until they found a girl to their liking. In another dastan, despite the fact that Lady Chichek and Bamsi Beyrek were betrothed in the cradle by their fathers, Bay Bijan and Baybora, Chichek did not marry Beyrek before testing him.[51]

However free the young were to exercise their wishes in matters of marriage, they did not ignore the customs of their families and tribe. After Beyrek and Chichek agreed to marry, Beyrek went home and informed his father, Baybora, of his decision. His father answered thus:

"Son, let us invite the nobles of the teeming Oghuz to our hearth-fire and let us act as they think advisable."[52]

Those invited to the council agreed to the marriage and resolved the matter of the envoy. Since the task of representation was carried out by the revered aksakal, the Oghuz Beys said:

"Let Dede Korkut request her hand."[53] Dede Korkut, designated as the emissary by the gathering, is greeted on his return with the query:

"Dede! Are you a boy, or a girl?"

Dede replied:

"I am a boy."

"The bearer of good tidings came to Beyrek and his mother and sisters and they rejoiced and were glad."[54]

This example of sending an emissary is reminiscent of the present-day tradition. In the same dastan, there are also references to *baslik* [presents or money given to the bride's family from the groom's side] and *cheyiz* [bride's dowry]. The brother of Lady Chichek demands a baslik for his sister thus: "Bring me a thousand horses that have never mounted a mare, a thousand male camels that have never seen a female camel, a thousand rams that have never seen a ewe, a thousand dogs with no tails or ears. . . ."[55] After Beyrek's father provides what was demanded, consent is received and the *kichik toy*[q] is held.[56] The term *kichik toy* found in *Dede Korkut* is encountered today in some regions, meaning a feast to commemorate the engagement. After the kichik toy, the young couple are *nishanli* [engaged, intended]. In the dastans, the word *nishanli* also has variants such as *yavuklu* [token of betrothal] and *adakli* [promised]. At the time the dastans were written, among Azerbaijan tribes there was also the tradition of *beshikkertme, yavuklu etme*[57] [betrothal at the cradle, token of betrothal] from childhood.[58]

In the dastans, as we noted, the term kichik toy was utilized for engagement, and the *ulu toy* was reserved for the grand feast [marriage ceremony]. "Yaltajuk, son of Yalanji held the kichik toy. He promised the ulu toy."[59] After the ulu toy, they repaired to the *bey otagi* [nuptial chamber], still called by this name), a distance from the bride's in-laws.[60] In the "Bamsi Beyrek Son of Baybora" it is noted: "At the time of the Oghuz, upon marrying, a young man would shoot an arrow. Where the arrow landed, there they erected the nuptial chamber."[61] This tradition, the establishment of the nuptial chamber some distance from the parents' home, was symbolic of the growth of the tribe, constituting a natural increase of population, leaving behind its limited scope.

The bride and young women wore simple ornaments and jewelry. "Her hair braided, wearing buttons of red, hands dyed with henna to the wrists,[62] ornate gold rings on her fingers, the girl was married."[63] The bride wore a scarlet veil. The groom would wear the "scarlet kaftan," which the bride had made and sent to him, for forty days. Afterward, it would be presented to a dervish.[64]

As we gather from the *Dede Korkut* dastan, divorce among the nomadic tribes was almost nonexistent during the ninth–eleventh centuries. In the twelve dastans comprising the book, we do not encounter a single divorce. Husband and wife are separated only by chance, when battles and conflicts necessitated a man's absence from his family. In such cases the men would say to their wives or fiancées: "Woman [girl], allow me a year! If I do not return by then, give me two years! If I am not back by then, allow me three years!"[65] Relations among family members are characterized by an even higher degree of loyalty and sacrifice. The love between husband and wife is placed above parents' affection for their offspring. In "Wild Dumrul Son of Dukha Koja," the principal character is defeated in a battle with Azrael. Azrael wants to take his life. He pleads, and Azrael gives him the option of substituting another soul. The young man asks his parents, but they do not want to die in their son's place. The young man loses all hope, and prepares to bid farewell to his wife, who says: "Your embalmed mother and father, what is in a life that they declined? ... May my life be sacrificed to yours,"[66] and declares her readiness to accept death in her husband's stead. A reading of the dastans reveals the wife to be the supportive, honored, and devoted friend of her husband.

During the ninth–eleventh centuries in Azerbaijan, Islam had still not attained a dominant position among nomadic tribes.[67] Religion was very weak. Even though there were references to Islam in the language, we do not encounter compliance with such precepts in deeds. In "Wild Dumrul Son of Dukha Koja," belief in God is reluctant. The character defies God. He does not entertain any thoughts of Azrael; he battles with and attempts to destroy him. Here, the character is presented as being much more powerful than Azrael in many respects. While their belief in God was weak, the heroes of the dastans often concluded compacts based on earthly objects. For example, they took oaths with the words: "May you be pared by my sword," "perforated by my arrow," "water the earth." Their prayers were not religious, but, like their oaths, consisted of elements from daily life.[r]

There was no compliance with the Islamic "precepts." Wine, prohibited by religion, was not absent from their tables. Statements such as "If there is a shadow on your pure heart, wine will clear it,"[68] "they drank wine in golden goblets,"[69] are often encountered in the dastans. The gatherings depicted in the dastans are not without "wine-filled cups." In these social occasions, one cannot escape a line of "golden-stemmed pitchers." Infidel girls fill the cups of the Oghuz Beys.[70] The names introduced by Islam, such as Mohammed, Ali, Hasan, and Hüseyin, had not found acceptance within this society. Music and dance, forbidden by Islam, were intertwined with the daily life of the ninth–eleventh century Azerbaijan people. The nomadic tribes in particular could not live their lives silently. Instruments and singers were not condemned, but on the contrary, the famed *ashiks* of the era were the respected *ozans* among the people. To be an ozan, to play the *kopuz*[s] was the aspiration of every tribal member, to the extent that tribal leaders, too, learned these skills. The son of famed Baybora, Beyrek, after obtaining his freedom, returns home in the guise of an ozan, in order to take stock of his friends and foes. This event is depicted thus:

> Beyrek came to the Oghuz land and saw a minstrel [*ozan*] journeying. "Wither away, minstrel?" said he. "To the wedding, young lord," the minstrel replied. "Whose is the wedding?" "Yaltajuk's, son of Yalanji." "And who is the girl he is marrying?" "The betrothed of the lord Beyrek," said the minstrel. "Minstrel," said Beyrek, "give me your lute [*kopuz*] and I shall give you my horse. Keep him till I come and bring you his price and take him. . . ." The minstrel gave his lute to Beyrek. . . . Beyrek took it.[71]

Kazan Khan, depicted as the principal character of the *Dede Korkut* dastans, also played the kopuz, composing poems.[72] Kopuz-players traveled widely, becoming a witness to people's sorrows and happiness. They discerned people's friends and foes, and were well acquainted with the brave and the contemptible. In the introduction to the fifteenth-century *Dede Korkut* dastans, it says: "Kopuz-bearing ozans traveled from land to land, tribe to tribe; it is the ozan who knows the brave and the coward."[73] To have your daughter marry an ozan, becoming related with the ozans, was also regarded as an honor. In popular poetry, this is summarized as:

> My daughter, my daughter
> May my daughter be resplendent[74]
> May the ozan earn silver
> I betrothed my daughter to an ozan.

According to the Turkish scholar M.F. Köprülüzade, as found in the eighteenth-century music book *Zubdetül Advar*, the *kopuz-saz* has three strings, is made of wood, and played with the plectrum.[75] In addition to the kopuz, *nagharalar* [kettle drums] and *burmasi altin borular* [golden knotted, as coiled horns][76] were among the musical instruments of the nomadic tribes in this era. The kettle drums and horns were largely used in battle.[t] The drummers would be accompanied by a group of *zurna*-players[u] at feasts.[77]

The information contained in the *Dede Korkut* dastans is very interesting for the study of the spiritual civilization of the Azerbaijan people in the ninth–eleventh centuries. In these dastans, we also encounter information on feast days, childrens' games, and entertainments. As we begin to study the dastans from an ethnographic point of view, it will be possible to obtain more knowledge about these matters.

Editor's Notes

a. See Peter B. Golden, *Khazar Studies* (Budapest: Akadémiai Kiadó, 1980); D.M. Dunlop, *The History of the Jewish Khazars* (Princeton: Princeton University Press, 1954); N. Golb and O. Pritsak, *Khazarian Hebrew Documents* (Ithaca: Cornell University Press, 1982).

b. See *Turks, Hungarians and Kipchaks: A Festschrift in Honor of Tibor Halasi-Kun*, P. Oberling, ed., *Journal of Turkish Studies*, 1984, vol. 8.

c. According to sources, Derbend is the location of first contacts between the Khazars and the Arabs, ca. A.D. 642–52. See D.M. Dunlop, *The History of the Jewish Khazars*.

d. It is stressed that Getran Tebrizi is an Azerbaijan poet, writing in Persian. His collected works have been translated into Azerbaijan Turkish. See Getran Tebrizi, *Divan* [Collected Poems], trans. by Gulamhuseyin Berdeli (Baku: Nizami Institute of Literature and Language, Azerbaijan SSR Academy of Sciences, 1967). The first eighteen pages of the introduction in this volume is devoted to the arguments and documentation that Getran Tebrizi was an Azerbaijan Turk and that he wrote his works in Azerbaijan Turkish. Tebrizi's works have long been available in the West, cited, *inter alia*, by E.G. Browne in his *Literary History of Persia* (London, 1902) and catalogued by Charles Rieu. See the *Catalogue of the Persian Manuscripts in the British Museum* (London, 1895), vol. 4.

e. The original quotation is in Persian and written in Perso-Arabic script, followed by its translation in Cyrillic "designed" for Azerbaijan Turkish in the Soviet era. See *Al-pamysh* for the "language reforms" leading to the formation of the "alphabets."

f. For the terms *ozan* and *ashik*, the composers and reciters of *dastans*, see Paksoy, *Alpamysh*, pp. 3–5, 14–15.

g. Literally "white-beard," the respected elder. See H.B. Paksoy, "The Traditional Oglak Tartis among the Kirghiz of the Pamirs," *Journal of the Royal Asiatic Society (of Great Britain & Ireland)*, 1985, no. 2.

h. Types of dwellings, with or without portable wooden structures. For a detailed discussion of the dwellings or homes of this type, see Z.V. Togan, *Türkili Türkistan*, p. 46. *DLT* also provides examples.

i. Dadashzade uses the architectural term *agban*, variant of *eyvan*: a three-walled, vaulted structure, usually open at the front.

j. The principal characters of the dastan *Dede Korkut*.

k. Also known as *qumiss*, etc. See, *inter alia*, *DLT* (p. 184). It is still an immensely popular drink containing natural alcohol, due to the fermentation process in its preparation (although it is not as strong as hard liquor). It is not plentiful year round because of seasonal factors. Russians became aware of the nourishing and rejuvenating qualities of kimiz after their occupation of Kazakhstan. Several sanatoriums are currently operating in the Kazakh steppe where kimiz is the primary dietetic and therapeutic prescription, especially against tuberculosis. This discovery of the beneficial effects of kimiz against TB is probably what caused Moscow to reconsider and relax sovhoz-kolhoz rules in the area, in order to ensure the maintenance of large herds of mares necessary to supply kimiz for the sanatoriums where party officials are treated.

l. Meat that is deep-fried to prevent spoilage.

m. Where food in containers, usually in clay pots, is buried in hot coals or ash for slow cooking.

n. The implication being that although he is not of noble lineage, he is able to tell off the adversary courageously.

o. Clearly an exaggeration for emphasis, worthy of the "pouch" of the slingshot he had. One *batman* was equal to 5–30 lbs., depending on the geographic location. As a weight-measure, the batman was in use until the 1930s in the region.

p. The word used here, *chöl*, means both "steppe-desert" and "farming," depending on context. While reading the next passage, one must keep this in mind.

q. *Toy* is the term used for ceremonies, including but not limited to weddings. For example, feasts of all manner found in *Dede Korkut* are called *toys*.

r. What appears to be an argument in compliance with the Communist Party of the Soviet Union's atheistic policies, therefore assured a sympathetic reading from the official censor, in actuality has a secondary agenda. According to I. Kafesoglu, there was an indigenous religion, Tengri, among the Turk groups before the arrival of Islam. See *Türk Milli Kültürü* (Istanbul, 1984). Throughout the 1980s, Central Asians began expressing similar thoughts, rejecting Islam as a usurper that sapped the vitality of the Turks. For example, M. Mahmudov, in his "Ölmez Kayalar" ("Immortal Cliffs," serialized in the monthly *Sark Yildizi* [Tashkent], October and November, 1981), underscores the struggle between the indigenous religion and Islam. See H.B. Paksoy, "Central Asia's New Dastans," *Central Asian Survey*, 1987, vol. 6, no. 1. That theme received attention even earlier in Azerbaijan. For example, in 1927, Jafar Jabarli wrote a novel with the title *Od Gelini* (Bride of Fire), which was reissued in the original, in the collective works of Jafar Jabarli, *Eserler*, vol. 1 (Baku: Azarbaijan Devlet Neshriyati, 1968). One of the main themes of this novel is the battle between the indigenous religion and Islam, introduced by Arab invaders in the eighth–ninth centuries. It was also translated into Russian, under the title *Nevsta ognia*, reference to which is found in N.A. Pashaev, *Pobeda kulturnoi revoliutsii v sovetskom Azerbaidzhane* (Moscow: Nauka, 1976), p. 118. See also *Ocherk istorii Azerbaidzhanskoi sovetskoi literatury* (Moscow: USSR Academy of Sciences,

1963), which contains a synopsis (pp. 145–46). Nor is this movement confined to the post-1917 period. Even earlier, Celil Memmedkuluzade began outlining and expressing this conflict in his immensely popular journal *Molla Nasreddin* during 1906. See H.B. Paksoy, "Elements of Humor in Central Asia: The Example of the Journal *Molla Nasreddin* in Azerbaijan," *Turkestan: als historischer Faktor und politische Idee*, Baymirza Hayit Festschrift, Erling von Mende, ed. (Cologne: Studienverlag, 1988). Moreover, this conflict has been receiving attention in the writings of others throughout Central Asia.

s. Lute. A representative specimen may be found in the Pitt-Rivers Museum. In Asia Minor, a direct descendant of this instrument, the *saz* and a slightly larger version, the *baglama*, is still enormously popular. For a full description with photographs, see Bolat Saribaev, *Kazaktin Muzikalik Aspaptari* (Alma-Ata, 1978); and G. Doerfer, "Turkische und Mongolische Elemente," *Neupersichen* 3 (Wiesbaden, 1967), 1546.

t. The main purpose was to transmit orders from the commanders to the troops, over distances of up to three miles. These orders involved direction of attack, regrouping, flanking, and specialized tactical ambush maneuvers. Later, under the Ottomans, a full military band evolved.

u. The *zurna* is a double-reed woodwind instrument, probably the grandfather of the modern-day oboe. It is still in wide use.

Notes

1. M. Rafili, *Drevnaiaia Azerbaizhanskaia literatura (do nachala XVI v.)* (Baku, 1941), p. 16.

2. Dr. Mehmed Cevad, *Tercüme Tarih Tabari az abvali balgay* (Tahran, 1332 [1914/1915]), p. 327 [in Perso-Arabic script].

3. *Materialy po istorii Azerbaidzhana iz Tarikh-al-Kamil ibn al-Asira* (Baku, 1940), p. 111.

4. Getran Tebrizi, *Divan* (Tabriz, 1333 [1916/1917]), p. 5 [in Perso-Arabic script]. [This is the volume from which the above-cited Azerbaijan Turkish translation of the same work was made.]

5. *Kniga moego Dede Korkuda: Oguzskii geroicheskii epos.* V.V. Bartold, trans. (Moscow-Leningrad, 1962), p. 120.

6. Ibid., p. 5.

7. *Azerbaijan Edebiyati Tarihi* [History of Azerbaijan Literature], vol. 1 (Baku, 1960), p. 53.

8. For detailed information on the language of the *dastans*, see E.M. Demircizade, *Kitab-i Dede Korkut dastanlarinin Dili* (Baku, 1959), p. 6.

9. *Azerbaijan Edebiyati Tarihi*, vol. 1, p. 54.

10. *Kitabi Dede Korkut* (Baku, 1939), p. 22 [see *The Book of Dede Korkut*, G.L. Lewis, trans., p. 31, "The Story of Boghach Khan"].

11. *Azerbaijan Halk dastanlari*, vol. 1 (Baku, 1961), p. 124. [The epithet Gurbani evokes images of "sacrificial." On the poet Gurban, see P. Efendiev, *Azerbaijan Sifahi Halk Edebiyati* (Baku, 1981), p. 168. This is a textbook for the Institute of Pedagogy. It is not unusual for parents to "pledge a vow, sacrifice" when they desire offspring. See Lewis, "Bamsi Beyrek," in *The Book of Dede Korkut*].

12. *Kitabi Dede Korkut*, p. 26.

13. *Esrük-sarhos.* [Dadashzade is providing the current-use equivalents for a number of words. In this case, the old Turkish word *esrük*, also found in the eleventh-century *DLT* (see above), is "intoxicated."]

14. *Kitabi Dede Korkut*, p. 87 [ellipsis by Dadashzade].

15. Ibid., p. 76.
16. Ibid., p. 35.
17. Ibid., p. 32.
18. Ibid., p. 130.
19. *Beyaz at cins at* ["white horse," symbolizing a thoroughbred].
20. *Tuman-chok saydi* [numerous].
21. *Gaytaban—deve yatagi* [specific place where the camel herd stays or is sheltered].
22. *Kitabi Dede Korkut*, p. 22.
23. *Kulun-at balasi* [colt].
24. *Köshek-deve balasi* [camel-colt].
25. *Kitabi Dede Korkut*, p. 39.
26. *Evliyayi seyahatnama*, vol. 3, p. 13 [in Perso-Arabic script].
27. *Ashiklar*, vol. 2 (Baku, 1960), p. 23.
28. *Kitabi Dede Korkut*, p. 144. [See Togan, *Oguz Destani*, for the earliest mention of "cart."]
29. Ibid., p. 34 [see the Lewis translation, p. 46].
30. Ibid., p. 36 [see the Lewis translation, p. 50].
31. Yoghurt—*katik*. In some places in Azerbaijan, the term yoghurt is still used.
32. *Kitabi Dede Korkut*, p. 157. [The original has two footnotes designated number 32 in the text, but only one footnote 32 is referenced at the bottom of the page. The second note 32 is not otherwise identified.]
33. The word *kaftan* was utilized in this context until the twentieth century.
34. *Yal—it yali* [dog slop].
35. *Zogal* [it appears that notes 35 and 36 were reversed during typesetting].
36. *Kitabi Dede Korkut*, p. 33.
37. Ibid., p. 36 [see the Lewis translation, p. 44].
38. *Tugulga—demir börk* [iron helmet] [see the Lewis translation, p. 49. The order of the original footnotes was scrambled, especially those pertaining to "dogwood" and "helmet"].
39. *Aya—sapanin tas koyulan yeri*.
40. *Kitabi Dede Korkut*, p. 40.
41. Ibid., p. 34.
42. Goat-hair [*kechi tükü*] is also called *gezil*.
43. *Kitabi Dede Korkut*, p. 129 [this word basically means "noise." Another term for this toy is "patlangach."]
44. Ibid. (Baku, 1939), p. 26 [see Lewis, p. 35].
45. Ibid., pp. 48–49 [see Lewis].
46. Ibid., p. 84.
47. Ibid., p. 94.
48. *Kitabi Dede Korkut* (Baku, 1939), p. 20. [See Lewis, p. 28. There are slight variations between lines provided by Dadashzade and the Lewis translation].
49. Ibid., p. 19 [Lewis, p. 28].
50. Ibid., p. 93 [Lewis, p. 117].
51. Ibid., p. 45.
52. Ibid., p. 49 [Lewis, p. 65].
53. *Kitabi Dede Korkut*, p. 51.
54. Ibid., p. 52 [Lewis, p. 67].
55. Ibid., pp. 49–51 [Lewis, p. 67].
56. Ibid., p. 55.
57. Ibid., p. 47.
58. This tradition was still alive until the revolution.

59. *Kitabi Dede Korkut*, p. 53.

60. The terms *gaynata* [*kayin-ata*: father-in-law] and *gaynana* [*kayin-ana*: mother-in-law] are still in use.

61. *Kitabi Dede Korkut*, p. 53.

62. The tradition of decorating hands with henna began during the Middle Ages.

63. *Kitabi Dede Korkut*, p. 137.

64. Ibid., p. 53.

65. Ibid., p. 137.

66. Ibid., pp. 90–91.

67. Said Nefisi, in his introduction to the *Nizaminin Kasideler ve Gazeller Divani*, basing himself on the works of the authors of the Middle Ages, states that even in the tenth century in Azerbaijan, Moslems do not constitute a majority.

68. *Kitabi Dede Korkut*, p. 55.

69. Ibid., p. 126.

70. Ibid., p. 31.

71. *Kitabi Dede Korkut*, pp. 58–59 [Lewis, p. 75].

72. Ibid., p. 145.

73. Ibid., p. 162 [see also Lewis, p. 190].

74. E.M. Damircizade, *Azerbaijan Edebi Dilinin Inkisaf Yollari* (Baku, 1958), p. 18.

75. *Azerbaijan Incesanati*, vol. 7 (Baku, 1962), p. 38.

76. *Kitabi Dede Korkut*, p. 42.

77. Ibid., p. 64.

Kahar Barat

Discovery of History
The Burial Site of Kashgarli Mahmud

Editor's Introduction

Kashgarli Mahmud was the author of *Divan Lugat it-Türk*,[1] completed ca. 1077 A.D. This unique text was discovered during the First World War in Istanbul, and the *Editio princeps* was made by Kilisli Rifat and published in Istanbul in 1917–19. *Divan Lugat it-Türk* has been translated into English, with an extensive critical apparatus, by Robert Dankoff, in collaboration with James Kelly.[2] Since its discovery, the *Divan Lugat it-Türk* continues universally and fundamentally to influence Central Asian studies. As very little was known about Kashgarli Mahmud's era, his outline of events in this study is most welcome for the recovery of history. Broadly viewed, that period was distinguished by struggles for the mastery of Central Asia with the Karakhanids in the east, the Seljuks in the west, and the Ghaznavids in the center, in the area from the Altai mountain range to the Oxus River.[3]

The news of the discovery of Kashgarli Mahmud's burial site was reported by the media in the People's Republic of China. The account below is a summary of information from contemporary Uyghur sources.

Notes

1. Kashgarli Mahmud, *Kitab Diwan Lugat at Türk* (Istanbul, 1917–19), 3 vols.
2. *Compendium of Turkic Dialects* (Cambridge, MA, 1982–84), 3 vols; no. 7 in the series *Sources of Oriental Languages and Literatures*, eds. S. Tekin and G.A. Tekin.

Kahar Barat, from Kulja, Xingjiang, completed doctoral studies in Harvard University's Inner Asian and Altaic Studies program. His report was first published in *AACAR Bulletin*, vol. 2, no. 3 (fall 1989).

3. For the applicable source material, see the notes to Muhammad Ali, "Let Us Learn About Our Heritage: Get to Know Yourself," in this volume.

DISCOVERY OF HISTORY:
THE BURIAL SITE OF KASHGARLI MAHMUD

After word emerged that work on the Uyghur edition of *Divan Lugat it-Türk* had begun in Xinjiang, Kashgarli Mahmud's name enjoyed a resurgence of popularity among the Uyghurs. When the news of this effort became public, it was heard that Kashgarli Mahmud's burial site was located in the village of Opal,[a] 45 kilometers west of Kashgar. In 1981, A. Rozi reported the discovery.

Details of Kashgarli Mahmud's life are scant. O. Pritsak suggested that Mahmud was a student of Husayn ibn Muhammad, the eldest son of Muhammad ibn Yusuf and mayor of Barsgan, and that Mahmud fled from a court revolt in Kashgar to Baghdad.[b]

During December 1982, the editors of the Uyghur *Divan Lugat it-Türk*, I. Muti'i and M. Osmanov, went to Opal to investigate the authenticity of the reports. Muti'i and Osmanov organized a forum to collect the recollections of the local populace. The people called the site "Hazrati Molla Mazari" (burial site of the venerable teacher), and spoke of a *Tazkire* (a written history of the shrine) that had been in their possession until 1956 and contained the name Mahmud bin Husayn, as Kashgarli Mahmud signed his name in the *Divan Lugat it-Türk*.

The shrine has been cared for by a Sheykh [hereditary caretaker] family, and they had had a *Tazkire* of it, but it "disappeared in the hands of archaeologists," stated people at the forum. "In 1956, Ismail Ibrahim (from Opal), now head of the cultural office of Kashgar Kona-Shahar, obtained the book from a man named Mahammat Congsa and gave it to Yusup Beg Mukhlisov." Ibrahim and Mukhlisov were both working in the Xinjiang Museum at that time. Thereafter, Mukhlisov moved to the USSR. In his notebook of 1957, which is kept in the Xinjiang Museum, Ibrahim made a record of the shrines in the Opal area and he wrote "Hazreti Mollam, name Kashgari, died in 477 Hegira." In 1981, Rozi wrote, "The book called *Tazkira'i Hazrati Molla* was written in 1791 by the historian Muhammat Abdul-Ali from Kashgar."

Before it was given away, the *Tazkire* was a sacred possession of the Sheykh family and local people. The people at the forum made many statements to Muti'i and Osmanov from their memory; all of these testimonies seem to have come from a single source and it is hard to imagine that the villagers could have made it up. Their interviews have been published [and are quoted here from Uyghur sources]. Among the interviews was one stating as follows:

> Fifty years ago I saw a document about that shrine from past Sheykhs. It was copied from the original document of "Hazreti Mollam," because while Badawlat (Yaqup Beg) was mayor of Kashgar, he collected all shrine documents in the Kashgar area. The preface of the document of "Hazreti Mollam"

read something like this: "I am Hazreti Mollam, Mawlana Shamsaddin Allam Mahmudiya. I have donated my . . . Patman* land. After I die, if some of my descendants become Sheykh and Mutawalla to my shrine, with permission, they must till my land without selling it, without making it their own property, without inheriting it, [they can] make [or use?] . . . oq* with grains, the Sheykh can use . . . oq of it, the Mutawalla can use . . . oq of it, use . . . oq for repairs, and spend for visitors from many places."

The information from these statements is, as suggested, consistent, and may be summarized as follows: (1) Hazreti Molla's name was Mahmud ibn Husayn al-Kashgari; his father, Husayn, was mayor of Barsgan with the title Amri Sab; his mother, Bubi Rabiya (or Bubi Rabiya Basri), was an intelligent woman; (2) Mahmud went to Iraq and Iran to study; he traveled through the dangerous pass "Muq Yolu"; (3) After he returned, Mahmud or his student killed a beast; Mahmud taught for eight years as a Mudderis. He died in 477 A.H. at the age of 97.

During this trip Muti'i and Osmanov also discovered another hamlet nearby, with the name of Sösar Agzi. It had originally been called Azikh. Azikh is recorded in *Divan Lugat it-Türk* as "the name of one of our villages." According to the local citizenry, the name change took place 100 to 150 years ago, after a flood. In an interview, Dawut Zumun, age 90, from Sösar Aghzi (Azikh), stated:

> My father died in 1952 at age 110. My grandfather's name was Kanji Ghojikam. The former name of the hamlet was Azikh. Later on it was inundated by flood waters from Sösar Aghzi, which left behind sand, so the name was changed to "Qumbagh" [sand garden]. "When we were growing up, it was Qumbagh," my father told me. Now it is called Sösar Aghzi."

A short time later, on January 6, 1983, an 80-year-old man, an intellectual, Emir Husayn Qazi Akhun, brought out from his home an old written document, a book titled *Masnawi Sirip*. It contains an inscription written in 1252 Hegira which states that this book is dedicated to the shrine. The importance of this inscription lies in the fact that the full name and title of the person in the shrine is indicated. It is the same name and title listed in *Divan Lugat it-Türk* and matches the claims of the villagers:

> On Rajab 14, 1252, the ox year (October 25, 1836 of the Common Era), I, the qadi of Kashgar court which was established on the basis of the law, Molla Sadiq Alam bin Shah Ala, have signed my seal as a document for this; in my healthy age of 114, with my love of and interest in knowledge, and with my polite manner, I have dedicated forever and I have donated perpetually my book which is the source of wisdom, replete with knowledge, six booklets bound together in one cover, written with embellishments by the careful pen on

---

*A unit of measure.

the pages, my expansive property, bought with gold, to the shrine of Hazreti Mawlam Sams al-Addin Chin Sahibi Qalam Mahmud al-Kashgari, buried above the pure spring, on the hillside of Opal in Kashgar.

I hope writers and scholars who sit at the stage of the shrine of Shams al-Addin Husayn Sahibi Qalam Mahmud al-Kashgari, who sit around the Süzük Bulag [the pure spring], read this book, pray to Sahibi Qalam Hazreti Mawlam Shams al-Addin Husayn Mahmud al-Kashgari; and teach knowledge to the Muslim people and our descendants and nations, making them superior in quality and excellence. I have appointed my leading student Molla Heyit Khalpat ibn Molla Ewaz to be the manager of it. I, Molla Sadiq Alam, have signed my seal below. . . .

Witnesses of the truth of my statement are Ulama-i Muddaris al-Nazar Akhunum, Secretary-General Molla Abdurrahim Nizari and secretary Navruz, secretary Turdus, Turdi Shaykh Akhunum, Molla Gojilaq, Zayidin Qorulbagi from Opal.

In June 1983 a united archaeological group from the autonomous regional bureau of cultural relics and the Kashgar regional bureau went to Opal and made further excavations. According to their report, the shrine is located at the latitude 37°, 30′ 75″ north and longitude 50° 18′ 39″ east. Some pieces of wood were sent for carbon dating. The expedition found many pre-Islamic relics, including pieces of Buddhist sculptures and hundreds of Sanskrit pages from Hazreti Molla Hill. Hazreti Molla Hill had been a flourishing Buddhist culture site before Islam. Local people frequently find Buddhist sculptures, figures, jars, and the like. One villager, Qasim Qazi Akhun remembered: "On the hill, there is an underground cave named 'Toqquz Qaznaq' [nine caverns]. When we were school children, we used to climb the Mazar and play there, entering through the top hole and getting out from another entrance" (*Kashgar Adabiyati*, 1983, I, p. 9).

Forty years ago, Qadir Haji, from the nearest Mollam Beghi village, and his father, Zordun Akhun, dug up a room by the hillside, and when they opened the door they found a big Buddhist copper statue weighing 25–30 kilograms. On a shelf on the left wall, there was a thick book which they believed was written in "Mongolian." Qadir Haji kept the book until the Cultural Revolution and then hid the book when he was accused, but now he cannot remember where he hid it (*Mahammat Zumum Sidiq*, 1983, p. 5).

Wei Liang-tao in pursuing his research on the Qarakhanids, had traveled to Hazreti Molla Mazar and reported that there was a stone inscription on the shrine. In his book *Sketch of the History of the Qarakhanids* (1983), he stated that, "According to comrade Li Kai, the great writer's inscription was found here during the Great Cultural Revolution, but soon after that it was moved to a new county cement plant and was used as a foundation stone, and now it is difficult to find it again."

The discovery of Kashgarli Mahmud's tomb produced much excitement. The journal *Kashgar Adabiyati* dedicated its first issue of 1984 to this topic. Kashgar Uyghur publications published a collection *Mahmud Kashgari*. The government declared it a protected cultural site and set aside 50,000 yuan to rebuild it.

According to the available materials and despite the seven-century gap in the evidence, the person mentioned by the villagers is apparently Mahmud al-Kashgari, the author of *Divan Lugat it-Türk*. Even if this is not a genuine shrine, it may still be true that it was the source of another copy of *Divan Lugat it-Türk* that was subsequently lost.

In *Divan Lugat it-Türk* it is recorded that the writing of the book was begun in the beginning of the Hegira Jumada I, 464 (January 25–February 23, 1072). We are told that Mahmud died in 477 Hegira at age 97. Calculating on that basis, Mahmud began his book at age 82. He was born in 380 Hegira (March 31 990–February 991) and thus the year 1990 will be the thousandth anniversary of his birth.

Translator's Notes

a. In *Divan Lugat it-Türk*, the name of this village is spelled "'Bul," and is called by Kashgarli Mahmud "one of our homelands." Dankoff notes that the spelling could have been "abul." In the *Masnawi Shirip* manuscript [see below], this name is spelled as "Uyfal" or "Oyfal." In the Arabic script, the letters 'b,' 'y,' and 'p' are distinguished from one another by one, two, and three dots, respectively, below the line.

b. See O. Pritsak, "Mahmud Kasgari Kimdir?" *Türkiyat Mecmuasi* X (Istanbul, 1953); reprinted in the same author's *Studies in Medieval Eurasian History* (London: Variorum, 1981).

Bahtiyar Nazarov

Kutadgu Bilig
One of the First Written Monuments of the Aesthetic Thought of the Turkic People

Kutadgu Bilig by Yusuf Balasagun (completed 1070 A.D.) is one of the first written literary monuments of the aesthetic thought of the Turkic people.

In the history of mankind, almost without exception, every state, every empire, every social formation is reflected not only in its historical works and scientific treatises but also in great art works of oral and written character that give the future generations rather vivid and clear representation of a detailed picture of the life of the society and the people of the previous epoch.

Among these is one of the first written masterpieces of the Turkic-language people. *Kutadgu Bilig* appeared in the period of the decline of the Samanid empire and the emergence of the Karahanid state, which existed from the middle of the ninth until the beginning of the thirteenth century on the territory of eastern and western Turkistan.

This wonderful work of Turkic and of world written literature has become the object of investigation by many scholars—Russian, Turkish, German, English, French, Hungarian, Uyghur, and others. Noteworthy are the investigations of

Bahtiyar Nazarov (Doctor of Philological Sciences), a Special Assistant to the President of the Uzbek Republic, was previously the Director of the Institute of Language and Literature of the Uzbek SSR Academy of Sciences. Dr. Nazarov read this paper to the 30th meeting of Permanent International Altaistic Conference, held at Indiana University, Bloomington, during 1987. It was later published in *AACAR Bulletin,* vol. 2, no. 1–2 (spring 1989). The couplets quoted from *Kutadgu Bilig* by Dr. Nazarov were in the original. English translations and references are substituted by the editor from Robert Dankoff, tr., *Wisdom of Royal Glory: Kutadgu Bilig* (Chicago: University of Chicago Press, 1983), indicated pages.

scholars of different generations, among whom should be mentioned A. Vambery, R. Radloff, S.E. Malov, V.V. Bartol'd, E.E. Bertel's, F. Köprülüzade, A. Kononov, R.R. Arat, A. Dilachar, A. Valitov, E.K. Tenishev, N.A. Baskakov, S.N. Ivanov, I.V. Steblev, D. Majidenov, U. Asanaliev, K. Ashuraliev, Fitrat, S. Mutalibov, G. Abdurakhmanov, N. Mallallaev, A. Kajumov, K. Karimov.

It should also be emphasized that the dissertations of the young specialists Bakijan Tukhliev and Kasimjan Sadikov in Tashkent are dedicated to the investigation of this work, which in itself attests that the problems of studying the literary heritage of our national cultural traditions takes one of the central positions at the present time.

Acquaintance with the ample literature dedicated to *Kutadgu Bilig* by Yusuf Balasagun shows that the specialists up to the present time addressed mainly the linguistic, literary, philosophical, political, social, and didactic aspects of the work. Special investigation from the point of view of aesthetic problems is still missing. If at all, they are touched extremely superficially, although *Kutadgu Bilig* is in its essence one of the first valuable sources of Turkic-language written literature, one in which the formation of the aesthetic thought of Turkic people is reflected most vividly and deeply. This consideration caused the choice of the subject of the present short communication. This is, of course, a very large theme, requiring the efforts of many specialists to solve it. Taking advantage of the case, I would like all colleagues to pay attention to this problem in their investigations. Such study is of both scholarly and practical importance in the cause of developing cultural and moral values in our present unique world. The aesthetic values of *Kutadgu Bilig* are considerable from our point of view because, being of a general humanist nature, they can have rather objective and direct influence on the development of moral basis of the nature of the modern personality irrespective of the social structure to which it belongs.

We are convinced that books like *Kutadgu Bilig* are necessary for us at the present time, since therein we can find answers to the urgent, exciting questions, answers that our ancestors left as their legacy to us. In our communication we are trying to enlighten the aspects of aesthetic problems reflected in *Kutadgu Bilig*.

One of the central problems in aesthetics is known to be the problem of beauty. Democritus saw beauty in the order, symmetry, and harmony of one part with the other. It must be noted here that Yusuf Balasagun's views in relation to the beautiful coincide in many aspects with those of Aristotle and Confucius.

According to Yusuf, in order to be beautiful, esteemed in society, a person, in our case the Grand Chamberlain (the post Yusuf Balasagun occupied at the Karakhanid court), must possess both inner and outer beauty. Thus, the beauty in the man acts as the whole category in Yusuf's conception. The harmony and symmetry of the mind, physical beauty, and the moral basis in a man, especially the man influencing the life of the society, is one of the central principles of the aesthetic conception of Yusuf. On this occasion he writes the following:

He should be handsome in appearance. . . . He should have a sound mind and a quiet demeanor. The man with a sound mind does not forget his word. . . . He should have a humble and quiet heart, full of compassion. And he should be skillful and knowledgeable about royal custom. It is skillful men who produce all the beautiful objects in the world. . . . He should have a cheerful face and smiling eyes. [pp. 119–23]

Here to some extent one cannot help but notice the nearness of Yusuf's conception to the classical understanding and treatment of the beautiful, known to us from aesthetic views of the ancient philosophers: the harmony of the beautiful in both spirit and mind.

In our opinion, Yusuf's understanding of the beautiful is one of considerable achievements of aesthetic thought of Turkic people, expressed in written form. This is simultaneously one of the significant treatments of the conception of man.

The understanding of this problem by the author is, of course, in the ideal rather than real attitude to existence, for one cannot forget that it matters to the chamberlain, whose class criteria were on the side of the ruling elite, to whom this highest title was given at that time. It should be emphasized, however, that Yusuf, developing his aesthetic views, states a number of important ideas, applicable to the present day.

The beautiful in man, the beautiful man cannot exist by himself, isolated from other people, from society; more specifically, these qualities of man can be evaluated positively only in the case when they are useful to other people. That is, as seen from Yusuf's conception, the beautiful acts, on the one hand, inseparably from utility, while on the other hand, it begins to acquire public and social significance. Here, in our opinion, it would be appropriate to make an analogy between these thoughts of Yusuf and those of Socrates, who spoke about the usefulness and purposefulness of the beautiful.

Yusuf Balasagun expresses his views in the following:

Do not give a job to someone simply because he happens to be in your service; rather take into your service men who will be of genuine use to you. . . . Remove useless men from your service. As for those who are of use and benefit, give them appropriate jobs and provide them with honor and reward. [pp. 219–20]

Thus, according to Yusuf, the beautiful in man, the beautiful in his deeds, consists not only in manifesting the individual but at the same time in the social significance of the manifested. Therefore, from our point of view, Yusuf approaches the understanding and treatment of the beautiful as a public and social phenomenon, which makes it possible to speak about the social purposefulness of his aesthetic views.

However, the author of *Kutadgu Bilig* does not stop here. He goes further. In his work, which consists of about 6,500 couplets written more than nine centuries ago, from the very beginning to the very end there is the leading, main idea about the harmonious beautiful man, and it is not by chance that the author names the main character (the hero) Küntugdi [Rising Sun], personifying Justice. Thus, in Yusuf's opinion, everything connected with social and personal life can be beautiful only if it is associated with justice in its high and ideal meaning. Without justice man's life will be as the sun eclipsed.

All this to some extent attests to the democratic purposefulness of Yusuf's views, though due to the narrowness of his outlook, he sometimes manifests a tendentious attitude toward simple people. In special sections of the book, dedicated to peasants, poor people, craftsmen, stock-breeders, blacksmiths, shoe makers, carpenters, carvers, and archers, the author gives tribute to the common people; nonetheless, the sympathy of Yusuf in the first instance refers to the representative of the ruling classes. In this, one can see, of course, the class narrowness of the author of *Kutadgu Bilig*. Yet this does not diminish the value of the basic, progressive conceptions and thoughts presented in the book of Yusuf Balasagun.

It is noteworthy that sometimes Yusuf evidences moments of realizing (not, of course, in the modern understanding, but on the level of thinking of his times) the class difference between people. He states [p. 141] that he who has riches, has "long" hands.

It should be emphasized that Yusuf is apt to associate the beauty in human deeds first of all with his attitude to labor, to skill. [pp. 130–31]

Naturally, one should bear in mind that in relation to the problem of human perfection, Yusuf is firmly connected with theological views of his time; it cannot be otherwise. Therefore, much, if not everything in human perfection is treated by Yusuf as the gift of the Most High to his obedient servants. In Yusuf's opinion, the whole of human nature, all the beautiful in man—his mind, his senses, and so on—is the gift of God. But not all the beautiful, the earthly is treated by Yusuf in this manner.

Strange as it may seem, the fact is that the praise of the hereafter, of its rewards and benefits, is virtually absent from *Kutadgu Bilig*. Yusuf mainly praises the earthly joy of life and the beauty of the real world in which man lives and works. The most beautiful for the poet seems to be the beauty of nature, which is limitless and endless. Accordingly, he praises this beauty with great strength.

It is known that under the rubric "word" is meant the polynomial attribute of human reason and thought. But the word alone, though very good and correct, is not the very essence of the subject arising from it. Yusuf writes that a good word should become a good deed. [p. 47] These words would seem to be addressed to us from the remote past. They sound so modern, they need no comment.

But the unity of words and deeds should express the wisdom in the decision of this or that problem. According to Yusuf this is not a result, but a purpose.

The real result is not only the display of wisdom, but its realization, in motion. That is why he says definitively: "Any man may don a cloak of honor, but true nobility belongs to the man of wisdom and intellect." [p. 49]

Really, these are beautiful, aphoristic lines, which can sound quite sharply today. "Speak knowledgeably, therefore, and your words will be an eye to the blind," he writes. [p. 45] In our opinion it is the word "art" that is meant here. The word "art" has to bear a social moral content that might help a person to overcome his personal defects and misfortunes. This should become a definite life guide.

Developing his thought in this direction, Yusuf puts forward the following beautiful words, which have not lost their meaning in our days and resound even more sharply: "The criminal is hanged by force of intellect, and civil turmoil is suppressed by means of wisdom." [p. 46] This means that, according to Yusuf's study, knowledge, the power of the word and the power of reason, is more powerful than weapons. To prevent evil and fault, it is necessary to be able to use this great power.

These words of our ancient ancestor impose a deep obligation upon us, inhabitants of the planet at the end of the twentieth century, to use the power of reason when solving any kind of conflict. Yusuf noted that the words of poets were sharper than a sword. Like art in Aristotle's works, according to Yusuf, the word is the means of refinement of people's souls from personal negative passions and one of the main sources of the joy of comprehension.

The main component of beauty is kindness. This opinion of Balasagun testifies to the unity of his point of view with that of Confucius. A person should always be kind in his thoughts and deeds; through kindness, he can comprehend the source of joy. Yusuf calls every person to be among people and to present one another with joy and happiness.

According to Yusuf Balasagun the ugliest thing in life is violence in any form. The poet compares violence with a burning fire [p. 106], which swallows everybody approaching it. Against violence Yusuf puts forward Justice and compares it to water, the source of life. Because of water everything is alive. It should be noted here that, in proving his aesthetic concepts, the author addresses the things and phenomena of the Earth, not the world of paradise or hell. He composes his artistic characters using the natural phenomena surrounding man. This fact emphasizes their nearness to life and their influence on the reader.

This is an important element in Yusuf Balasagun's aesthetics. The traditions of his aesthetics influenced greatly the development of the artistic and aesthetic thought of the Turkic people of the following ages. In his poetry Yusuf addresses the problems of justice, comparing it to living water, and he addresses oppression, comparing it to burning fire. For example, Yusuf says to his ruler that he put out the burning fire of oppression by his living water of justice. [p. 142] These opinions of the author expressed his ideals and somehow exalted the ruler. In other couplets Yusuf wrote about injustice and ignorance existing in the society of those times. There is no truth in life, there is no justice and understanding, he says bitterly in his book.

There are some lines in *Kutadgu Bilig* in which the poet speaks about justice as the most beautiful thing and about oppression as the ugliest not only in the Karakhanid's empire but throughout the world. He continues:

> Speech is descended from blue heaven to brown earth, and it is by means of speech that man ennobles his soul. Man's heart is like a bottomless sea and wisdom is the pearl that lies at the bottom: if he fails to bring the pearl up out of the sea it could just as well be a pebble as a pearl. . . . As long as the wise man does not bring out wisdom upon his tongue, his wisdom may lie hidden for years and shed no light. Fine things indeed are wisdom and intellect: put them to work, if you possess them, and you will soar to heaven. [p. 46]

Kutadgu Bilig was created in Kashgar and dedicated to Tabgach-Bugra Karakhan, describing the events of the Kagan's life and including his education. In its artistic content and philosophical direction, the work goes beyond the confines of this limited purpose and in general the work is of universal humanistic and human character. The same can be said about the aesthetic value of the work.

From the excerpts quoted above, one can see that Yusuf pays special attention to the problems of justice and oppression, prosperity and destruction. Hence, Yusuf's aesthetic opinions have the character of an aesthetic ideal. The progressive people of his time dreamed of this ideal and strove for it.

Thus Yusuf Balasagun's appeals to justice and oppression represent contrasting forces, manifesting themselves first in beauty, and then in ugliness. It is necessary to note that the great son of his time calls his rulers to follow the first force and to deny the second one. These ideas of Yusuf are very progressive for his epoch. One can say that they have not lost their meaning even in our days. The aesthetic views of Yusuf, keeping in step with every period of human development, are powerful and modern.

In conclusion, I want to say to my colleagues, to the participants of all international forums, that we should pay more and more attention to study the artistic heritage of remotest times, for example to the investigation of *Kutadgu Bilig*.

It is sufficient to remember that the Fourth Special Conference on Turcology, held in Leningrad in 1970, was devoted to the nine hundredth anniversary of *Kutadgu Bilig*'s creation. During the last two years, two poetical translations of *Kutadgu Bilig* were made in Uzbekistan. The translations into modern Uzbek were made by Sadulla Ahmad and Bakijan Tuhliyev. Fifteen years ago this work was published in transcription with interpretation by K. Karimov. Two years from now, we are going to celebrate the nine hundred and twentieth anniversary of this unique masterpiece of Turkic people. In this connection I have a proposal. Perhaps it would be reasonable for the international scholarly community to begin preparations to mark this date. And it would not be inappropriate if a group of experts were to meet in Tashkent where one of three extant manuscripts of Yusuf Balasagun is preserved.

This measure would promote further strengthening of international scholarly cooperation working in the difficult but very noble branch of modern social sciences.

Deceivers
Observations Pursuant to Judicial Proceedings

Editor's Introduction

"Adabiyatchi" is a pseudonym. Literally, the name means "one who is involved with literature," and is sometimes loosely employed to refer to a "philosophizer." The name was often utilized by the editorial board to sign editorials in the daily *Sovyet Uzbekistani*, which was the organ of the Uzbek Communist Party Central Committee. Recent information suggests that the Uzbek KGB may have "borrowed" the "Adabiyatchi" pseudonym from time to time.

DECEIVERS

I cannot deny that I am writing this commentary reluctantly. I ask myself whether it is necessary to write about persons who commit acts that violate customs and have brought shame to themselves.

One of the characters in this essay is a false healer type—a personality reminiscent of the movie comedy *Evliya Yorgen Bayrami* about the class struggle in the Ferghana Valley. Remember the charming deceiver (portrayed by artist A. Ktorov) who "cures" the depressed and the limbless with a crutch?

Our personality belongs to the same category. When his professional deficiencies are accepted and viewed with indulgence, it becomes evident that he has a female nature. . . . He believes that he has "discovered the existence" of a second spinal cord, which causes ailments. . . .

"Firibgarlar—Suddan Keyingi Mulahazalar," *Sovyet Uzbekistani* (Tashkent), September 26, 1982. This translation by H.B. Paksoy was published in the *Journal of Muslim Minority Affairs*, vol. 9, no. 2 (July 1988).

Yet another manipulative Mullah of Tashkent opened a "school" in his house to conduct instruction on religious books!

And why should it not be so, when in various quarters some graybeards are inclined to take their children to such "schools" and are endlessly joyful when they are accepted. The graybeards believe that their sons will try to emulate their "teachers" in leading a completely spiritual life.

Why would people in the twentieth century—an era of intellectual achievement—not respect the clear, documented, humanitarian [achievements of the] scientific-technical revolution?! Why would young people who embark upon a university education and succeed in passing the infinitely difficult final exams not serve as an example to those who are not similarly educated?! Humanity tames atomic energy for its own purposes and lives in space for months at a time, foreseeing the future benefits of its investigations, studies artificial intelligence and the secrets of life, prepares to divert a portion of the waters of the Siberian rivers for use in Central Asia and Kazakhstan. . . .

Contrast these great accomplishments to the revered medieval period. I forbear to pursue the comparison further. Most contemporary readers are, I hope, able to evaluate events objectively and realize, moreover, that one must attend to the known facts.

. . . This discussion leads down the following path. Let us meet the perpetrators of an unusual event that took place in the "October" Bazaar in Tashkent on June 5 of this year. . . . In the midst of all the people who were shopping for various colorful goods, the police apprehended a person named A. Saidkorihojaev.

He was selling—to people who place their trust in God first and last and who unfailingly say their daily prayers—an authorless book called *About the Muslim Religion*, which advocated shunning the "Godless."

This politically harmful booklet was being promoted to the shoppers in spite of the prohibition in Article 52 of the USSR Constitution, which bans "incitement of hostility or hatred on religious grounds."

"Don't you know that this activity is forbidden?" Saidkorihojaev was asked. "You should be severely punished for this."

"May God strike me, I didn't know that before," he swore.

He confessed, out of fear, that he had bought the books cheaply in hopes of selling them at high prices, for speculative purposes.

The police arrested Saidkorihojaev, and his identity was checked out at the Investigative Division of the Internal Affairs Department in Tashkent. He was questioned about the incident. During the investigation, much was learned. Slowly, all of his secrets were unraveled. It became apparent that Saidkorihojaev was buying these books from Mahmudjan Ruziev. The latter was procuring them from Abduzokir Rahimov, who was printing them clandestinely on his own handmade press.

In the beginning, Rahimov was printing the books alone in a cellar under his backyard. Later, as he tasted success, he took on his close friend Yuldash

Muhamedov as a partner. In Muhamedov's house they expanded their activities. Later, flush with money, they rented two rooms, for which they paid very little to the owners, in which to print the books. Rahimov was paying salesmen from the "Shuhrat" Department Store to supply him with paper, and others such as Z. Mahkamov who used their "Zhiguli" cars for distributing the printed pamphlets to customers. Rahimov coaxed sellers to work for him by giving them money or vodka, and collected the proceeds.

What would induce Rahimov to such an occupation, punishable under Article 179 of the Uzbek SSR penal code? Who drove his partner Ruziev into selling not only the brochure *About the Muslim Religion* but also cassette tapes of *namaz* prayers, the Koran, and similar books? Eleven like-minded persons who were engaged in speculation were sentenced under Article 175 of the penal code.

What is more, two of this group had previously been tried for similar activities under the same articles!

We asked F.A. Danilian, the Internal Affairs Department investigator who has been conducting the inquiry, about Rahimov, Ruziev, and their band of undesirables. He suggested that we examine the prosecution documents, saying: "You will be mistaken if you take these people for religious conservatives seeking to propagate their teachings through their publications. True Muslims never made commerce out of religious books, because this is against their belief and the shariat. The collection of Muslim laws forbids that." The motives of Rahimov and his partners in this activity were a hunger for wealth and a desire to cheat others of money!

On one occasion Rahimov gave Muhamedov one thousand rubles out of bookselling proceeds—and this was repeated many times over.... They did not just enjoy a cursory benefit from this activity; they led a magnificent life on earth, freeloading without a single day's job of work. Moreover, Rahimov gave the appearance of being destitute, having only an insignificant job within the "Vtorchermet" administration. In actuality, however, he had bought a plot of land and was building a house!

Perhaps it was his awareness of the ultimate investigative powers of justice, and fear that his secret would eventually be uncovered, that drove Rahimov to serious drinking to chase these worries out of his mind. For example, in fear of discovery, he attempted to mislead a possible future investigation. Although he published *About the Muslim Religion* in 1981, he stamped the book with the inscription "Isfara, 1976." Apparently he had learned this despicable gambit during his first imprisonment.

Rahimov, like his partners, had no regard for the truth in his everyday life; that is, a dishonorable occupation is not compatible with goodness. In the course of the investigation, Muhamedov confessed to jointly publishing books of a religious nature with Rahimov from 1980 until July 1981, displaying his partner's shame. This confession was completely confirmed by the discovery of unauthorized equipment and supplies in his brother Musaev's house—including a printing press, chemicals, and other materials.

It was discovered that the proprietor of the place where the printing press was located was A.H. Chemevatenko, a nurse from the Tashkent pediatrics hospital, who took advantage of the 130 rubles offered by Rahimov and rented him one of the four rooms in her large, western, Russian-style house, thereby abetting him.

This is a group of people whose hearts were full of wrath, involved in criminal matters in one way or another, driven to money making year after year, forgetting their honor, conscience, and the future, unable to face their own children, whose innocence cannot be defended in a courtroom. . . . To sum up: a link in the chain of criminal treachery and deception. . . .

When one familiarizes oneself with the investigation and the court documents, and reads the decision of Tashkent's Kirov Raion people's court, one fully understands the fact that they deserve the sentences they received. Rahimov's punishment is to spend seven years in a hard labor camp. Ruziev will not be free for four years. The remainder of this group of eleven like-minded people did not go unpunished.

It made us very happy to learn that the samples of the great Eastern literary works that were confiscated from these people have been turned over to the Manuscripts Institute of the Uzbek SSR Academy of Sciences. There, perhaps for this first time in a long time, these works will used in the service of knowledge. . . .

Now, a lesson: The strong demand for this type of publication is surprising.

One of the protagonists of the incident described above, a former engineer from "Uzmedtekhnika," P. Gaffarov, wanted to print the books more efficiently. For that purpose, he initiated relations with the production sections of several establishments and asked for "help."

They provided him with the latest technical assistance and—with the good resources of the state, ink and paper, and electrical power (used during business hours!)—prepared thousands of these misdirected and harmful books.

I do not understand why the supervisor of the production facility that gave them this assistance turned a blind eye to the ambitions of those entrepreneurs— P. Gaffarov and his associates S. Bakihojaev and S. Umarov. Their business was unusual, a sort of private criminal activity, and upon discovery should have been reported to the legal authorities.

Another question: What is the attraction of these secretly produced books? What is in these books, other than an invitation not to be in amity with those who do not believe in religion?

While I was leafing through *About the Muslim Religion*, I tried to find an answer to this question. . . . The appearance of the pamphlet was ordinary, and the picture on the cover was in only one color. . . . The inside pages contain some poems by the great poets—Sadi, Bedil, and Navai—and excerpts from the works of Abu Ali Ibn Sina. . . .

These pieces were masterfully selected so that readers would be unwittingly trapped into reading portions that pertain to religion. These passages primarily provide historical information about the Muslim religion, the duties of a Muslim, what is acceptable for Muslims to do and what is not. Interspersed among these were the texts of prayers and suras from the Koran.

Two pages of the book were printed in Arabic, in the Arabic script; the remaining twenty-eight pages in the Uzbek language. Presumably, the editor-author was being considerate. Considering that most of us do not read Arabic, he wrote the instructions on Muslim practices in Uzbek.

Thus the author displays consideration for the majority of readers. What would prevent such people from achieving their goals?

Since the schools in Uzbekistan do not teach religion, even the children say, "We will not accept this: we are not taught in this manner."

We cannot accept it because we have not been informed about the Muslim religion in the schools, institutes, and, after graduation, in the political indoctrination sessions at the workplace.

In this manner they have produced a forbidden fruit, whose sweetness becomes more alluring by the temptation to "taste it."

Let us resume our consideration of why these people are interested in religious literature. For this purpose, we do not need to refer to books like *About the Muslim Religion*, which was printed clandestinely, to gather detailed information.

Over the past decade, the Department of Muslim Religion [the Muslim Spiritual Board, in Tashkent] has printed the Koran six times. The seventh edition is in preparation for publication. The library of the Religious Department is open to all. In this place it is possible to select and read any books one wants and to get to know the journals published for religious people.

Perhaps some people have believed the lies and disinformation being circulated in the West, according to which religious literature is "forbidden" in our country. They are then interested in buying these books which were not published by the state.

The following fact must be taken into consideration as well. The contemporary Muslim religion is totally different from its previous form. Now the dogmas of the religion do not frighten people; on the contrary, these principles invite believers to be acquainted with the present era! Influential great men of religion advise people to learn about space, and urge Muslims not to fall behind the West in this field. Some of these religious leaders have even announced that they are ready to fly to the moon—supposedly because they want to be close to "Great God and away from a place that is submerged in sin."

While on the topic, it would be appropriate to think about improving the mission of the Museum of Atheism in Tashkent. Its exhibitions can be filled with materials about the present day, and narrate the tragic as well as sometimes bloody history of struggles between enlightenment and darkness, between religious ignorance and scientific efforts, and between idealism and materialism, by writing skillful commentaries on the exhibited materials.

Perhaps we should also think about the nature of our ideological work in the collectives (and not only there); about political activities not confined to recitation and praise of our past accomplishments, so that political agendas seem to be clogged with matters of trivial importance. Insufficient concern is attached to progress in solving problems that require detailed and complex discussion. . . .

It should not be forgotten that in advanced socialism the struggle between new and old is abating. Ignorance, religious demagogy, and the class approach to life are disappearing.

It should not be forgotten, it seems to us, that knowledgeable people who went to the "October" bazaar in Tashkent should have been incensed at the efforts to sell booklets *About the Muslim Religion* and condemned the attempt by those speculators, egoistic peddlers, and editors to exploit [people] and make three rubles for their "literature."

Among ourselves we encounter the sort of people who act as if they are "Soviet workers" but bark chapters from the Koran without knowing the prayers anywhere near the proficiency of the Mullahs, and recite prayers at burial and other ceremonies. They do not personally honor the religious customs, do not fast, ignore religious holidays, do not offer thanks to God before meals, yet they criticize others who do not utter Fatiha [a short sura from the Koran] at the proper times. People in the know make fun of these persons.

Are we simply nitpicking? Do they not have any good qualities in their characters, relative to their station in life, that might evoke esteem and respect? To some extent, they do.

But most importantly: It should not be forgotten that what comes after this invitation to adherence and respect for customs is [an invitation to] conscious, secret submission to sharia and religious dictates, with no deviation from these religious precepts. . . .

Abbas Alovulla, an official scholar of the Muslim religion who completed his studies in four madrasas and spent many years studying the Koran and its interpretations and thus became a specialist on the subject, was at one time prepared to "enslave the antireligious or even exterminate them."

Then, twenty years ago I read an article by Abbas Alovulla that was published in the newspaper Sovetskaia Karakalpakiia and I was pleased to note that he had severed his ties to religion; I thought that religious people would want to follow his lead.

No, they did not learn or take heed. There is no shortage of lessons about the doings of religious people. As an example, I can cite incidents from the newspaper *Pravda Vostoka*. An elderly member of the Telman Kolkhoz took her twenty-five-year-old daughter to the sixty-year-old Mullah of the "Hoja Urba" *mescid* . . . so that the daughter could be treated for paralysis and cured. . . . The girl stayed on and became the fifth wife of the old man, who likes to have retainers to enhance his life. . . .

In order to pass judgment, let us bring to your attention the following example. In 1976, Ali Tukanbaev, People's Poet of the Kirgiz SSR and a Hero of
Socialist Labor, published an article in *Komsomolskaia pravda* commenting
about the bride-price tradition of the Muslims. He said the following:

> Nowadays the bride-price is favored under various guises, and in addition
> there are various hidden costs are associated with it. We may assume that the
> parents of an educated girl receive much, but a wealthy and esteemed person's
> daughter, according to tradition, commands a much higher amount. This secret
> monetary bride-price "increases the honor" of the girls as the sum rises. Thus
> "the greater the bride-price, the higher the rank and dignity of the bride."

It is regrettable that educated, knowledgeable comrades and their parents,
who adhere to the latest fashions and wear contemporary clothes and neckties,
accept this bride-price as a national tradition handed down for centuries and
agree with it. Actually, these "traditions" are nothing but a cover that masks
opportunism.

Further, there are certain bizarre persons who have resorted to accumulating
wealth through "activities" that hide behind the curtain of the name of God. The
activities of the false mullah Saidkerim Azamov may be cited as an example of this.

. . . He opened a religious learning "school" in a quarter of Tashkent. As soon
as they heard this news, some teenagers were attracted to his doorstep under the
guidance of their parents. The parents obligingly brought their children to his
clandestine "school" so that they could learn the religious precepts.

Contrary to the general educational laws governing the separation of school
from church in the Soviet system, which abolished this type of schools from the
curriculum, this instruction took place daily.

Azamov, approaching middle age, determinedly pursued his efforts to increase his wealth without considering that he would one day be called to account
for his crime. He continued to poison the minds of the young children with
religion under the threat of the hereafter. He succeeded in attaching his hopes to
the taste and existence of a hereafter.

He accepted presents from the parents of his students without hesitation. In
his courtyard he tethered many heads of cattle and forty sheep. The mullah
bought six magnificent pieces of real estate; but, fearing that his treachery would
be uncovered, he registered them under the names of his siblings and other
relatives, to legitimize them.

At this writing, Azamov's property has been confiscated. I heard that he is
currently away from our sunny country, "cleansing his sins."

Now, in evaluating the behavior of Azamov, honesty requires consideration
of the help received by individuals, whose fathers are honorable, from those who
published religious books and sold tape cassettes containing Koran and prayers,
through which they speculated for "easy" money in order to accumulate wealth.
Did Habibulla ever consider the error of his ways when he pursued the mirage of

increasing his wealth? Did Azamov's "students" understand the purely harmful nature of their clandestine endeavors? As they fell victim to a manipulator, blindly believing in the lies, did they consider the consequences of their actions?

These questions are not asked in vain. The illegal "activity" of the false healer Devran Buronov provides verification. Currently it is difficult to determine exactly how, when, and on whom this "healer" performed his cures. However, it is true that the spread of his fame is unequaled. As a result of this success, he assumed the title "miracle healer" and was praised to the heavens by the sick people who placed their trust and faith in him. No one was concerned about the legality of his status, or curious about the manner in which he performed his "miracles." Actually, since he did not even have intermediate medical training, they should have realized that he was a deceiver. Buronov was at one time the work brigade leader of the 17 Sovkhoz in Sariderya Oblast, where he embezzled three thousand rubles from the state. He escaped to Sovkhoz 18, where he committed thievery and finally attempted to hide in Ferghana.

He was found out and sent to court. Buronov escaped from prison, his shame revealed one more time, and he once again, as before his imprisonment, set out to amass wealth through the practice of "healership," and he let this fact be known by word of mouth. In fact, ill people from Andijan, Namangan, and Osh oblasts of the Kirgiz SSR, and blind people suffering from eye disease and other afflictions came to him, bypassing state clinics and hospitals in order to appear before him. Ill women and girls who sought cures from him spent time and lived in his house. From the Hojaabad Raion, a twenty-year-old medical nurse named Etibar M. spent half a year in Buronov's house! An eighteen-year-old tenth-grade student, a girl named Ugilay H., was "treated" in his house for five months. At the time he was imprisoned, it was discovered that he had a list in excess of one hundred male and female patients.

Buronov was married three times; the womanizer's third wife was an ill woman from Namangan. He had an eye for young girls, coerced them into submitting to basically false "massage," and "aided them to a cure." The patients should have thought about what he was doing and told their own parents, so that his shamelessness could have been exposed. Since this was not attempted, the rat amassed one hundred thousand tanga [an old monetary unit]! But no, it was not done. Rather, they unresistingly "served" and lived in his rented home. The fraudulant "doctor" continued to busy himself with "cures" until the officers of the relevant organs were astonished to discover him.

Now, it is too late for the parents of the patients to worry about the predicament in which they find themselves. I cannot imagine the intensity of their sorrow, but neither can I sympathize with them. One view is that they brought it upon themselves. The parents did not teach their daughters, in a timely manner, the necessity of using logic to distinguish unacceptable behavior, not trampling on the values of humanity, and resisting the inclination to submit to societal pressures blindly.

It is possible that they are calmed by the fact that Buronov has been deservedly and appropriately punished. But this is no real reason to be calmed, since this needless injustice was punished without the participation of the victims.

At this point, it is appropriate to remember an old proverb: "If God wishes to punish a person, He first takes away that person's mind. . . ."

Certainly, religious persons now oppose these types of activities, but in order to educate them in the end, it is necessary to bring them up to date. Against maladies like these it is necessary to mount a coordinated attack, from all fronts, utilizing all available means.

3

REDISCOVERY OF POLITICAL HISTORY

Yusuf Akchura

Three Types of Policies

Editor's Introduction

Yusuf Akchura's famous treatise "Three Policies" was first published in Cairo in the newspaper *Türk* (nos. 24–34). Due to Ottoman censorship under the rule of Abdülhamid II, a number of oppositionist periodicals opposing[1] were printed in Cairo, then under British rule. Among these were not only *Türk*, but also *al-Nahdah*, published by Ismail Bey Gaspirali (1854–1914),[2] who was related to Akchura by marriage. In 1912 "Three Policies" was reprinted in pamphlet form in Istanbul. It was reissued in 1976 with an introduction by the late E.Z. Karal and two of the original responses to the work, by Ali Kemal and Ahmet Ferit (Tek). The issues discussed in "Three Policies" have engaged wide attention over the decades and hold no less interest today. A brief biography of Akchura is provided by David Thomas.[3]

* * *

Yusuf Akchura was born in 1876 in Simbirsk (Ulyanovsk) on the right bank of the middle Volga. His father died when he was two; five years later he and his mother emigrated to Istanbul. Akchura received his early education in the schools of the Ottoman empire and in 1895 he entered the *Harbiye Mektebi* (War College) in Istanbul. Upon graduation he was assigned to the General Staff Course (*Erkan-i Harbiye*), one of the most prestigious posts for young and ambitious cadets and an essential step up the ladder of the Ottoman military hierarchy. Before he completed his training, however, he was accused of belong-

---

"Üch Tarz-i Siyaset" (Three Types of Policies), first published in *Türk* (Cairo), nos. 24–34, 1904; reprinted in 1912 and 1976. This translation by David S. Thomas was published in *AACAR Bulletin*, vol. 5, no. 1 (spring 1992).

ing to a secret society opposed to Abdülhamid and was sent into exile at Fezan in the interior of Libya. In 1899 Akchura and Ahmet Ferit (Tek), his close friend since their days together in the War College, escaped and made their way to Paris.

Akchura remained in Paris for four years, a period that exerted a decisive influence on his thinking and reoriented him for the remainder of his life toward intellectual and academic pursuits. He gained firsthand experience of European, specifically French, culture, and perfected his knowledge of French. At the same time he became politically conscious and began to understand the motive forces and power of nationalism.

In 1903 Akchura left Paris and returned to his ancestral Tatar home in the Russian domains, where he composed what was to become his best-known work, "Three Types of Policies." In this essay, which appeared in 1904 in the newspaper *Türk*, published in Cairo, Akchura advanced a number of arguments which, when taken together, were in fact a proposal to the Turks of the Ottoman empire, urging them to recognize their national aspirations, to forget about being Ottomans, and to adopt Turkish nationalism as the focus of their collective loyalty and identity. For their time these ideas were revolutionary. Among the Ottoman Turks they were either universally ignored or rejected. It was only during the period of the Second Mesrutiyet (Constitutional Monarchy) (1908–1918) that such notions were taken seriously and elaborated by Akchura and others into an ideology of Turkish nationalism.

In pursuit of this cause, Akchura founded the journal *Türk Yurdu*, which, from 1911 to 1917, became the foremost publication in the Turkish cultural world advancing the cause of nationalism "for all the Turks of the world." In it, Akchura elaborated his own comprehensive doctrine of Turkism, which was radically different from that advanced by Gökalp. His ideology of Turkish nationalism was distinguished by its definition of the Turkish nation in terms of ethnicity, its recognition that the Turks needed to develop a national economy to sustain national consciousness, and its insistence on reform of all institutions of Turkish society in accordance with a program of total Westernization.

In the Turkish Republic, Akchura assumed a position of intellectual leadership. He continued to influence the ideological evolution of the new Turkish political entity, the Turkish Republic, through his position as an influential university professor and popular teacher, and through his ideas on the writing of history as well as his historical studies. Akchura died in Istanbul in 1935.

David Thomas

Notes

1. To place the events of the era into perspective, see, for example, Y.H. Bayur, *Türk Inkilabi Tarihi*, 3 vols. (Ankara, 1940–1967); A.B. Kuran, *Inkilap Tarihimiz ve Jön*

Türkler (Istanbul, 1945); T.Z. Tunaya, *Türkiyede Siyasi Partiler, 1859–1952* (Istanbul, 1952); Sherif Mardin, *Jön Türklerin Siyasi Fikirleri, 1895–1908* (Ankara, 1964); A. Bennigsen and Chantal Lemercier-Quelquejay, *La presse et le mouvement national chez les musulmans de russie avant 1920* (Paris, 1964); E.E. Ramsaur, *The Young Turks* (Beirut, 1965); Feroz Ahmad, *The Young Turks: The Committee of Union and Progress in Turkish Politics, 1908–1914* (Oxford, 1969); Sina Aksin, *31 Mart Olayi* (Ankara, 1970); S.S. Aydemir, *Makedonya'dan Orta Asya'ya Enver Paia*, 2d ed. (Istanbul, 1976), vol. II, esp. pp. 443–94; Stanford J. and E.K. Shaw, *History of the Ottoman Empire and Modern Turkey* (Cambridge, 1977), vol. II; M. Sükrü Hanioglu, *Bir Siyasal Örgüt Olarak 'Osmanli Ittihat ve Terakki Cemiyeti' ve 'Jön Türklük' 1889–1902* (Istanbul, 1985), vol. I; Masami Arai, *Turkish Nationalism in the Young Turk Era* (Leiden, 1991). Most contain extensive bibliographies.

2. Thomas Kuttner, "Russian Jadidism and the Islamic World: Ismail Gasprinskii in Cairo, 1908," *Cahiers du monde russe et sovietique*, 16 (1975); Edward Lazzerini, "Ismail Bey Gasprinskii's Perevodchik/Tercüman: A Clarion of Modernism," in *Central Asian Monuments*, ed. H.B. Paksoy (Istanbul, 1992); idem, "Gadidism at the Turn of the Twentieth Century: A View From Within," *Cahiers du monde russe et sovietique*, 16 (1975); idem, "From Bakhchisaray to Bukhara in 1893: Ismail Bey Gasprinskii's Journey to Central Asia," *Central Asian Survey*, vol. 3, no. 4 (1984); idem, "Ismail Bey Gasprinskii and Muslim Modernism in Russia, 1878–1914" (Unpublished doctoral dissertation, University of Washington, 1973); Ismail Bey Gasprinskii, *Russkoe musul'manstvo: mysli, zametki I nabliudeniia* (Simferopol, 1881) Society for Central Asian Studies (Oxford, 1985), Reprint No. 6; Cafer Seydahmet, *Gaspirali Ismail Bey* (Istanbul, 1934).

3. For further details, see David Thomas, "Yusuf Akchura and the Intellectual Origins of Üch Tarz-i Siyaset," *Journal of Turkish Studies/Türklük Bilgisi Arastirmalari*, vol. 2 (1978); idem, "The Life and Thought of Yusuf Akchura 1876–1935" (Doctoral dissertation, McGill University, 1976).

THREE TYPES OF POLICIES

It seems to me that since the rise of the desires for progress and rehabilitation, spread from the West, three principal political doctrines have been conceived and followed in the Ottoman dominions. The first is the one that seeks to create an Ottoman nation through assimilating and unifying the various nations subject to Ottoman rule. The second seeks to unify politically all Muslims living under the governance of the Ottoman State because of the fact that the prerogative of the Caliphate has been a part of the power of the Ottoman State (this is what the Europeans call Pan-Islamism). The third seeks to organize a policy of Turkish nationalism (*Türk Milliyet-i siyasiyesi*) based on ethnicity.

The first of these principles had an important influence on the general political policy of the Ottoman empire, whereas the last appeared only recently in the writings of certain authors.

I

The desire to bring into being an Ottoman nation did not aim at a lofty objective or high hopes. Rather, the real purpose was to grant and impose the same rights and political duties on the Muslim and non-Muslim peoples of the Ottoman dominions, and thus to realize perfect equality between them and to grant complete freedom of thought and worship. The aim was thus to create an Ottoman Nation (*Osmanli Milleti*), a new nationality united in a common country, similar to the American nation in the United States of America, by blending and assimilating to each other the above-mentioned peoples in spite of the religious and racial differences existing among them. The ultimate result of all these difficult processes was to be the preservation of the "High Ottoman State" in her original external form—that is, within her old boundaries. Although the continuance and strengthening of the power of a state whose majority was Muslim and Turkish was beneficial to all Muslims and Turks, this political principle would not directly serve them. For this reason the Muslims and Turks living outside the Ottoman lands could not be so interested in this policy: the point is that it would be only a local and internal matter.

The policy of creation of an Ottoman nation arose seriously during the reign of Mahmut II.[1] It is well known that this ruler said: "I wish to see the religious differences among my subjects only when they enter their mosques, synagogues, and churches." Around the beginning and the middle of the nineteenth century it was natural that this policy was thought preferable and practicable for the Ottoman dominions. At that time in Europe the idea of nationalism, through the influence of the French Revolution, accepted as the basis of nationality the French model based on the principle of conscience rather than that of descent and ethnicity. Sultan Mahmud and his successors, self-deceived by this principle which they could not thoroughly comprehend, believed in the possibility of blending and molding the subjects of the state, who were of different ethnicities and faiths, into a united nation, by means of freedom, equality, security, and fraternity. Some examples that could be observed in the history of the integration of nationalities in Europe also strengthened their conviction. In fact, did not the French nationality originate from a compound of German, Celtic, Latin, Greek, and other elements? Were there not many Slavic elements digested in the German nationality? Is not Switzerland a nation despite differences of ethnicity and religion? It is not improbable that these Ottoman statesmen, through an inadequate understanding of the nature of the policies pursued by the Germans and the Italians, who were striving for their political unity at that time, presented these movements as evidence to support the correctness of their policy.

The idea of an Ottoman national unity was observed especially during the time of Ali and Fuat Pasha. Napoleon III, the apostle of creating nations according to the French principle of the plebiscite, was the most powerful supporter of these Westernized pashas. The French-inspired reforms during the time of Sultan Abdüaziz and the lycée at Galatasaray which this reform symbolized were all results of the time when this system was fashionable.

When Napoleon and the French empire fell in 1870–71, symbolizing the victory of the German interpretation of nationality—one that assumed ethnicity as the basis of nationality, which, I believe, is closer to reality—the policy of Ottoman unity lost its only powerful supporter.

It is true that Mithat Pasha was to a degree a follower of the two famous ministers mentioned above, but his political program, which was more complex than theirs, disappeared very quickly. As for the program of present-day Young Ottomans, who pretend to follow the work of Mithat, it is very vague. I believe, therefore, that it would not be a mistake to assume that the illusion of organizing an Ottoman nation passed away with the French empire and, like it, can never be revived again.

When the policy of creating an Ottoman nation failed, the policy of Islamism appeared.[2]

This idea, which the Europeans term Pan-Islamism, was recently developed out of Young Ottomanism, namely by a group who partially adopted a policy of forming an Ottoman nation. The point at which many Young Ottoman poets and politicians ultimately arrived, having begun first of all with the slogans "Homeland" and "Ottomanism," that is, Ottomanism embracing all the peoples living in the homelands, was "Islamism." The most influential cause of this metamorphosis was their experience of Europe and their closer observation of Western ideas. When they were in the East they stuffed their heads with the ideas of eighteenth-century political philosophy—one of them was a translator of Rousseau—but they were unable to comprehend completely the importance of ethnicity and religion and, especially, they were unable to understand completely that the time had passed for creating a new nationality; that the interests, if not desires, of the various elements under the rule of the Ottoman state were not in accordance with such a unity and blending, and hence that the application of the French conception of nationality was impossible in the East. When they were in foreign countries, however, they saw their own country with greater clarity from afar, and they were successful in understanding the gradually increasing political importance of religion and ethnicity for the East. As a result they realized that the desire to create an Ottoman nation was an illusion.

Thereupon they became convinced of the necessity to unify completely all Muslim peoples using all possible means, starting first with those living in the Ottoman dominions and then with those living in the remainder of the world, without regard to differences of ethnicity, but taking advantage of their common faith. In accordance with the rule that "religion and nation are one," which every Muslim learns from his earliest years, they believed that it was possible to join all Muslims in the form of a unified nation in the sense given to a nation in recent times. In one respect this would lead to dissolution and separation among the peoples of the Ottoman dominions: Muslim and non-Muslim Ottoman subjects would now be divided. On the other hand, however, this would be the means of uniting all Muslims in an even greater unification and assimilation. This policy, in comparison to the previous policy, was more extensive; in current terminology, it was worldwide (*mondiale*). This idea, which in the beginning was purely theoretical, appearing only in the press, gradually began to have practical application as well. During the last years of Sultan Abdülaziz's reign the word Pan-Islamism was frequently heard in diplomatic conversations. The establishment of diplomatic relations with certain Muslim rulers of Asia was undertaken. After the fall of Mithat Pasha—that is, after the complete renunciation of the idea officially of creating an Ottoman nation—Sultan Abdülhamid II strove to follow this policy. This ruler, in spite of the fact that he was the irreconcilable adversary of the Young Ottomans, was, to a degree, their political disciple. The Young Ottomans, once they realized that the non-Muslim subjects did not want to stay within the Ottoman commonwealth, even if they were granted complete equality in rights and freedom, had begun to express their enmity toward these non-Muslim subjects and toward their Christian protectors. The present-day policy of the Padisah exhibits a striking resemblance to Young Ottoman ideas after this change in their outlook.[3]

The present-day ruler tried to substitute the religious title of Caliph for the terms Sultan and Padishah. In his general policies, religion, that is, the religion of Islam, held an important place. In the curricula of the secular schools the time allotted to religious instruction was increased; the basis of education was religious. Religiosity and pietism, even if external and hypocritical, became the most important means for attracting the protection of the caliphal favor. The imperial residence of Yildiz was filled with hojas, imams, seyyids, sheikhs, and sherifs. It became a custom to appoint men with turbans to certain civil posts. Preachers were sent among the people to inspire firmness in religion, strong loyalty to the office of the Caliphate—to the person who occupied that office rather than the office itself—and hatred against the non-Muslim peoples. Everywhere tekkes, zaviyehs, and jamis were built and repaired. Hajis won great importance. During the pilgrimage season, pilgrims passing through the city of the Caliphate were honored by the blessing and favor of the Ruler of the Muslims. Their religious allegiance and loyalty of heart to the office of the Caliphate was sought. In recent years envoys have been sent to the lands of Africa and China that are thickly populated by Muslims. One of the best means of carrying out this policy has been the building of the Hamidiye–Hijaz Railway.

Yet, with this political policy the Ottoman empire resumed the form of a theocratic state that it had tried to abandon in the period of the Tanzimat. It now became necessary [for the state] to renounce all freedom, freedom of conscience and thought and political freedom, as well as religious, ethnic, political and cultural equality. Consequently, it was necessary to say farewell to a European-type constitutional government; to accept an increase of the already existing enmities and antipathies arising out of the diversity of ethnicities, religions, and social positions, which ultimately led to an increase of revolts and rebellions as well as to an upsurge in Europe of enmity against the Turk. In fact that is just what occurred.[4]

The idea to bring about a policy of Turkish nationalism based on ethnicity is very recent. I do not think this idea existed in either the Ottoman empire up to now or in other former Turkish states. Although Léon Cahun, the partisan historian of Chinggis and the Mongols, has written that this great Turkish Khan conquered Asia from end to end with the ultimate intention of uniting all the Turks. I am unable to say anything concerning the historical authenticity of this assertion.

Furthermore, I have not encountered any trace concerning the existence of an idea to unite the Turks during the Tanzimat and in the Young Ottoman movements. Probably the late Vefik Pasha, when he showed interest in a pure Turkish language by writing his Dictionary, was fascinated for a while with this utopian idea. It is true, nevertheless, that recently in Istanbul a circle, scientific rather than political, has been founded to pursue the idea of Turkish nationalism. It seems to me that an increase in the relations between the Ottomans and the Germans, and the growing acquaintance among Turkish youth with the German language and especially the historical and philological studies done by the Germans, have been very influential in the formation of this circle. In this new group, rather than the light, frivolous, and political style characterized by the French tradition, there exists a soundly based science which has been obtained quietly, patiently, and in a detailed fashion. The most prominent members of this group are Semseddin Sami, Mehmet Emin, Necip Asim, Velet Chelebi, and Hasan Tahsin; *Ikdam*, up to a point, seems to be their organ. The movement is developing rather slowly because the present-day government apparently does not look with favor on this mode of thinking.[5]

I do not know whether followers of this idea exist in places other than Istanbul in the Ottoman empire. Yet Turkism, just like Islamism, is a general policy. It is not limited to the borders of the Ottoman empire. Consequently it is necessary to look at the other parts of the world inhabited by the Turks.

In Russia, where most of the Turks live, I know of the existence in a very vague form of the idea of the unity of the Turks. The nascent Idil literature is more Turkish than Muslim in character. If external pressure had not existed, the regions of Turkistan, Yayik, and Idil, wherein the great majority of the Turks are found, could have provided a more favorable environment than the Ottoman dominions for the flourishing of this idea.

This idea may also exist among the Caucasian Turks. Although the Caucasian Turks have had an intellectual influence on the Azerbaijan Turks, I do not know to what degree the Turks of northern Iran have embraced the idea of Turkish unity.

In any case, the formulation of a policy of nationalism based on ethnicity is still in its infancy and not widespread.

II

Now let us investigate which of these three policies is useful and practicable.

We said useful, but useful to whom and to what purpose? To this question only our natural instincts—in other words, our sentiments, which reason is still unable to analyze and justify—can give an answer. "I am an Ottoman, a Muslim, and a Turk. Therefore I wish to serve the interests of the Ottoman state, Islam, and all Turks." But are the interests of these three societies, which are political, religious, and ethnic, common? That is to say, does the strengthening of one imply the strengthening of the others?

The interests of the Ottoman state are not contrary to the interests of Muslims and Turks in general, inasmuch as both Muslim and Turkish subjects would become powerful by its gaining power, and at the same time other Muslims and Turks [outside] will also have support.

But the interests of Islam do not completely coincide with Ottoman and Turkish interests, because the strengthening of Islam would lead in the end to the separation of some non-Muslim peoples from the state. The rise of conflicts between the Muslims and the non-Muslims would lead to a partition of the present-day Ottoman commonwealth and its weakening.[6]

As for the interests of the Turks, they also do not completely coincide with the interests of the Ottoman state or with Islam, since the division of Islamic society into Turkish and non-Turkish parts will weaken it, with the result that this would unleash discord among the Ottoman Muslim subjects and lead to a weakening of the Ottoman empire.

Therefore, a person belonging to each of the three societies must work for the interests of the Ottoman state. Yet in which one of these three *policies* that we are discussing lies the interest of the Ottoman state itself? And which one of these is practicable in the Ottoman commonwealth?

III

The creation of an Ottoman nation is the sole means for preserving the Ottoman empire within its present-day borders. Yet, does the real strength of the Ottoman state lie in its preservation within its present-day geographical form?

In the case of an Ottoman nation, it is believed that a composite nation will come into existence from among the various religions and ethnic groups on the basis of liberty and legal equality. They will be united only by the ideas of homeland (The Ottoman Dominions) and nation (The Ottoman Nation). The conflicts and animosities arising from religious and ethnic differences will cease, and in this fashion the Greeks and Armenians, like the Arabs, will be fused into a unity. The Ottoman Turks who are the basic foundation of the Ottoman state will be content with the spiritual benefits of attributing the name of Osman Bey, their first leader, to their homeland and nation and especially of seeing the empire which came into existence through the efforts of their ancestors not partitioned any further. Perhaps they may even be forced to drop this name altogether because in this free state, in which the former conquered peoples constitute a majority, the name "Ottoman," which to them is a symbol of their former subjugation, may be abolished by their will!

The Ottoman Turks may continue their actual predominance for a limited duration of time thanks to their sovereignty exercised through past centuries, yet it must be remembered that the duration of the force of inertia in the social realm is no greater than that observed in the realm of nature.

As for the generality of Muslims who live in the Ottoman nation, since they will constitute the majority, the complete power of rulership in the administration of the state will pass into their hands. Consequently, if it is recognized that spiritually and materially the Islamic element will derive the greatest benefit from this composite society, then we also must admit that in this Ottoman nation religious conflicts remain, a real equality does not exist, and the various elements have not truly been merged into one.

To say that in the creation of the Ottoman nation the Turkish and Muslim population and their power will not be increased is not to say that the power of the Ottoman state will be decreased. Nevertheless, our basic question is the power of the state. Power will certainly be increased. The people of a state organized in a rational, closely knit fashion, in short, as a bloc, rather than being in the state of continuous disputes and conflict (anarchy), will certainly be more powerful.

But the basic problem is whether or not the elements belonging to different ethnicities and religions, which up to now have never ceased being in conflict and contention with one another, can now be united and assimilated?

We have seen above that experiments of this nature in the past have ended in failures; in order to understand, then, whether or not success is possible, let us survey the causes of this failure.

1. Muslims, and especially Ottoman Turks, did not themselves wish this combination and assimilation. Such a policy would have put an end legally to their six-hundred-year-old sovereignty, and they would descend to the level of equality with reayas whom they had become accustomed over many years to regard as subjugated peoples. As the most immediate and material result of it they would be forced to let the reayas enter the governmental and military positions that they had customarily monopolized up to that time. In other words, leaving an occupation looked on as honorable by the aristocratic peoples, they themselves would be forced to enter into trade and industry, which they looked down upon and with which they were little acquainted.

2. Likewise, the Muslims did not wish this, inasmuch as this powerful religion, which looked after the real interests of its followers from a very material and human point of view, did not accept complete legal equality of Muslim and non-Muslim: the Zimmis were to remain always on a secondary level. As for liberty, although it is true from every aspect that Islam, among all the religions, has been the most liberal, nevertheless as a religion, having its origin in the supernatural, it regards every custom not entirely of its own principles and customs, derived [as they are] from absolute truths, as contrary to the true path. It would not accept, therefore, merely for the goal of human happiness, complete freedom of thought and conscience.

3. The non-Muslims, too, did not want it, because all of them had their own past, and their own independence and their own governments in that past, which was now being glorified because of the revival of national consciousness. Muslims and especially the Turks had ended their independence and had destroyed their governments. And under the Ottoman rule, they believed, they had experienced injustice and not justice, contempt and not equality, misery and not happiness. The nineteenth century had taught them their past, their rights, and their nationality on the one hand, and had weakened the Ottomans, their masters, on the other. And some of the fellow subjugated peoples had already won their independence. Now their weakened masters are extending their hand of brotherhood unwillingly and hesitantly. They wanted them to share sovereignty; they wanted to equalize the privileges. These invigorated subjects, whose wisdom was now brighter than their masters' and who understood that some of the hands extending toward them were really sincere, did not fail to recognize the role played in the formation of this new policy by the pressure of Western powers, who, for their own interests, sought the maintenance of the integrity of the Ottoman empire. The interests of some of them were probably with the idea of the Ottoman nation, yet they were also prone to exalted emotions rather than cool calculations. Thus, literally none of them wanted to form a new national unity by letting themselves merge with those whom they looked upon as their enemies.

4. The greatest enemy of the Ottomans, Russia, as well as its satellites, the Balkan states, also did not want it. Russia wanted to get possession of the Straits [Bosphorus and Dardanelles], Anatolia, and Iraq, Istanbul, and the whole of Balkans, and the Holy Lands, and thus to realize its political, economic, national, and religious aims. By occupying the Straits, Russia would obtain a large and protected port for its naval fleet, [and could thus] freely roam the important trade routes of the Mediterranean. From that position, Russia could, at any time, ambush the British naval and commercial fleets, the caravans of our time, and thereby at will sever the British lines of communication with her wealthiest colony. In short, Russia could flank India, which it has coveted for a long time, again, this time from the West. By occupying Anatolia, Russia would be in a position to control totally the most fertile and productive continent on earth. By expanding into Iraq, Russia would complete its conquest of Asia, thus tilting the age-old competition with Britain for the control of the Islamic Holy Lands and populations in its own favor. As a result, by gaining the Straits and a substantial portion of Ottoman Asia, Russia would reap important political and economic benefits.

By annexing the Balkans to its already wide lands, [Russians would] unify the South Slavs, and, by planting the Cross on St. Sophia, gain control of the lands from which the Russian Orthodox religion originated. This would allow the extremely devout Russians to claim with all their hearts their highest religious and emotional objectives.

The realization of these aims depended upon a weak, troubled, and divided Ottoman state. Therefore, Russia could never tolerate the rise of an Ottoman nationality.

Then, those Serbian and Greek states, which had recently gained political life, would want to increase their populations "that have been left under the yoke of the Turks." This could only be attained by segregating the Ottoman communities. They would have striven toward that [objective].

5. The idea was not well received in some sections of European public opinion. Some of those who manipulated European public opinion were still under the influence of the age-old religious quarrel between Christianity and Islam. They were still following the tradition of the Crusades. They wanted to rescue Christians from the Muslim yoke, to clear the infidels out of Europe and the lands of the Christians. Some of them, giving a more humane and scientific color to their claims, wanted not only to rescue the "European nations capable of progress" from the yoke of the half-barbarian Turanians who knew nothing but waging warfare, but also to push these Asiatics back to the deserts of the continent from which they originated. Frequently these two theses became mixed and confused with each other so that it was not clear which one was derived from the other.

We see, therefore, that in spite of the desires of all peoples living in the Ottoman lands and in spite of all external obstacles, only a few persons who were at the top of the Ottoman government wanted to create an Ottoman nationality simply by relying upon the support of certain European governments (especially the France of Napoleon III)! It was an impossible task. Even if these men at the top were great geniuses, it would not in the least have been possible to overcome so many obstacles. In fact, their efforts ended in failure.

Those obstacles have not decreased since then. On the contrary, they have become more numerous. Abdülhamid's policy increased the enmity and the gulf between the Muslims and the non-Muslims. Additional numbers of non-Muslim peoples were gaining their independence and this doubled the enthusiasm of the others. Russia increased its power and became more aggressive. European public opinion turned more bitterly against the Turks. France, the most powerful supporter of the idea of Ottoman nationality, lost its greatness and became a follower of Russia. In short, both inside and outside, the conditions became more and more unfavorable to the scheme. It seems, therefore, that from now on to follow the policy of Ottomanism is nothing more than a waste of time.

Now let us see whether the policy of Pan-Islam is beneficial and practicable for the Ottoman state.

As has been suggested above, the application of this policy would increase the already existing rivalries and animosities among the peoples of the empire and thus would mean the weakening of the state. Moreover, the Turks would find themselves separated into Muslims and non-Muslims and thus the common affinity based on ethnicity would be destroyed by religious conflicts.

Against such disadvantages, however, this policy had the advantage of unifying all Muslims, and consequently the Turks would create an Islamic commonwealth more solid and compact than the unity of the Ottoman nation. More important than this, it would prepare the ground for the rise of a larger unity, based on religion, which would be able to survive alongside the great powers arising out of Anglo-Saxon, Germanic, Slavic, Latin, and perhaps Sino blocs.

The realization of this ultimate aim would undoubtedly take a long time. In the beginning it would suffice to strengthen the already existing spiritual relations and to set down the outlines of future organization. But gradually the outlines will begin to take a clearer and more definite form, and then it would be possible to create a stable spiritual unity extending over the greater part of Asia and half of Africa which would serve to challenge the above-mentioned great and formidable blocs.

But is it possible to pursue this policy successfully in the Ottoman lands?

Islam is one of the religions that puts much importance on political and social affairs. One of its tenets may be formulated by the saying that "religion and nation are the same." Islam abolishes the ethnic and national loyalties of those who embrace it. It also tends to do away with their language, their past, and their traditions. Islam is a powerful melting pot in which peoples of various ethnicities and beliefs produce Muslims who believe they are a body with the same equal rights. At the rise of Islam there was within it a strong orderly political organization. Its constitution was the Koran. Its official language was Arabic. It had an elected head and a holy seat.

However, the changes observable in other religions can be seen in Islam, too. As the result of the influences of ethnicity and various events the political unity achieved by religion became partly disrupted. A century had not even passed since the hijra before the national conflicts between the Arabs and the Persians (taking the form of the struggles between the Umayyad and Hashemite dynasties) had opened an unbridgeable rift in the unity of Islam. It created the great schism between the Sunni and Shii Muslims. Later on various other elements like the Turks and Berbers appeared in addition to the Arabs and the Persians. In spite of the great leveling, assimilating, and unifying power of Islam, the unity of the official and religious language, too, disappeared. Persian claimed equality with Arabic. A time came when the power of Islam began to sink to its lowest ebb. Part of the Muslim lands and then gradually a great part of them (more than three-fourths) passed under the domination of the Christian states. The unity of Islam became more disrupted. And, in recent times, under the impact of Western ideas, ethnic and national feelings, which previously had been subsumed by Islam, began to show their force.

In spite of all these forces that have weakened the power of Islam, religious beliefs are still very influential. We can safely say that among the Muslims skepticism toward their faith and the doctrine of atheism are not yet widespread.

All followers of Islam still seem to be faithful, enthusiastic, obedient believers, who can face every sacrifice for the sake of their religion.

Although the new legislations of some Muslim states have diverged from the sheria of Islam, these states still pretend to maintain the Islamic law as the basis of legislation. Arabic is still the only religious language of science and literature among the Muslims of certain lands. Many Muslim madrasa, with a few exceptions, still teach in Arabic and follow the same scholastic programs. Still many Muslims are saying "Thank God, I am a Muslim," before saying "I am a Turk or an Iranian." Still the majority of the Muslims of the world recognize the Emperor of the Ottoman Turks as their Caliph. Still all Muslims turn their faces to Mecca five times a day and rush from all corners of the world, enthusiastically confronting all kinds of difficulties, to the kabah of Allah to kiss the Black Stone. Without hesitating, we can repeat, therefore, that Islam still is very powerful. Thus, it seems that the internal obstacles against the policy of Pan-Islam may more or less easily be overcome.

The external obstacles, on the other hand, are very powerful. On the one hand, all of the Islamic states, with one or two exceptions, are under the influence of the Christian states. On the other hand, all of the Christian states, with one or two exceptions, have among their subjects, Muslims.

These states believe that their Muslim subjects' allegiance to a foreign political power—even if this allegiance is only in a spiritual sense—is contrary to their interests and is something that might prove dangerous in the future. Therefore, these states would naturally use every means within their power to prevent the realization of a Pan-Islamic unity. And, through their influence and might over the Muslim states, they are in a position to prevent it. Therefore, they can follow and eventually succeed in the materialization of a policy contrary to the Pan-Islamic program of the Ottoman government, which is the strongest Islamic power today.

Now, let us survey the benefits of the policy of Pan-Turkism (tevhid-i Etrak). By such a policy all Turks living in the Ottoman empire would be perfectly united by both ethnic and religious bonds and the other non-Turkish Muslim groups who have been already Turkified to a certain extent would be further assimilated. Those who have never been assimilated but at the same time have no national feelings would be entirely assimilated under such a program.

But the main service of such a policy would be to unify all the Turks who, being spread over a great portion of Asia and over the eastern parts of Europe, belong to the same language groups, the same ethnicity, and mostly the same religion. Thus there would be created a greater national political unity among the other great nations. In this greater national unity the Ottoman state as the most powerful, the most progressive and civilized of all Turkish societies, would naturally play an important role. There would be a Turkish world in between the world of the Caucasian and the East Asian ethnicities. Recent events suggest that such a division of the world into two great blocs is imminent. In between these two blocs the Ottoman state could play a role similar to that which is played by Japan among the East Asian ethnicities.

But, over these advantages, there are certain disadvantages that may lead to the partition of the non-Turkish Muslims from the Ottoman empire. These peoples cannot be assimilated with the Turks, and therefore this policy would lead to the division of the Muslims into Turks and non-Turks and thereby to the relinquishment of any serious relations between the Ottoman state and the non-Turkish Muslims.

Moreover, the internal obstacles against this policy are greater in number than those that were unfavorable to the policy of Pan-Islam. For one thing, the Turkish nationalistic ideas, which appeared under the influence of Western ideas, is still very recent. Turkish nationalism—the idea of the unification of the Turks—is still a newborn child. That strong organization, that living and zealous feeling, in short, those primary elements which create a solid unity among Muslims do not exist in Turkishness (*Türklük*). The majority of the Turks today have forgotten their past!

We must remember, however, that a great majority of the present-day Turks who seem to be amenable to unification are of Muslim religion. For that reason, Islam may be an important factor in the realization of a Turkish unity. Religion is admitted as an important element in various definitions of nationality. Islam, however, to play such a role in the realization of the Turkish nationality, has to face a change so that it can admit the existence of the nationalities within itself—a recognition achieved recently in Christianity. And such a transformation is almost inevitable. The dominant current in our contemporary history is that of nations. Religions as such are increasingly losing their political importance and force. Religion is increasingly becoming less and less social and more and more personal. Freedom of conscience is replacing unity of faith. Religions are renouncing their claims to being the sole director of the affairs of the communities and they are becoming spiritual forces leading hearts toward salvation. Religion is nothing more than a moral bond between the Creator and the created. Religions, therefore, if they are to maintain any of their social and political importance, can do so by becoming a helper and even a handmaiden to the national unities.[7]

External obstacles against the realization of the Turkish unification, on the other hand, are less strong in comparison with those working against Pan-Islamism. Among the Christian states the only power to work against this policy will be Russia. As to the other Christian governments, they may even encourage this policy because they will find it against the interests of Russia.

The following conclusions seem to emerge from our discussion. The policy of Ottoman nationality, though implying many advantages for the Ottoman state, seems to be impracticable. Other policies aiming at the unification of the Muslims or of the Turks, on the other hand, seem to imply advantages and disadvantages of almost equal weight. As to the practicability of these two policies, we see likewise that the favorable and the unfavorable conditions are equal.

Which one, then, should be followed? When I saw the name of your publication, *Türk*, an uncommon name to be used [by the Ottomans], I hoped to find in your columns an answer to this question which used to occupy me continuously, and I hoped that this answer would be in favor of the policy of Turkism. But, I see that the "Turk" whose rights you are defending, the "Turk" whom you are trying to enlighten and move, is not anyone of that great ethnicity who lives in the lands of Asia, Africa, and Europe, extending from Central Asia to Montenegro, from the Timor Peninsula to the Karalar Ili, but rather one of the western Turks who is a subject of the Ottoman state. Your newspaper *Türk* knows and sees this "Turk" only as a Turk living since the fourteenth century and whose history is known only through the eyes of the French historians. You are trying to defend the rights of only the "Turk" against the pressures of the foreign nations and the non-Muslim and Muslim peoples who are subjects of the same [Ottoman] state but who belong to a different [non-Turkish] ethnicity. For your newspaper *Türk*, the military, political, and civil history of the Turks is nothing but the history of Murat I, Mehmet the Conqueror, Selim I, Ibn Kemal, Nef'i, Baki, Evliya Chelebi and Namik Kemal. It does not and cannot be extended to the names of Oghuz, Chinggis, Timur, Ulugh Bey, Farabi, Ibn Sina, Taftazani, and Navai. Sometimes your opinions seem somewhat close to the policy of Pan-Islam and the Caliphate, leaving the impression that you are supporting the policies of Pan-Islamism and Turkism at the same time. You implicitly seem to believe that both groups, being Muslims, have common interests on vital questions. But you do not even insist upon this view.[8]

In short, the question that is in my thoughts and inviting an answer is still unanswered. The question is: Of the three policies of Islamism and Turkism (*Türklük*), which one is the more beneficial and practicable for the Ottoman state?

Yusuf Akchura
Village of Zoya, Russia
15 (28) March 1904

Notes

1. Although it can be claimed that this policy had been followed in a natural fashion by certain Ottoman rulers up to the time of Selim I, it was not because of imitating Europe. Rather, it originated from the needs of the time and from the fact that Islam was not yet well established. Consequently it is not relevant to our discussion.

2. This policy had been followed several centuries before by the Ottomans. Bayazit the Lightning, Mehmet the Conqueror, and Mehmet Sokollu pursued this idea. The desire to unify the world of Islam is obvious in almost every action of Selim I. These periods, however, do not fall within the scope of this article.

3. It must not be forgotten that this article was written over seven years ago. [Editor's Note to the 1912 reprint].

4. My intention must not be misunderstood. There are several reasons for the hostility which exists among the diverse peoples and the conflicts between Europe and the Ottoman empire. The cause I have mentioned above forms only one of several varied causes.

5. If I am not mistaken the government did not permit publication of the second volume of the *Turkish History* [which this group prepared].

6. Because the non-Muslim Turks are very few [in number], this last danger is not important.

7. Examples are: the Orthodox church in Russia, Protestantism in Germany, Anglicanism in England, and Catholicism in various countries.

8. "Makam-i Celil-i Hilafet," *Türk*, 18 Kanunevvel 1319 (1903).

The Program of the Turkic Federalist Party in Turkistan (1917)

Editor's Introduction

The Turkistan national liberation movement had its beginnings in the context of resistance to conscription of Central Asians into labor battalions in the Russian Army during World War I, beginning in 1916. One of the first political parties to emerge during this period was the Turkistan Turkic Federalist Party. The party's program was published in 1917, but its translator, Professor Hisao Komatsu of the Tokyo University of Foreign Studies, has established that the text duplicated that of the program of the Azerbaijan Musavat Party, thought to have been established in Baku in 1911.[1] The Azerbaijan party program was probably brought to Tashkent as a medium for compromise among the principal political groups vying for preeminence there. Komatsu provides a preliminary analysis of the program preceding his translation proper.

Note

1. The program of the first Musavat Party appears to have been published in 1912. See Audrey L. Altstadt, *Azerbaijani Turks* (Stanford: Hoover Institution Press, 1992); see also Society for Central Asian Studies, *Programs of the Muslim Political Parties 1917–1920* (Oxford, 1985).

This translation with preceding commentary by Hisao Komatsu of the Tokyo University of Foreign Studies was first published in the *AACAR Bulletin*, vol. 5, no. 1 (spring 1992).

"History resembles a book with pages missing." One who is acquainted with
our history books will agree that this idea of the Japanese writer Akutagawa is
true. . . . It is necessary for us to understand, more seriously than ever, why
our history was erased intentionally.
—Said Murad (1990)

Recent Central Asian publications contain many new facts and source materials
relating to issues and individuals that were previously absolutely neglected or
treated as a taboo subject.[1] In this paper, I would like to discuss an interesting
document presented last year by Uzbek scholars and suggest its interpretation
from a historical perspective.

This document is the program (*maramnamasi*) and regulations (*nizamnamasi*)
of the Turkic Federalist Party (*Türk Adam-i Markaziyat Firqasi*) adopted on
August 23, 1917. It was published as a lithographed pamphlet in Tashkent in the
same year and reprinted in the Cyrillic alphabet in the journal *Fan ve Turmush*
(1990, no. 7) through the efforts of Ahmadjan Madaminov and Said Murad. I
regret that I have not yet obtained the original of the pamphlet; as far as I can
determine, that document remained unknown to the rest of the world until now.

To begin with, it is appropriate to provide a glimpse of the political circumstances in Turkistan between the February and October revolutions. The February Revolution encouraged the nationalist movement among the Turkistan
population against Russian colonial rule. The Turkistani political awakening was
observed in every major city where a number of newspapers and journals were
published. In addition to the periodicals, the first political organization, the
Turkistan Muslim Central Council (*Turkistan Müslüman Merkez-i Shurasi*) was
established mainly by the reformist intellectuals (Jadids) in Tashkent in April of
the same year. However, the leadership was in fact divided into two political
groups. The first was the Islamic Council (*Shura-i Islam*), established by the
liberal reformists in March 1917. The second was the Ulama Society (*Ulama
Jamiyati*), founded by conservative Muslim intellectuals in June. In the first
phase, there was hostility and sharp conflict between them over doctrines and
tactics. While the first designed an autonomous republic for a future Turkistan,
the latter stressed autonomy only in the realm of Islamic law. At the all-Russian
Muslim Congress held in Moscow in May 1917, the varied orientations among
the Turkistan delegates were in evidence. However, before long, the political
situation in Turkistan—including the negative Russian attitude toward the
Turkistani population—brought about a compromise and union of the two political groups, which was completed on the occasion of the Fourth Turkistan
Muslim Congress convened in Khoqand in November, just after the October
Revolution.

Now I would like to examine the above-mentioned document. First of all, its
content. The program consists of a Preamble, or Special Remark (*Ikhtar-i
Mahsus*), and of nine chapters, which are titled as follows: State and Autono-

mous Organization; Nationality Issues; Religious Issues; Human Rights in Autonomous Segments; Economic and Financial Matters; Land Issues; Labor Issues; Juridical Matters; and Educational Affairs.

The aim of the party is shown in the Preamble. It states: "In order to bring about an autonomous and federative administration in Turkistan, there are no other means than to create an effective Federalist Party in Turkistan." Accordingly, the new Russian state should be based on a federal system. Such major national segments as Turkistan, Kirghizistan (Kazakistan), Caucasus, Bashkurdistan, and others were to enjoy national and territorial autonomy, while other scattered or small nations, for example, the Volga and Crimean Tatars, would enjoy national and cultural autonomy within Russia. In general, the program proposes establishment of a democratic, secular, and, with respect to domestic affairs, an independent Republic of Turkistan. For instance, its secular aspect is evident in the article that states: "No religions or sects are to be preferred to others by the government." However, at the same time it should be noted that the aspiration for Turkic and Islamic unity in Russia is clearly expressed. There was to be an all-Russian Turkic Union for national and cultural affairs and an all-Russian Muslim Spiritual Board, presided over by a selected *Shayk al-Islam*, for oversight of religious affairs. The program also states that a common Turkic written language should be learned and used in higher education. This is not to say that the program denied linguistic pluralism in multiethnic Turkistan. A local language or dialect was to be used along with the official language in the administrative affairs of every province and district. The local language or dialect spoken by the majority of the population was to be used in the classrooms of elementary and secondary schools.

The next question pertains to the identity of the authors. At the end of the document, we find a list of fourteen coauthors. Let me introduce some of them. Mullah Kamaluddin Qazi Damulla Rahmanberdiogli of Khoqand was one of the delegates of Turkistan Ulama at the all-Russian Muslim Congress in Moscow. Their conservative attitude was severely criticized by reformist- (and socialist-) minded delegates from Turkistan. He and some mullahs named on the list are thought to have been members of the Ulama Jamiyati. Mullah Abidjan Mahmudyar, a merchant of Khoqand, and Mir Adil Mirza Ahmadogli, a merchant of Skobelev (Margilan), were reformist intellectuals and later entered the cabinet of the short-lived Turkistan Autonomous Government. Munavvar Qari Abdurrashidhan Ogli and Mullah Mahmudkhoja Bahbudiy were rather famous Jadid leaders. It may be noted that Behbudiy's early project of autonomous Turkistan, presented in 1909, is enlarged and incorporated in this party program. Sadriddinhan Mahdum is one of the most remarkable Turkistan nationalists. After the collapse of Turkistan autonomy [under Red Army occupation], he went to Istanbul with the purpose of establishing a Turkistan Representative Committee in Switzerland.[2] Although he left for Switzerland with Köprülüzade Mehmet Fuat, having been assisted by Talat Pasha, the revolutionary conditions in

Eastern Europe prevented him from accomplishing his purpose. Later returning to Turkistan, he joined the Basmachi movement. In short, we can find on the list the leaders of the two opposite political groups and also the most eminent nationalist leaders in Turkistan. And one more person not to be forgotten is Muhammad Amin Afandizada, an ulama from the Caucasus.

The list indicates that the program was drafted by Turkistani nationalists themselves. However, it seems not without help. Zeki Velidi Togan, who himself participated in the Turkistan national movement, writes as follows:

> In the summer of 1917, the Turkistan reformist intellectuals were engaged in establishing their own political party in preparation for the coming election of the all-Russian Constituent Assembly. Formerly there was among the Uzbeks the Turan Society for Spreading Education. At first they tried to reorganize it on Social Democratic principles, but later, under the influence of an Azerbaijani, Mehmet Emin Efendizade, they transformed it into the Turkic Federalist Party and published a definitive program. It presented a socialist version of the Azerbaijan Musavat Party's program. They also published newspapers titled *Turan* (April–September) and, later, *Türk Ili* (September).[3]

Togan's statement is very instructive for our interpretation. When we compare the program with that of the Azerbaijan Musavat Party, it turns out that the former is essentially the same as the latter except for a few alterations. Not only the framework of the two programs but also most of the articles are identical. Thus the program is considered the result of the cooperative work of the Turkistan and Azerbaijan reformists. The work was carried out under the effective guidance of Muhammad Amin Afendizada, who was supposed to have been sent by the Musavat Party at the Turkistanis' request. Objectively speaking, it was inevitable that the Turkistani intellectuals, who lacked political experience, would take the Musavat program as a model. On the other hand, some differences are found between the two programs. In general, the Turkistan program appears more moderate than the Musavat's. Presumably, the Turkistan reformists had to modify it in some respects to persuade their conservative colleagues to form a united national front against the Russians. They seem to have compromised with the Ulama Jamiyati with respect to such problems as expropriation and distribution of large tracts of private land, women's rights, and so on. We know that the delegates of the Turkistan ulama had made a strong protest over those issues during the Moscow Congress. Therefore, we cannot agree with Togan, who pointed out that the Turkistan program presented the socialist version of the Azerbaijan Musavat Party program. On the contrary, some radical articles in the Musavat program, for example, workers' and women's rights, disappeared in the Turkistan version. The reformists' concession to the ulama, who were conservative yet influential among the population, appear also in the party organ *Türk Ili*'s motto: "Holding on to Islam, we work hard to defend autonomous rights."

The biggest difference between the two programs may be found in the articles relating to land issues. As to this subject, the Turkistan Party had its own claims. First, the Turkistan program omitted the Musavat principle of expropriation and distribution of large tracts of private land. Second, the Turkistan program claimed the recovery of land and villages confiscated by the Russians as a result of some incidents; we know, for instance, of the Andijan uprising and the Kazakh revolts in Semirechiye in 1916. Third, the Turkistan program states that the whole waqf lands confiscated unlawfully should be returned to the rightful owners according to the waqfnames concerned. In short, as to the land issue, the Turkistan Party was radically against the previous colonial rule, but moderate as to the traditional Muslim land ownership.

Unfortunately, we have not sufficient knowledge about the party's real aspects. The party's organ, *Türk Ili*, was at the same time the organ of the Turkistan Muslim Central Council, and it is supposed that the party included almost all the members of the Islamic Council. The very short life of *Türk Ili* suggests that the party could not enjoy great success. On the other hand, Nurshirvan Yavshev did not hide his disappointment after observing the activities of the Second Turkistan Muslim Congress held in September, just after the birth of the party. Nevertheless, it is undeniable that the Turkic Federalist Party attempted to draw up the first and systematic political program independent of the Russian political parties in Turkistan, and promoted the autonomous Turkistan idea among the population, even if in a limited sphere. And around it, such talented young intellectuals as Fitrat began to search for Turkistan national history and traditions. When the Musavatists in Azerbaijan decided to adopt the Ilkhanid's blue banner as their symbol, Fitrat remembered the golden age of the Timurids.

Hisao Komatsu

Translator's Notes

1. A. Madaminov and S. Murad, "Turkistanda Khalq Jumhuriyati," *Fan ve Turmush*, 1990, no. 7, pp. 6–8; Mahmud Khoja Behbudiy, "Turkistan Idaresi," *Shura*, 1908, no. 23, pp. 720–23; idem, "Turkistan Mukhtariyati," *Hürriyat*, December 19/22, 1917 [reprinted in N. Avazov, ed., "Mahmudkhoja Behbudiy," *Yashlik*, 1991, no. 10, pp. 40–41]; Nurshirvan Yavshev, "Qurulyat," *Shura*, 1917, no. 20, pp. 462–65; Ziya Said, *Özbek Vaqtli Matbuati Tarihiga Materiyallari, 1870–1927* (Tashkent-Samarkand, 1927); S.M. Dimanshtein, *Revoliutsiia i natsional'nyi vopros* (Moscow, 1930), vol. 3; Mehmet-zade Mirza Bala, *Milli Azerbaijan Hareketi: Milli Azerbaijan "Musavat": Halk Partisi Tarihi* (Berlin, 1938); A.Z.V. Togan, *Bugünkü Türkili Türkistan ve Yakin Tarihi* (Istanbul, 1947); Society for Central Asian Studies, *Programs of the Muslim Political Parties 1917–1920* (Oxford, 1985); Kh. Ismailov, "Turkistan v epokh dvukh revoliutsii," *Istoriia SSSR*, 1990, no. 5, pp. 211–19; R. Abdullaev, "Turkestanskie progressisty i natsional'noe dvizhenie," *Zvezda Vostoka*, 1992, no. 1, pp. 106–13.

2. According to a recent publication, the famous Uzbek linguist Ghazi Alim Yunusov

(1893–1938) came to Istanbul with nationalist ideas and met Talat Pasha at the same time. See I. Tursunov and H. Uzakov, "Tilshunas Alim Fajiasi," *Sharq Yulduzu*, 1992, no. 1, pp. 203–6.

   3. Togan, *Türkistan*, p. 362.

THE PROGRAM OF THE TURKIC FEDERALIST PARTY IN TURKISTAN

Preamble

Undoubtedly, in order to bring about an autonomous and federative administration in Turkistan, there is no other means than to create an effective Federalist Party in Turkistan. Now, this Party began to organize in every place and recruit members. It is necessary for every Muslim desiring national-territorial autonomy in Turkistan to join the Party and make every effort for its strength and growth.

I. Organization of the State and Autonomy

1. The aim of the Party is to establish a Republic in Russia based on national-territorial federal system.
2. The Party demands national-territorial autonomy for each segment, such as Turkistan, Kirgizistan (Kazakistan), Caucasus and Bashkurdistan, and a national autonomy for the Volga and Crimean Tatars and other Turkic groups living in Russia.
   Note: When other Muslim compatriots demand autonomy for themselves, the Party provides them with every assistance.
3. Every member of the Assembly, local autonomies and all other organizations established in autonomous segment is to be elected by universal, equal, secret and direct balloting.
4. Every adult who has reached the age of 20 has the right to elect and to be elected, regardless of sex, class, religion and sect.
   Note: Muslim women's suffrage is to be determined in the realm of the Islamic law.
5. The whole of the above-mentioned autonomous segments is dependent on the central government as to national defense, currency, customs and diplomatic relations with foreign governments.
6. Autonomous segments are independent in their domestic affairs.
7. Every governmental seat of autonomous segment will establish a legislative assembly and a representative committee as an administrative organ.
8. Every autonomous segment is to be divided into provinces, prefectures and districts enjoying broad privileges and rights.
9. Although the majority language or dialect is adopted as the official language in every autonomous segment, local language or dialects are to be used in provinces and prefectures.

10. Every autonomous segment will establish a militia for national defense, and abolish the former military organization.

II. Nationality Matters

1. In order to resolve and advise common issues relating to all peoples of respected Turk nation living in Russia, their national and cultural union is established.
2. The method of organization, authority and responsibility of this union will be decided on the occasion of the first Congress of the autonomous segments.

III. Religious Issues

1. In order to supervise simply religious affairs; in the center the Sharia court; in the provinces, its branches, and in every city, village and clan office judgeships are to be established.
2. In order to resolve and advise religious problems of all Russian Muslims regardless of their ethnicity and sect, there will be established a spiritual board that is presided over by an elected Shaykh al-Islam, and consisting of the representatives of all Muslim segments and peoples. In this board, representatives of non-Turk Muslim peoples will be present as well.
3. For the election of the representatives, their numbers are to be determined (proportionally) according to the Muslim population of each segment.

IV. Human Rights in Autonomous Segments

1. All inhabitants are equal before law, regardless of religion and sect.
2. Freedom of conscience is protected in the complete sense of the word, and no person can be persecuted or pressured on the bases of religion, sect or conviction.
3. No religions or sects are to be preferred to others by the government.
4. Every individual is free to publish and announce one's own thoughts and ideas in the press or elsewhere.
5. Every individual has the right to gather and convene at any location in order to consider and resolve problems in which he/she is interested.
6. There is no need to obtain permission from anybody to establish an association or society.
7. Civil liberties and the sanctity of the home will be applied universally, and without a court order, no house can be searched nor can anybody's papers be inspected.
8. It is necessary for an arrested individual to be brought before the concerned court within 24 hours.

9. The former passport system is abolished, and anyone has the right to travel internally or externally without requiring permission.
10. The above-mentioned human rights are included in their entirety in the constitution and their protection is entrusted to the Higher Courts.

V. Economic and Financial Matters

1. The Party favors the abolition of all former taxes and proposes to levy taxes only on land, water, commercial income, and taxes on other usages. These taxes will be proportional to revenues and usage.
2. The Party deems reduction necessary in the customs/taxes to increase the usage of equipment and machinery necessary for the crafts and agriculture, and the indispensable necessities of the population, to keep their costs low.

VI. Land Issues

1. The Party regards the expropriation necessary, in their entirety, of the imperial property and the emperor's private lands and the domains of the aristocratic families without compensation, to be sold or leased to the local population engaged in their cultivation, as much as needed.
   As to private lands:
2. Whatever land law is enacted in Russia other than Turkistan, they are autonomous. Since in Turkistan there are few partnerships and other *olpovitlar* who have extraordinarily large lands, private ownership in Turkistan is to be left as is.
3. The Party endeavors to return to their former owners lands forcibly confiscated and distributed to others as the result of some incidents.*
4. Henceforth, necessary measures are to be set into motion to return the waqf (foundation) lands, that have been confiscated by the government, to their original purpose set forth in their trusts.

VII. Labor Issues

1. The Party does not prevent workers from forming or joining unions or associations, and when necessary, their taking actions to protect their own rights by means general or specific actions.
2. The Party demands that the labor standards, laws, and concessions ceded to workers should also apply to private employees, and the admittance of labor representatives to those offices charged with the administration of the protection of labor laws.

---

*For instance, the Andijan uprising headed by Ishan Madali of Mingtepe. [Uzbek editor's note]

3. It is necessary to defend the legal rights and health of women and child laborers, and administer the protection of all laborers from hazardous conditions with special regulations.
4. The disputes and discords occurring between laborers and capital holders, that are not subject to particular laws and regulations, are to be mediated by a committee consisting of delegates from both sides.
5. The Party demands: (a) that the government oblige capital holders to pay [social] insurance premiums for their workers; (b) that workers who are retired due to age or infirmity should be insured at the National Treasury's expense; (c) protection of the inviolability of the labor laws.

VIII. Juridical Matters

1. The law courts are only subject to law and sheria, and should be free from any interference and outsiders' intervention.
2. No one may be punished without the decision of the concerned court, legally confirmed.
3. Executive organs are not allowed to interfere in the appointments and dismissals of judges, and particularly in juridical procedures in courts.
4. Sentences are handed down in accordance with the laws enacted by the constitutional procedures, namely, by the Representative Assembly.
5. During interrogations, the presence of advocates will be established.
6. Criminal law courts will be divided into two categories. The first is a court of first instance, judges of which are elected by the population or community. The second is a court of appeals composed of select judges which will hear the cases acted upon by the courts of first instance.

IX. Educational Affairs

Educational affairs are to be organized based on laws in accordance with the federative system.

1. In educational affairs all inhabitants are equal regardless of religion, nationality and gender.
2. School management carried out by private or local autonomy's initiative cannot be proscribed.
3. Instruction in schools should be free from any restriction.
4. Consistent educational system is to be so that students can advance easily from elementary school to middle school, to high school, and to university.
5. Universities and other institutions of higher learning are independent in their internal affairs and they enjoy academic freedom.
6. Educational and cultural activities undertaken by institutions of higher learning among common people should not be prevented.

7. Local autonomy's educational efforts should not be prevented.
8. Elementary education should be public, free, and compulsory.
9. Local autonomy is encouraged to open schools, libraries, and public reading rooms for the adult population.
10. It is necessary to make every effort to develop craft and industries.
11. In elementary and high schools, the majority language or dialect of each autonomous province is used.
12. In secondary and high schools it is compulsory to teach in Russian and common Turkic.
13. In higher institutions lessons are given in common literary Turkic.
14. When there are over forty pupils in elementary schools for the minorities, it is compulsory to teach in their own language.
15. When there is a sufficient number of students among the minorities, middle and high schools are opened on the condition that the lessons are given in their own languages.

In order to achieve the aims mentioned in the program, the Party relies and trusts first in God, and second in the suffering nationalist compatriots.

* * *

The co-authors of the Turkic Federalist Party Program are the following:

> Molla Kemaluddin qazi damulla Rahmanberdi oghli, Khoqand
> Molla Muhiddin makhdum a'lam molla Muhammad, Andijan
> Molla Baqi akhund damulla Adilbai oghli, Andijan
> Molla Nuriddin a'lam Yoldashhoja eshan oghli, Andijan
> Molla Muhammadjan baibiche Kamalkjanbaev, merchant, Andijan
> Mirza Abdulkadirbek Mirzaahmad Qushbegiyev, Andijan
> Mulla Abidjan Mahmuduyar, merchant, Khoqand
> Mir Adil mirza Ahmad oghli, merchant, Skobelev
> Munavvar qari Abdurrashidkhan oghli, Tashkent
> Molla Mahmudkhoja Behbudiy, mufti, Samarkand
> Abdulqasim Muhammad Aminzade
> Muhammad Amin Afandizada, ulama from Caucasus
> Sadriddinkhan makhdum Muhammad Sharifkhoja qazi oghli, Tashkent
> Molla Mir Abdullah molla Shahmirza akhund oghli, student, Tashkent.

5 Zulqada 1335 A.H. (23 August 1917)
11 Sumbula 1917 A.D. (1 September 1917)[a]

Translator's Note

a. The dates given do not coincide, even if we consider the Julian calendar used in the Russian empire.

H.B. Paksoy

Excerpts from the Memoirs of
Zeki Velidi Togan

Introduction

Ahmet Zeki (Validov) Velidi Togan (1890–1970)[1] published two comprehensive accounts of the revolutionary and early postrevolutionary period and the Basmachi movement.[2] One account was historical (*Türkili Türkistan*); the other, more personal (*Hatiralar*). Both were based on diaries Togan kept during the period. The diaries were smuggled out of Turkistan, via various persons and routes, before and after Togan's own departure in 1923. The two accounts are complementary and contain ample material to aid the reader in reconstructing events.[3]

In completing the final versions of these works for publication, Togan indicates that, in addition to his own field notes, he utilized secondary sources to refresh his memory. These included materials deposited at the Hoover Institution Library which he consulted in 1958, along with newspaper collections pertaining to the period he chronicles. As Togan later recalled, he and Alexander Kerensky (1881–1970) "sat down at the microfilm machine and together read the newspapers dating back to the times when we knew each other." Togan also cites various histories written in the Soviet Union after his departure.[4]

The account below is largely based on excerpts from pp. 399–474 of *Türkili Türkistan* (1981 edition) and pp. 365–463 of *Hatiralar*.[5]

Notes

1. Togan's "The Origins of the Kazaks and the Özbeks" appears in part 1 of this collection.
2. See H.B. Paksoy, "Basmachi," in *Modern Encyclopedia of Religions in Russia and the Soviet Union* (Gulf Breeze, FL: Academic International Press, 1991), vol. 4, pp. 5–20.

3. Togan was fluent in quite a number of dialects used in Turkistan, both historical and modern. At times he writes in an amalgam of these, not only when he is quoting from manuscripts, but also when he mentally travels to a particular location, recalling an incident. Togan gives the impression that the memory was etched in his mind in that particular dialect. Togan had strong views about the "language and dialects" issue and confronted Bolshevik claims that the dialects of Central Asia are separate languages. Togan discusses the politics of language in detail in a special section of his *Türkili Türkistan* (pp. 486–526).

4. Although Togan's memoirs cover the period up to and including the year 1925, he often interrupts the narrative to provide information on the repercussions of a particular event up to the time he was writing the memoirs themselves. On the other hand, Togan does not introduce issues that arose after 1925.

5. Togan's writing style requires comment. It is not always an easy task to unpack his highly elaborate, detailed, information-laden, and lengthy sentences. At times it has been necessary to break his paragraph-long statements into a number of smaller ones. This factor and others mentioned above may be holding back potential translators and publishers of Togan's works. Indeed, several attempts have been made to translate his *Türkili Türkistan* into English and German over the past decades. Almost all of these remain in manuscript form, some complete. Togan reports that one draft English translation of *Türkili Türkistan* was distilled by Olaf Caroe and incorporated into one of his books, and indeed, Caroe acknowledges his indebtedness to Togan. See Olaf Caroe, *Soviet Empire and the Turks of Central Asia* (London, 1953).

Background

Togan was born December 10, 1890, in Bashkurt-Eli, the Kuzen aul near Isterlitamak. His family had for some generations been involved in agriculture, most prominently apiculture and animal husbandry. Togan received his elementary education from his parents, both of whom were literate in several languages in addition to the Bashkurt dialect and well read in related literatures. Togan also studied in the village medrese of his own father and of his maternal uncle at Utek, a few miles away from his home. By age 18, Togan had a command of his native Bashkurt, Chaghatay, Persian, Arabic, and Russian. He accompanied his father on travels to Troitsk and neighboring cities and became familiar with a wide geographic region.

In the summer of 1908, he unceremoniously left his home to further his education. At Kazan, he met several prominent Orientalists including N. Katanov (1862–1922) and N. Ashmarin,[1] and attended lectures at the Kazan University and the Kasimiye Medrese. He notes that in Kazan, Merjani's (1818–1889) circle was very much alive.[2] By 1911, Togan published in Kazan his *Türk ve Tatar Tarihi* (Turk and Tatar History), meant to be a textbook for the course he began teaching at Kasimiye.

During the summer months of ensuing years Togan returned to Utek, on the way stopping at various cities, such as Orenburg, Astrakhan, and Kemelik to visit historical sights and meet with individuals with whom he was corresponding. He began learning German, French, and Latin. His aim was to sit for the necessary examinations to qualify as a teacher in higher institutions of learning within the Russian empire. He was reading voraciously, both Eastern and Western authors, especially works on the history of the Turks.

His *Türk ve Tatar Tarihi* was well received, and Togan was elected a member of the Kazan University Historical and Archeological Society. He also received invitations from a number of medreses to teach, with offers of "satisfactory stipends." In 1913, the Kazan University Historical and Archeological Society officially charged Togan with the task of collecting primary documents pertaining to the indigenous history, language, and literature of the Ferghana region. In Tashkent, he was invited to join the Turkistan Military Governor's administration. He declined.

The following year, the Imperial Academy of Sciences (St. Petersburg) and the International Central Asian Historical Society, with the recommendation of Katanov and Bartold (1869–1930), jointly sponsored Togan to conduct a similar study and collection tour in the Bukhara Khanate. Upon his return to St. Petersburg, Togan, with Bartold's encouragement, began publishing the results of these missions in related journals.

Bartold also introduced Togan to General Pisarev, the director of School of Oriental Languages, where Bartold was attempting to secure a position for Togan as an instructor. Again on the advice of Bartold, Togan went to Kazan and sat for the examinations to qualify as a Russian language teacher at the "non-Russian Seminaries." Although he passed the test, the schedule of which was expedited by Ashmarin, Togan dryly notes that, "since I did not have an appointment, the diploma was useless." He continues:

> Bartold did not approve of the war efforts of the Tsardom. He told me: "You are not suited to be cannon fodder." But the efforts of Bartold, who had lost a number of his students at the front during the first months of the war, and of Samaylovich bore no fruit. I was inducted into the army. Fifteen days after I had settled into the barracks as a soldier, a law was passed to exempt the teachers of the non-Russian schools. I returned to Ufa.

At the end of 1914, Togan started teaching at Ufa. In 1915, he was elected a deputy from that city to the St. Petersburg Duma. Togan continued his scholarly endeavors in St. Petersburg and helped Bartold with the preparation and publication of *Ulugh Bey*.[3]

He became a member of Radloff's (1837–1918)[4] circle and worked on the corrections of Bartold's *Timur's Indian Expedition*. He worked with Samaylovich at the Imperial Geographic Society and also at the Asiatic Museum. He continued publishing.

All the while, Togan maintained his contacts with the educated and the students from all over Turkistan who were living and working in St. Petersburg. He also made the acquaintance of a number of political figures, especially those belonging to the Socialist Revolutionary Party (SRs). Kerensky was one such individual. He had grown up in Tashkent as the son of an Education Inspector. With the aid of Kerensky, Togan and Mustafa Chokay visited the front to observe the conditions of the laborers conscripted from Turkistan.[5]

During this period, Togan also met Maxim Gorky (1868–1936) and the writers working at Russkii Letopisets:

> Gorky had decided to publish a *Sbornik* [collection] of the "nations imprisoned by the Russians," stressing their cultures. Histories of Ukrainian, Finnish, Armenian, and Georgian literatures were being written. Gorky asked me to prepare the volume of the Russian Muslims. During the winter of 1916 I devoted much time to this project. I read all pertinent publications printed in Russia, such as those written by Gaspirali (1854–1914),[6] Hasan Bey Melikov (Zerdabi; 1842–1907) of Azerbaijan, and Fettah Akhundov (Mirza Fath Ali Akhunzade; 1812–1878);[7] also those Russian works printed in Turkistan. Old Professor V.D. Smirnov, who was the director of the Oriental Section of the St. Petersburg General Library, rendered extensive help. I evaluated those works written by Russian Muslims but not published. Smirnov was very interested in the topic, from the Russian point of view. I finished the draft of this large volume during winter of 1916, in Russian, and gave it to Gorky. He gave it to Gurevich, a Ukrainian, to read. Then the revolution took place. The volume was left in the hands of Gurevich, who was killed after he became Minister of Education in Ukraine.

February–October 1917

The February 1917 revolution found Togan living in St. Petersburg, across from the Preobrazhenskii Military Barracks. He immediately plunged into organizing for the political meetings that were "called to discuss the legal and social status of the Turk population of Russia under the new developments." These endeavors took Togan to Tashkent, where he opposed the largely Russian Tashkent Soviet. He joined the Socialist Revolutionary Party in Tashkent, but resigned within a month upon learning of the complicity of that party in inequitable food distribution.

The majority of the educated Russians in Tashkent were members of the Constitutional Democratic Party (Kadets), which was headed by the mayor of the city. The Kadets planned to establish two categories of municipal districts (one for the local people, the other for the Russians), with the Russian side ultimately wielding all power. Togan, "having read the relevant literature for the past few years," vehemently and publicly objected to the plan, exposing the hidden purposes behind it in a series of meetings: "I knew that the structure proposed was translated into Russian and published from the [British] Indian Government laws. The aim was to have the minority rule over the majority Turkistanis. I brought the books to the meeting."

In preparation for the forthcoming Moscow Congress of Moslems of Russia (May 1917), Togan "everywhere demanded that the Turk populations should have territorial autonomy, thus forming a federative system within the new regime." He was in favor of "including all Turk regions of the Russian empire into this autonomous Turkistan." Togan faced opposition not only from the Bolsheviks but also from some "unitarists" among his own people who rejected the federation idea in favor of a single Russian state. Likewise, the *kadimist ulama* (the orthodox clergy), in some regions a part of the Spiritual Board, a salaried Russian bureaucracy, objected to demands for territorial autonomy or the formation of a Turkistan as a part of a federated Russian state.

Bashkurt Autonomy

Since the Moscow and Tashkent soviets were opposed to anything but "Russianism," Togan continued his efforts among the Bashkurts, and there he met with success. In November 1917, after several *kurultays* (congresses), Bashkurt autonomy was declared under the presidency of Yunus Bekov, with Togan as Minister of Interior and Defense. Bashkurt government affairs began to be formalized and the Bashkurt Army was reestablished.[8]

On January 18, 1918 (new style), Bolsheviks occupied Orenburg, where the autonomous Bashkurt government was headquartered. For the first few days the Bolsheviks were solicitous toward the Bashkurt government, but on February 3 they arrested and jailed its prominent members, including Togan. Togan's followers led an uprising to secure his release, and he was freed during the night of April 3–4. Quickly organizing his friends, Togan began a guerrilla movement for the purpose of protecting the Bashkurt population and property.

On May 27, 1918, the Czech Legions revolted against the Bolsheviks and joined the Whites. Togan and his Bashkurt organization established contact with the Czechs. The Bashkurt government was reestablished in Cheliabinsk on June 7 and Bashkurt regiments were mobilized.

In cooperation with the West Siberian and Kazakh Alash Orda governments, Togan and his Bashkurt army units began engaging Red forces and succeeded in driving them out of Orenburg and traditional Bashkurt lands. In collaboration with the Samara government, the Ural Cossacks, and the Kazakhs, an intelligence department was established with representatives and contacts in various cities around Turkistan.[9]

On November 21 Admiral Kolchak declared himself Supreme Ruler and began preparations to disband the Bashkurt-Kazakh armies. He captured Samara, a principal munitions supply point for the Bashkurt army, thus dashing the chances of Togan's forces to resist the Reds. Togan and his friends concluded that they would have to come to terms with Moscow in order to save the native population from further losses. Upon announcement of the Western Allies' cease-fire with Central Powers, the Bashkurts and Kazakhs sent representatives to the Bolsheviks to negotiate terms. Togan asked his old friends Fedor Chaliapin

(1873–1938) and Maxim Gorky (1868–1936) to assist in the establishment of contacts with the Bolshevik leadership.

"Affiliation" with the Bolsheviks, especially after vigorously fighting them, had to be undertaken with the greatest care. During the ensuing negotiations, the Bolsheviks dispatched Mirsaid Sultangaliev (1895–1939?)[10] from Moscow to Ufa to expedite matters. Sultangaliev secured conditions favorable to the Bashkurt-Kazakh forces and their leadership. Finally, on February 18, 1919, Togan officially entered into cooperation with Lenin and Stalin, an alliance that was to last fifteen months.

Lenin, Trotskii, Stalin, and the rest of the Bolshevik leadership sorely needed the propaganda victory afforded them by the Bashkurts' "joining" the Bolsheviks (Lenin immediately wrote an article on "Developments of the Eastern Question," published in the March 2, 1919, issue of *Pravda*). The Bashkurt army was reconstituted under its previous leadership and some of its units were sent to the Western Front. This decision revealed differences of opinion among prominent Bolsheviks: Lenin ordered arms and ammunition to be provided to the Bashkurt Army; Stalin reversed the directive; then Trotskii overruled Stalin's orders and provided the Bashkurt army with ample war materiel.

Whatever his expectations may have been, Togan quickly became disillusioned with the Bolsheviks. It became increasingly clear to him that the Russians did not intend to share power, despite their promises. Talks with Trotskii, Plekhanov, Lenin, Stalin, Preobrazhenskii, Artium, and a score of others did not produce a resolution in support of maintaining the union and autonomy of the Bashkurt-Kazakh lands and populations. Instead, a Russian province was to separate the Kazakhs and the Bashkurts.

On February 25, 1920, the Bashkurt Revolutionary Committee elected Togan chairman to succeed Haris Yumagulov, who had been "called to Moscow." Shortly afterward, Togan, too, was called to Moscow where, according to both Lenin and Stalin, he was to undertake "Soviet state-wide affairs" as opposed to "looking after such a small tribal matter as the Bashkurts."

Toward the end of May 1920, Togan came into contact with Jemal and Halil Pasha (of the Committee of Union and Progress),[11] who were visiting Moscow. During a dinner given in honor of these individuals at "Bashkurt House" in Moscow,[12] and probably to force the hand of the Russians, Togan suggested a Congress of the Peoples of the East of "Russia." Togan repeated the idea to Stalin and the Party Secretariat, and it was also relayed to Lenin and Stalin by Jemal and Halil Pashas.

Lenin personally invited Togan to sit down with him to discuss the issues pertaining the Eastern question and "decolonization" policies. Lenin insisted on receiving Togan's comments in writing. In this last meeting, Lenin rejected the requests and demands contained in the joint resolutions of the Turkistan leadership, submitted to him through Togan. This may have been the final incident that caused Togan to break with the Bolsheviks and redouble his earlier efforts to devote himself to the affairs of what he called the "Secret Organization." During March 1919, just after the Bashkurt-Bolshevik alliance, Togan and others in the Turkistan leadership had proposed to establish the Erk Party for Central Asians, with the idea that this party would become a member of the Comintern directly and thus avoid total domination by the Russian Communist Party. The idea was vetoed by Stalin. Togan and the others then concentrated on introducing their members into the upper levels of the communist parties being established in Central Asia (probably with the involvement of the Intelligence Department of the Bashkurt government). This amalgam must be the "Secret Organization" to which Togan refers.

Following the last rebuff of national aspirations by Lenin in spring 1920, Togan resolved to join up with the Basmachi movement in Central Asia. On June 29, 1920, he left Moscow.

The Break with the Bolsheviks

Togan spent the summer months on the Central Asian *bozkir* (prairie) planning the next phase of his group's activities. In early September 1920 he surreptitiously attended the Congress of the Toilers of the East in Baku, where intermediaries kept him informed of the proceedings. He "participated" in the congress through motions and resolutions that he relayed via the same channels.

During the conference Togan learned of a resolution that had been passed by the Comintern after he had left Moscow. It was prepared by the Commissariat of Foreign Affairs under the guidance of its Middle Eastern specialist, Pavlovich, and was intended for the Bolshevik operatives assigned to work in the Middle East and Central Asia. The resolution was not distributed to the representatives of the indigenous populations. The copy in question was handed to Togan's organization by a sympathetic Polish delegate.[13] In summary, the resolution stated:

> Since class differentiation among the Arab, Turk, Iranian, and Afghan populations of the Near East is almost nonexistent, as is capitalism, it is necessary to exploit other cleavages already in place. It will be useful to keep alive *tarikat* and sectarian differences and competition among rival commercial interests and merchants even after elimination of some among their brethren. These rivalries ought to be supplemented through the use of differentiated languages, as the educated strata among the target populations is a thin one and it would not be difficult to break the population free of their influence.

From Petrovsk, Togan sent the following letter to Lenin, Stalin, Trotskii, and Rykov, dated September 12, 1920:

> It is apparent from the policy of the Central Committee of RKP(b) which is currently being implemented that you, like Artium and his friends, have accepted Russian national chauvinist ideas as the basis of your policy toward the

Eastern nationalities. Actually, Comrade Trotskii elaborated on this while he was investigating such matters in Ufa, and he pronounced the activities of the aforementioned as a series of provocations. Undoubtedly, he also made the same statement to the Central Committee. Nevertheless, Russian imperialism remained the policy. In the same session held after I and Ryskulov had departed, comrades Frunze and Kuibyshev—like Trotskii—stressed that this policy of the Central Committee was nothing but hypocrisy and deceit. In the same Turkkomisia [Turkistan Commission] sessions, those members of the party who wish to perpetuate Russian imperialism behind a mask openly stated their objectives: to fan the flames of artificial class distinctions among the Turkistan populations; to declare such nationalists as Ryskulov and Validov as the enemies of the laborers; and to create loyal servants among the local educated under the category of "Octobrists" and crush us with their help.

On the other hand, you must know that we cannot become the artificial class enemies of the local farmers and cannot allow ourselves to become the target of general mocking. You can find the required sacrificial lambs. But we cannot be those victims. The Congress of the Toilers of the East has clearly shown our fellow-countrymen in attendance that the attacks on the rights of Turkistanis are not simply the machinations of the local Russian Communists, but rather are the policies of the Central Committee. The attitude of the Central Committee representatives toward the Easterners in attendance is the same as that of the commissars at the beginning of the 1917 revolution toward the peasant congresses, whose members were regarded as ignorant. The Central Committee representatives not only prevented, by shouting down, those resolutions prepared by the delegates in their homelands, but also utilized Red Guard soldiers in silencing them. The delegates were forced to accept only those resolutions written in Moscow and sent for the purpose.

The fact that the Central Committee regards the Eastern nationality issues principally as a matter of land disputes, a peasant problem, indicates that the Central Committee has taken a wrong turn. The Central Committee can keep alive this artificial class differentiation among the Eastern peasants only by the force of terror. Our comments written in relation to these theses of Comrade Lenin, before he addressed the Comintern on colonialism issues, stressed that the social revolution in the East cannot be confined to [class] stratification, that this is a more complex matter. Since the European capitalist and the laborers of the East are going to act jointly as the rulers of the colony, then the Eastern peasant will have to join forces with the wealthy Easterner. When you determine that stratification is not taking place among the indigenous population, you will blame the local educated and declare a portion of the latter "class-enemy petty bourgeois" and the rest as the left-Octobrist "class enemy," and liquidate them. In their stead, you will conjure new left Octobrists. Finally, you will be left solely with the illiterate peasant who is only familiar with his donkey, ox, and spade. I do not believe that you can alter your distrust toward the native educated of Turkistan. You can at least allow the educated Turkistan elite the opportunity to renovate and populate Soviet Bukhara, whose Emir has fled.

Togan sent another letter from Petrovsk, this time to Krestinskii and Preobrazhenskii, secretaries of the Central Committee and members of the Politburo:

Since you and I have our differences in our understanding of socialism and nationalism, we cannot reconcile our positions with regard to the application of socialism in the development of great nations; as a person wishing to remain honorable, I have been honest with you two and many other Party members. I did not deceive you while I took the path of fighting against the Soviets and Communism. Those I have deceived are the likes of Stalin and other state officials who have deceived me. Those friends who complain of the masked Dictator's travesty of the dignity and the self-determination of human beings inform me of the severe terror that is yet to come within the party. Like them, I fear that one day your heads may fly. I did not wait for my head to fall. Even if I am to die, I must do so while engaged in open struggle.[14]

From September 12 until December 31, 1920, Togan traversed the lands between Petrovsk and Bukhara. Along the way, traveling incognito, he investigated historical sites, made contacts with local leaders, and further studied the terrain and its inhabitants.[15]

The Turkistan National Unity Society

Upon arriving in Bukhara,[16] Togan met with other members of the Turkistan National Unity Society as previously arranged. Their first task was to establish a Bukharan national army and bring in representatives from Khiva, Turkmenistan, and Kazakistan to establish the Turkistan National Union. The educated Kazakhs and individuals from other Turkistan locales who were sent to contact all groups in Kazakistan returned to join Togan after establishing channels with the Japanese and with Basmachi leaders operating in Ferghana. A number of the officers from the Bashkurt army were appointed to command garrisons in Karshi, Shehrisebz, Nur, Guzar, and Kermin. Their objective was to accomplish what the Russians were preventing: autonomy.

In addition to these "undercover" efforts, there were other officers working openly in "legal" positions known to the Bolsheviks. Although a Bukhara government was in existence in name, most affairs of state were in the hands of the Revolutionary Committee, a portion of it operating as the Central Committee. Togan describes the complexity of the political spectrum during the last stages of the Bukhara Emirate:

> There were three types of Basmachi: "Emirists," "semi-Emirists," and "anti-Emirists." The political spectrum of the Basmachi did not end there. Jemal Pasha wished to manage the problems of Turkistan and the Basmachi from Kabul. Enver Pasha, on the other hand, was conducting propaganda from Moscow for a pro-Bolshevik "Union of Islam." This had some effect. There were also others who tried to insinuate themselves, seemingly eager to join us. . . . Further, it was necessary to establish contacts with the Russian parties that were struggling against the Bolsheviks. In Bukhara and Khiva the government was passing into the hands of those nationalist friends whose administration,

though temporary, was moving away from "communism" toward "populism." It was necessary to formulate the economic and social theories of all. The political spectrum had earlier stratified as: (a) Kadimists, (b) Jadids, and (c) Socialists, and showed a propensity to crystallize around Jadids and Socialists after the disappearance of the Emir of Bukhara. However, thoughts were scrambled.

During the first week of January 1921, the matter of programs was debated by the Turkistan National Unity Society. Those involved were primarily individuals from among the "Islamic Unionists" and the Bukharan Jadids. Populist socialism was represented by Abdulhamid Arif[17] and myself. Since there was no previously prepared program before the general assembly, the Socialist Party Program was presented. It was first read in Bashkurdistan in 1919, then in Moscow in 1920, and finally at the 1920 Baku Congress. Few of those in attendance were prepared to accept it.

A few days later, Mirza Abdulkadir Muheddinoglu, representing the majority among those present, proposed a program comprising nineteen statutes. These pertained to the retention of the women's veil, continuation of the *Sharia kadis*, reverence for religion, and application to the League of Nations.[18] However, these were not acceptable to the other side.

As a result of their discussions, the two sides were able to agree upon the seven-point platform; subsequently, the two parties developed their own platforms. The contents of the seven-point program were further discussed and refined at a September–October 1921 congress in Samarkand and a September 1922 congress in Tashkent. The seven items are as follows:

1. The Society's aim is to have a free Turkistan and that the Turkistanis take charge of their own destiny.
2. Free Turkistan's form of government is a democratic republic.
3. Freedom can only be obtained through a national army. National government can only be based on a national army.
4. Turkistan's freedom is dependent on economic freedom. Turkistanis must have control over the decisions concerning: the general outlines of the economic policy; deciding the balance of vocational and agricultural training and the level of importance to be accorded to each; designating the locations and the directions of future railroads and irrigation channels.
5. Contemporary and professional education must prevail. Acquaintance with European civilization should be undertaken directly and not through Russians.
6. Nationality issues and the exploitation of the nation's natural resources will be organized according to census and prevailing proportions.
7. There will be freedom of religion. There will be no mixing of religious and state affairs.

It will be noted that the program is primarily secular in character and demonstrates religious tolerance. According to Togan, the aim was to accommodate a full spectrum of political views then prevailing in Turkistan under a single umbrella (in today's terms, something akin to a popular front).

During this period, the *Sosyalist Tüde* (Socialist Party) was formed, which later changed its name to Erk Party. Its program was shortened from 27 statutes to nine:

Erk Party Program

1. *On the economic plane*: In order to accomplish socialism, land, water, and mineral wealth must be nationalized and village life collectivized.

2. The labor organization of industrial countries is to be adapted, in a planned manner, to Turkistan. The farmers must also be regarded, from an organizational standpoint, as laborers.

3. Turkistan must free itself from colonizers and become self-governing. This is the first and fundamental step for stratification and the acquisition by the farmers of means to fight for their own rights.

4. The government in free Turkistan will be the democratic system supporting the farmers and those supporting self-renewal without barriers. The Turkistan parliament and provincial and city councils will be established and elected by the general population directly.

5. Establishment of the national army will aid the governance and the application of socialism.

6. In Turkistan, nationality and minority affairs are governed according to census figures and in representative proportions.

7. *On the educational plane:* Affairs are to be arranged so that the native population will have direct control of the country's governance; the national government will undertake all contemporary governmental services, modern transportation, railroads, post and telegraph, agricultural and industrial organization. Cultural affairs must be organized to reflect the strong national local culture, to remove foreign, meaning Russian, influences. To establish business and trade schools and to effect general education are among the principal objectives of education.

8. Religious affairs are kept totally separate from the affairs of the government.

9. The Turkistan Socialist Party can participate in an "International" provided that such a gathering is composed, in principle, of parties like itself, for the purpose of fighting for the freedom of oppressed nations.[19]

Counterbalancing the socialists were those "modernists" in Central Asia whose origins can be traced to the movement known as Jadidism, associated with such figures as Shihabaddin Marjani (1815–1889),[20] Kayyum Nasiri (1825–1902),[21] and Gaspirali Ismail Bey (1854–1914).[22]

Jadid Terakkiperver Party Program

1. To live as an independent nation, based on native culture, is the principal precept of life. This is the ideal of all nations. We aim to have an independent Turkistan with a national government. Nationality is based on the unity of language, religion, tradition, literature, and custom.

2. The nature of government in free Turkistan is republican. Sovereignty is in the hands of the national assembly and councils for the provinces and cities, elected according to democratic precepts.

3. Members of the central government are appointed by the president with the approval of the national assembly. Governors of the provinces are appointed by the central government. Chairmen of the provincial and city councils are elected by the members of those assemblies. The regulations governing the election of the members of the provincial councils are established by the first congress [*kurultay*] of independent Turkistan.

4. In Turkistan, non-Turk minority communities will have full civil rights. Turk elements must work rigorously and collectively to preserve the Turkistan culture.

5. Turkistan national government will depend on its national soldiers. Military service is mandatory.

6. Provincial governments will establish local police forces, which will be under the jurisdiction of the national defense organization.

7. There will be freedom of religion in the country. The state guarantees the freedom of the exercise of religious rights. Foreign [religious] missions will not be permitted to operate in the country.

8. Freedom of the press and publication and personal freedoms will be secured through the constitution.

9. Taxes will be proportional to income. So will inheritance taxes. In Turkistan, taxes that are the remnants of medieval times will be abolished.

10. Principles of land ownership will be based on the fact that water, land and the mineral wealth under and on the land, and the forests belong to the state. Land will be given to villagers as private property.

11. Private persons cannot engage directly in buying and selling of water and land to one another. These transactions can only be enacted through the state. Laws pertaining to ownership are determined by local custom and jurisprudence.

12. Turkistan's freedom can only be ensured with economic independence. In this vein, Turkistan will strive to establish and develop modern economic relations with neighboring countries.

13. The principal issue of land in Turkistan requires that the whole nation work with all its might to irrigate and expand cultivation. Water management must be handled with great care.

14. In Turkistan, especially the Kazak, Kirgiz, and Turkmen provinces, the most important issue is the transition from nomadic to settled life. This problem can be solved by irrigating regions alongside large rivers. No immigrants can be brought to Turkistan other than ethnic Turks and Moslems.

15. The solution to the problem of workers in Turkistan is dependent on the development of industry. Working conditions of the workers, working hours, and the rights of child and women laborers are determined according to methods prevailing in developed countries.

16. Equal justice for everyone shall prevail. This will be accomplished, without regard to differences in religion and sect, by accepting and applying modern laws.

17. General free education is to be striven for. Citizens can establish private educational institutions, provided that they are not against the interests of the state.

18. Importance shall be attached especially to the establishment of trade schools and to sending students to Europe.

19. Turkistan being the hearth of an ancient civilization, those monuments of civilization accumulated through the centuries will be preserved and organized to serve the development of the national civilization.

Togan observed:

> It must be categorically stated that the proposed future administration of Turkistan by two parties, one radical national and other socialist, was not influenced by any outside thought. This developed due to local conditions and in 1921 through consultations with the educated leadership representing the local population of Turkistan. The Alash Orda was added to the others to form a three-party system. At the time, during deliberations, Turkistan nationals were not aware of the existence of the two-party systems in England and in the USA.

The Turkistan National Unity Society and the Basmachi

Until the establishment of the Society, and while the Emirate of Bukhara was still in existence, the educated Turkistani were not in contact with the Basmachi. Basmachi units were largely based on the *Kadimist ulama* and elements of the Özbek bourgeoisie. During the 1917 Representative Council elections, the educated were vigorously opposed by the *ulama*. But, as the hopes of the educated were dashed by the Bolsheviks during 1920, they joined the ranks of the Society. At the same time, the abolition of the Bukhara Emirate eliminated the reasons that had prevented the youth from acting. Collectively, these developments diminished the influence of the *ulama* on the Basmachi.

Togan discussed the origin of the term Basmachi:

> *Basmachi* is derived from *baskinji*, meaning attacker, and was first applied to bands of brigands. During tsarist times these brigands existed when independence was lost and Russian occupation began in Turkmenistan, Bashkurdistan, and Crimea. Bashkurts called them by the Khorasan term *ayyar*. In Crimea (and, borrowed from there, in Ukraine), *haydamak* was used. Heroes gained fame, such as Buranbay among the Bashkurts; in Crimea, Halim; in Samarkand, Namaz. They did not bother the local indigenous population; they sacked the Russians and the Russian flour mills, and distributed their booty to the population. In Ferghana, these elements had also been active during the tsarist times. . . . After the proliferation of cotton planting in Ferghana [under the tsarist policy, replacing grain production], economic conditions deteriorated. This increased the brigandage.
>
> Among earlier Basmachi, as among the western Turks, the spiritual guidance of the Özbek and Turkmen bands was *Köroglu*.[23] Basmachi of Bukhara, Samarkand, Jizzakh, and Turkmen gathered at night to read *Köroglu* and other dastans.
>
> What has the external appearance of brigandage is actually a reflection and representation of the thoughts and spirit of a wide segment of the populace. Akchuraoglu Yusuf Bey[24] reminds us that the *Hödük* during the independence movements of the Serbians, and the *Kleft* and *Palikarya* of the Greeks were half nationalist revolutionaries and half brigands. . . .
>
> The majority and the most influential of the Basmachi groups founded after 1918 did not follow the *Köroglu* tradition; they were composed of serious village leaders and sometimes the educated. Despite that, all were labeled Basmachi. Yet in Turkistan, these groups were regarded as "partisans"; more specifically, as guerrilla groups fighting against the colonial power. Nowadays in the Özbek and Kazakh press, one reads about Chinese, Algerian, and Indian *basmachi*.[25]

The Society established contacts with the Basmachi in Samarkand, Khiva, and Ferghana. The objective was to shape the Basmachi into a real national movement infused with spirit, coupled with modern organization, to form military units under the command of educated individuals. To this end, educated advisers and some instructor officers were sent to them.

The Basmachi leaders Shirmehmet and Rahmankul themselves sought to establish contacts with the Society. Shirmehmet had sent two of his men, who were working within the Bolshevik apparatus, to the Baku Congress. Recounting a conversation with Shirmehmet, Togan recorded the impact of "a very interesting rumor pertaining to the Bolshevik policies concerning the East":

> The information arriving from Baku suggested that the Russians wished to kill fourteen and a half million of the inhabitants, only to retain two million under their rule. In the Baku Congress, the Turkistani decided not to lay down their arms and sent word to intensify the struggle. At the end of the Baku Congress, the Basmachi movement caught fire.

Togan also discusses the relationships between Enver and Jemal Pashas and the Society:

Even before I became chairman of the Central Committee of Turkistan National Unity [the Society], I was a member of that body. Therefore, it is necessary to delve into the relations between Enver and Jemal Pashas and the Society. They sought to join forces with the Bolsheviks by forming the "Islamic Revolutionary Society" for the purpose of liberating the Islamic world from European imperialism. First Halil and Jemal and later Enver Pasha arrived in Moscow with this aim and began their propaganda. We [the Bashkurt Movement leadership] spoke with Halil and Jemal during June 1920 in Moscow [see above]. Jemal Pasha explained his ideas and urged us to work with him, but we left Moscow.

On August 20, Jemal Pasha arrived in Tashkent. His goal was to secure the environs of Punjab and to establish an Islamic state there. He was going to prepare in Afghanistan. With 15–20 Ottoman officers in his retinue, he left for Afghanistan. In the meantime, Halil Pasha and Haji Sami[26] thought of establishing a truce with the Bolsheviks, to cross over to eastern Turkistan via Yedisu and Narin [rivers]. But they could not trust the Bolsheviks, nor could the Bolsheviks trust them. Finally, they returned to Moscow. Jemal Pasha told the Bolsheviks that he could use the Basmachi for a campaign to overthrow the British regime in India. But the Bolsheviks did not believe him in the least. We knew all this and the real intentions of the Russians through our friends working within the Communist central committees of Moscow and Tashkent. The Russians thought that Jemal Pasha was actually preparing an organization to control Turkistan, and wanted to keep the Pasha between the Indian and Afghanistan borders as a last resort for their own policies.

The personal representatives of Jemal Pasha, sent to enter into discussions with various Basmachi groups, were arrested by the Bolsheviks. This event, notes Togan:

Showed that Jemal Pasha did not have influence among the Bolsheviks. . . . Jemal Pasha's advice to the Basmachi was rather strange: "make peace with the Bolsheviks, without giving up your arms or dissolving your organizations." Although the Bolsheviks had previously tried that method on many occasions, we were now strictly against it.

On January 25, 1921, the Central Committee of the Turkistan National Unity sent a letter to Jemal Pasha, then at Kabul, via a courier of the Bukhara Foreign Ministry. The letter summarized the objectives of the organization (as noted above) and continued:

We ask that your Middle East policies be drawn so as not to sacrifice the future of old Turkistan to plans in preparation for the deliverance of the Islamic world. It is to the benefit of all concerned that all initiatives concerning Turkistan, including contacts with the Basmachi, be entered into via the

[Turkistan National Unity] Central Committee. Likewise, no aid should be extended to the Emir of Bukhara, currently in eastern Bukhara. Any support given to the Emir [by the Afghan government] will be taken as enmity toward our Committee. Even if we were to accept, for a moment, that the Bolsheviks remain sincere in their avowed position of liberating the colonies from European imperialists, Turkistan cannot subsume its future to the as yet unknown outcome of forthcoming struggle between capitalism and socialism. Thus, policies pertaining to Turkistan must be based on these principles.

Togan comments on this letter:

With these words, it was requested of Jemal Pasha that he not seek to utilize the political and military resources of Turkistan for the dreamed-of purpose of liberating India from the English. The Pasha did not like this. [Meanwhile] the Society steadily worked toward its goals, despite the paucity of politically experienced personnel among its ranks. Active elements of the Moslem Communists were channeled into the activities of the Society. In all of these provinces, members of the Society entered into the Soviet congresses and Communist Party meetings. Everywhere, the police [militia] organizations and administrative organs were under the influence of the Society. The labor organizations of Bukhara, Tashkent, Samarkand, and Kokand were under the influence of the members of the Socialist Tüde [Erk Party] branch of the Society. This was a monumental success and promise for the future of Turkistan and her inhabitants, who were relatively inexperienced in such matters. Although the individuals working within the government and party machinery of Khiva, Tashkent, and Orenburg were not members of the Society, they were completely cooperative. For that matter, they were not aware of the details. Such success of the Secret Organization could not have been dreamed, for example, during 1917.

Togan relates details of other matters weighing on the minds of the Society's Central Committee members:

The national flag was decided upon, having been earlier debated and reconstructed from historical elements, emblems, and colors, at the Samarkand sessions.... Teachers were sent in the retinue of each *Korbashi* ... [and] ten mounted troops were requested from in each *Korbashi* in Ferghana, Samarkand; to be sent to the Ferghana and Samarkand Commands. The purpose was to conduct preliminary preparations for the formation of a Turkistan-wide unified military command; experiment with military operations.... All existing disagreements between tribal units were resolved.... Those battalions in the barracks of the Bolsheviks were arriving to become units of the Turkistan forces. The Society was in constant contact with those high-level Russians who were against the Bolsheviks and supplied the Society with critical intelligence, thus preventing Bolshevik surprise attacks. In sum, the Central Committee of Turkistan National Unity was taking all precautions for a Turkistan-wide general and final assault. The final stage would have been accomplished by establishing military superiority and disrupting traffic and communications of the opposition with their center. The Moslem reactionaries,[27] as usual, were those Emirists and the *ulama* who had not yet lost complete credibility. These were still propagandizing against all our efforts. The hope was to reform them in a year or two. The arrival of Enver Pasha in Turkistan at year's end and the attitude of the Emirist recidivists toward him turned all precautions upside-down.

Togan and Enver Pasha

Enver Pasha[28] arrived in Bukhara and sent word that he wished to speak with me. On October 2, 1921, I met him for the first time, and at his request provided him with the details of the circumstances in Turkistan, especially the status of the Society. Since he was particularly concerned with the conditions in eastern Bukhara, I related to him the difficulties we were facing there, and the lack of progress due to the remnants of the Emirists. He indicated that he was aware of those conditions, that it would take an inordinate time to standardize the general organization through the Society, and that this would be a waste of time. He stated that he was going directly to eastern Bukhara and then to Ferghana with the intention of giving a different form to the Basmachi movement; he had made preparations to that end, had obtained horses and equipment, and had brought officers with him for the purpose. He would be leaving Bukhara on the pretext of a hunting expedition.

Enver Pasha's arrival in Bukhara, especially his plans, were a totally unexpected development for us. A few months ago this person was engaged in propaganda through the pamphlets of the "Union of Islam" and others, in connection with Jemal Pasha, advocating cooperation with the Bolsheviks against imperialism. He was now not only taking a position against the Bolsheviks, but actually had brought plans to attack them. . . . Enver Pasha told me that he had been in Soviet Russia for over a year now; [he had seen] that the Bolsheviks were despicable people and he had come to the conclusion that it was necessary to liberate the Moslems from Red Imperialism before any other Imperialism. . . . But his joining the Basmachi or even his going to eastern Bukhara was not acceptable. I stressed that point during our first meeting. He asked me what he could do to be of service to Turkistan. Truthfully, he appeared bewildered. We could not meet every day, since he was under Bolshevik surveillance. I wrote down fourteen reasons why he should not join the Basmachi, and sent it to him. The main points were: The Russians are about to wash their hands of external matters. Henceforth they can concentrate all their resources in Turkistan. Our organization, in proportion to its duties, is very weak. This year Turkistan is suffering from a great famine. Ferghana is experiencing a crisis in its attempts to feed the Basmachi. After joining the Basmachi, you would want to fight with regular fronts. At present, it is not feasible to keep a standing army larger than five to six thousand strong. It is only possible to conduct guerrilla warfare. As for the Basmachi in eastern Bukhara, it is not possible to cooperate with them unless agreements are entered into with the Afghans, and the Emir will not allow you to be recognized [as a leader]. Hence, they [the eastern Bukhara Basmachi] will not accept you as such. Until today, the Turkistan question, the Basmachi movement, and the secret political activity have remained an internal issue of Russia. . . . If you

join this struggle, the Turkistan movement may assume a Pan-Islamist character. . . . This could cause the Russians resident in Turkistan to unite with the
Bolsheviks, for their national objectives, against us. The best course of action
available for you is to cross over to Afghanistan and aid the Turkistan movement from there. . . .

Pasha was consulting with others on the topic. Some individuals, whose
names it would not be prudent to reveal as yet, received Pasha's joining the
Basmachi with a positive attitude. Haji Sami was another who was advocating
this course.

Togan describes Enver's consultations and vacillation and finally his decision
(possibly on October 28):

On the night of the following day, he sent word asking me to meet him. He
indicated that he was going to eastern Bukhara, to convene a congress of the
Basmachi and the educated. He asked me to send men to Khiva, the Kazakhs,
Ferghana, and the Turkmen for the purpose of relaying his decisions in the
name of the Society and inviting representatives. I again objected and re-
minded him that his crossing over to Afghanistan would be the most suitable
path. He was most annoyed. I gathered that Enver Pasha was not at all fond of
objections. Apparently he was not going to change his mind. The next night
five or ten of us met in someone's home. Enver Pasha related his decision in
careful phrases. Tears were streaming down his face. Others were somber as
well. . . . He was wearing German-made sports boots. He was giving the impression of a sportsman ready to jump into competition. He related his most
sincere thoughts. . . . That day I learned that this person was a great idealist,
who had not squared himself with events and life, and he had not equipped
himself with the geography and the statistics of Turkistan even from the Russian and the European publications. . . . Ten days later a special courier
brought a verbal message from Enver Pasha in Bukhara: "Decided to go to
eastern Bukhara. We will be Ghazi if we win, martyr if we do not. Let the
Turkmens (of Burdalik) not await our arrival."

Togan records Enver's imprisonment by the "frighteningly bigoted" Ibrahim[29]
of the Emirist Lakay clan. The hasty attack induced by Ibrahim of the Lakays
upset the carefully laid plans of the Society. Further, Enver caused the premature
emergence of a Turkistan army unit, an orderly force of 600 rifles, that had been
under "Bolshevik" cover. The skirmish was lost to the Bolsheviks, who were
openly aided by the Emirist Lakays. Enver Pasha and a few of his followers
crossed over to Afghanistan. By May, Enver Pasha had 7,000 troops. Volunteers
from Afghanistan had turned the tide. But, he was not without opposition. Togan
relates an assessment meeting after the latest event:

Enver Pasha was a fait accompli to the Society. The Central Committee met in
the vicinity of Samarkand to discuss the state of affairs. It was decided to
regard this development as specific to Bukhara border regions and not to
change the rest of the plans, not to declare an uprising in the name of the

Society, but to continue guerrilla warfare as before and to provide support for Enver Pasha. But the early failures of Enver's every initiative had a negative effect. This was also true of Enver's propaganda.

Togan proceeds with the details of his war preparations, listing the units, commands, commanders, troop strengths, and armaments under the Society auspices. He quotes from the memoirs of other combatants, members of the Society and participants in compiling this section.[30] Togan also states that between April and July of the same year he participated in the battles against the Bolsheviks:

> Between April and June, people and combatants of Turkistan were cheerful and the Bolsheviks were unable to leave the railroad lines. Comrades of Stalin, Eliava, and Ordzhonikidze arrived from Moscow in May. They could visit the Ulugh Bey observatory,[31] two kilometers from Samarkand, only in the company of a strong Bolshevik military detachment. For that matter, if they had not taken extreme precautions, they could have been thrashed by the Basmachi who were waiting in ambush.

The Beginning of the End

> During mid-March, Feyzullah Hoja brought a secret order from Moscow Communist Party headquarters, consisting of a few articles about "serious struggle against the Enver Pasha and Validov [Togan] Group." Stalin himself published an article in *Pravda*, under the title "Validovshchina," seeking to mobilize the nationalist youth against us. The Red Army's first action, after settling in Bukhara, was to employ the Emirists. The Red Army charged a high-level official of the Emir, one Nusreddin Aghalik, who had killed Mahmud Hoja Behbubi on March 25, 1919, with the administration of the Karshi province. Since this man was also in contact with the Emirist rebels, he was in a position competently to quash all our undertakings. As soon as he arrived in Karshi, Aghalik detained some individuals who would have been instrumental in carrying out the rebellion of the Shehrisebz, Guzar, and Karshi garrisons. These preparations were set and prepared for March 23 by War Commissar Abdülmamid Arif. Those of our essentially lax Jadid friends of Bukhara, who were in contact with the military organization in Karshi, became needlessly frightened, stating: "Nureddin Aghalik has heard of our intentions." . . . I personally traveled for two weeks between Karshi, Shehrisebz, and Katta Kurgan, but was unable to break the "Nureddin Aghalik" bands. In Kashan and other regions, some troops, fourteen educated Tatars and officers, Kashanli Behram Bek, Jure Ishan, and others were able to join the Basmachi, but they could not carry with them the stockpiled rifles and the ammunition. Molla Mushtak, a chieftain under Molla Kahhar, approached the Bashkurt army officers who were under the direction of Heybetullah Suyunduk. Disguised as Basmachi, Mushtak killed twelve men during a rest period on April 10.

Togan proceeds to answer a question oft misunderstood both in and out of the region:

Now, let me illustrate the complexity of the Turkistan question and the impossibility of conducting these affairs only on the basis of Turkism or of Islam, as Enver sought to, by way of an incident in Samarkand: A group of Russians—Socialist Revolutionaries—working in the cooperatives and food-distribution administration, and some officers under their influence, were in contact with the Society and provided us with ammunition. An individual occupying one of the highest positions in the General Staff [in the Turkistan Military District] was giving us help. On May 10, I met with an officer representing this group in Bag-i Bala of Samarkand. This group was seriously frightened of Enver Pasha's operations. A friend accompanying me stressed that Enver Pasha was in Turkistan temporarily, but the officer could not be persuaded. On that day, in a garden near Ab-i Rahmet, I spoke with an educated local Turk who had arrived from Tashkent. Although an intellectually committed Communist, he was rendering important aid to the national movement through the agency in which he was employed. He and his friends were frightened by the documents reaching their hands, signed by Enver Pasha as "Deputy of Bukhara Emir, Son-in-Law of the Caliph of Moslems, Seyyid Enver," and the news that Enver was cooperating with the Emir. I told this man: "Enver Pasha cannot serve the Emir. He is not a monarchist. No one in the Society will be permitted to lean toward monarchy. You can relay this to your friends." The same day, Yusuf Ziya Bey of Azerbaijan arrived from the side of Enver Pasha with the title of "Commander-in-Chief of the Northwest Front." He further claimed to bring a verbal order from Enver Pasha, to the effect that "The Society should not be involved in military affairs, but ought to confine its efforts to propaganda." Yusuf had the seeming intention of derailing the Zarafshan Basmachi movement, which had been reorganized only by the efforts of the Society. The next day, the young man from Tashkent [referred to above] saw Yusuf Ziya Bey in Kanigul. Yusuf Ziya Bey continued at length on the necessity of having an autocrat for the martially inclined Turks and that it would be very beneficial for such a person also to be a "seyyid." Next, he related that he had heard from Enver Pasha that there were 30 million Turks in western Turkistan and another 25 million in eastern Turkistan. On the issue of Kazakistan, Yusuf Ziya Bey rejected the proposals we put before him, which were done in cooperation with the young man. Yusuf Ziya's words and behavior entirely negated the guarantees I gave to this young man the day before. The young man was seriously grieved. In the letters we received from Enver Pasha after that incident, we found no confirmation of the words spoken by Yusuf Ziya. Nonetheless, it was clear that the statement of Yusuf Ziya, who had no idea of the spirit of this generation educated in the colonial psychology of Russian schools, was going to leave a negative impression on this young man and his cohorts. And so it was.

Those of us who noted the actions of the Emirists and their intentions thought that the Society was in a difficult position. Two days later we convened the Central Committee at a location outside the city to discuss the developments in detail. We regretfully observed that some Basmachi groups were attempting to enter into separate peace agreements with the Bolsheviks due to the crisis at hand. To prevent the united front from dissolving and to preserve the Society, we decided to take immediate action. In our opinion, the only solution to save the national armies from being routed and exterminated was to gather those Basmachi leaders in difficulty and Enver Pasha in Bukhara, and to have them cross over to Afghanistan freely. Troops were to give their arms to those going to Afghanistan and then they were to be sent back to their villages. To this end, we decided to write two letters: one to Enver Pasha, to persuade him to cross over to Afghanistan and to facilitate his opening communications with the Russian Commander-in-Chief, General Kamenev, who was expected to arrive in Bukhara. The other was to be signed by me, as Chairman of the Central Committee, to the Moscow Soviet government, containing the conditions of peace, on May 12. Both were to be sent via special couriers. The letter we sent to Moscow was delayed due to the mistakes of our friends in Tashkent. Enver Pasha, rather than accepting our suggestion (or perhaps before our courier arrived), sent an ultimatum to the Russians demanding that they withdraw from Turkistan, Bukhara, and Khiva. He signed it "Commander-in-Chief of the Turkistan, Bukhara, and Khiva National Armies."

A disciple of Enver Pasha arrived and visited Togan at the headquarters of Achil Bey:

The Akhund was a Shii theologian. He liked to talk on that topic. Akhund lectured the new arrivals on the necessity of fortifying the national movement from the religious aspect, and that they must provide information to the troops on the politics of Islam. He also looked around, on the way to preparing for *namaz*, as if to imply that everyone should be following him. But, only some individuals regularly performed *namaz* in the retinue of Achil Bey, and none could pressure the others to do so. After the event, I told the Akhund: "Among Samarkand Özbeks, the traditions of Timur are still dominant. Beys will not consult with the *ulama* and the *sheyks*, even those they greatly respect, on affairs of religion and military. The *hoja* and the *sheyks* do not even think of requesting such. Beys will go to *namaz* once a week, on Fridays. If I and my Bashkurt officers feel like it, we will perform *namaz*. If we do not, nobody will question us. Therefore, while you are in Samarkand, in the retinue of Achil Bey, it would be very commendable for you to be attentive to these matters."

Akhund Yusuf Talibzade, who had the objective of uniting the Turks with other Moslems on the basis of Islamic political plane, did not like my words. On another occasion, my friend Kaari Kamil brought kumiss [*kimiz*]. It was plentiful. The spirit of the ensuing conversations were based on the dastans of *Köroglu* and *Yusuf Ahmet*. In the afternoon, an Özbek played the *ney* [a woodwind instrument] and I recited a couplet in Persian. Kaari Kamil and other friends repeated in Özbek. Akhund said: "There is *ney* but no *mey* [wine]" and I responded "In this land of ours, kumiss is consumed during summer. Your not being satisfied with kumiss and asking for wine, though you are an educated Islamic scholar, will not be received well in this society, because we do not prefer wine to kumiss. Akhund asked: "Do you not drink wine?" I said: "Why not? But that is not the issue. Since you are a representative of Enver Pasha, there may be those in these *yaylaks* [summer pastures] who might disapprove of your drinking wine instead of kumiss. Kaari Kamil added: "We know you as a religious scholar, a Koranic commentator," and prevented wine being offered to the Akhund.

After these events, Togan chronicles the battles in which he took part. He provides political and military repercussions of each, as well as details. He was receiving intelligence from Moscow to the effect that large formations of Bolshevik troops from the Western front were on their way to Turkistan. There were attempts on his life. After numerous meetings of the Central Committee, a decision was made to fall back and regroup. The "above-ground" members of the Society were being pursued by Russian military formations. They dispersed, preparing to cross the Russian lines incognito, to meet in Tashkent. Togan, along with two of his friends, chose a mountainous route. After much difficulty, they arrived in Tashkent. According to the decisions taken in a series of further meetings, Togan was to leave Turkistan. He left, after sending a final letter to Lenin:

February 20, 1923

Dear Vladimir Ilich,

Due to your illness, it is possible that you may have been prevented from reading this letter or it might not have reached you. But since I sent copies of it to some other friends, it is now a historical document. Comrade Stalin ostensibly stated that under Comrade Rudzutak's auspices I could return to the Party. In other words, they [the Party] would disregard the letter I sent to the Central Committee from Baku in 1920, outlining my opposition to and initiatives against Moscow by joining the Rebellion. However, who can believe that and return? Especially since, by your order of May 19, 1920, signed only by you and Stalin, you have abrogated the March 20, 1919, agreement which was signed by you, Stalin, myself and my friends? When I personally protested that order, you characterized our March 20, 1919, agreement as "only a piece of paper." However, that agreement announced that Bashkurts would retain the right of maintaining their own army and that army was going to be under the command of Soviet headquarters without intermediary stages. With your May 19, 1920, order, you deprived the Bashkurt army of those provisions and assigned it to the trans-Volga army, disbursing the Bashkurt units as the trans-Volga headquarters saw fit among its formations. Indeed, that is what happened, and today there is no physical Bashkurt army. Similarly, in the same order, what was deceivingly termed "attaching Ufa to Bashkurdistan" turned out to be the reverse, attaching Bashkurdistan to the Ufa province. Consequently, what was conceded to the "Russian Moslems" on December 20, 1917, "the right to secede from Russia," should they choose, has been destroyed from its foundations by your order of May 1920. From now on, following the defeat of Bashkurts, Kazakhs, and Turkistanis in the southwest and my departure from Soviet Russia as of tomorrow, a new era shall begin in their history; that is, rather than seeking their legal equality with the Russians (in the Russian context), that experiment having failed, a transition to the international arena is being made. My task will be to familiarize the world with the history of those struggles.[32]

The Great Russian nation has already decided on the specific policy to be applied to the nations and tribes they are holding captive, not only in economic and social matters, but also in cultural affairs. The "Eastern University" which you established last year is operating as a center for these policies. A specialized "Eastern affairs" group, comprised of Great Russian personnel around the Central Committee, has also been formed. The Central Committee has brought in certain individuals of the Eastern nationalities of the Soviet domains and charged them with the specific duty of preparing material for these "Eastern specialists." Those Eastern nationals even published certain books and pamphlets. But, the topics they are to work on are assigned by your Great Russians. These non-Russian intellectuals are not even being admitted into the debates on the "constitutions" which are being prepared to govern them. Today, the main task on which the Central Committee's Eastern affairs specialists are working is to prepare separate alphabets and literary languages for each nationality and tribe, based on the extant local "phonetic" differences between them. In principle, the non-Russian communists are said to be serving only as consultants in this endeavor. The latest issue of the journal *Kizil Shark*, published by the members of the Eastern University, contained a commentary by one Ömer Aliyev of Dagestan. According to him, if the Cyrillic alphabet were to be accepted for the North Caucasus Turkish dialects, this would lead to Christianization. Further, he has reportedly said, it would be necessary to borrow the Latin alphabet in use in Azerbaijan.[33]

It is imperative that the issues of alphabet and literary language [according to Aliyev] not require Russian help, but the aid of those governments formed on the basis of national political freedom, and should be accomplished by native scholars. These writings and the efforts of the Azerbaijanis to gather the intellectual communists of the Turk tribes around *Kizil Shark* and one literary language is said to be making the Great Russian specialists nervous and angry. When Shahtahtinskii and Jelal Guliev of Azerbaijan defended a single alphabet based on Latin, Professor Polivanov and other Russians are said to have stated that even if the Latin alphabet were accepted, this would be replaced by the Cyrillic and a special subset would be created for Turkish dialects, whose number was approaching forty. Shahtahtinskii retorted that the aim of Russians was not to allow standard literary language to live. It is now understood that, when the Great Russians' friends begin playing with the language and the syntax of a people, you will not let their collars free until they, too, become complete Russians.

It is impossible not to be surprised in observing the differences between your current policies and your writings in "Against the Tide" and in your other writings where you state that, ideally, the rights of nations should be placed in their hands. Your representative Comrade Zeretskii gave numerous conferences to our people, during the summer of 1919, while we were refurbishing our army in Saransk, in which he said in effect that the Soviet government was the first in history to base the freedoms of captive nations on their own national armies. I myself published an article in *Pravda* in the same vein. It has not been four years since those events and it appears that your policies will be developing in the opposite direction. The Russian Communist Party may continue to claim, in Asia and countries far away from Russia, such as Africa, that it will liberate them. The truth is, your Great Russians become angry when people such as Gregori Safarov display the colonial policies of the tsar in Turkistan. Those Great Russians enjoy hearing the native Communists liken themselves to small fish being eaten by the whale—better if that argument were presented as a proverb. When Comrade Artium was visiting us, he used to state his belief that the Soviet Russian culture would become dominant in all of Asia except for China and India. Those native languages and cultures attempting to prevent this would not be worth dwelling upon, since they are only going to be used to spread communism. These and similar words were repeated elsewhere. Without a doubt, this will be carried out, and as a result all those nations who wish to retain their independence but have become your prisoners will view Soviet Russia as their foremost enemy. I mentioned these matters to you while you and I were discussing your theses on "Colonialism and the Nationality Question." Later, I reread your aforementioned theses in the journal *Kommunisticheskii Internatsional* (no. 11). You have suggested that even after the establishment of the worldwide dictatorship of the proletariat, "it would be obligatory for the vanguard nationalities to actively participate in the establishment of socialist regimes in the less developed countries." This translates into perpetuating the colonial regimes in India by the British, in Turkistan by Russia, in Africa by the French and the Belgians, through their labor organizations.

When I spoke with you and your friends in Ufa during 1919, never was there a mention of the use of terror to destroy human self-determination. What happened? Was that the object of those revolutions? Piatakov was correct when he directed this question to you while debating the "trade union" issues. You were beseeched not to take revolutions away from the labor unions whose sweat and blood were spilled for them. It is said that even Rosa Luxemburg was of the opinion that no good would come of socialism if it became a prisoner of imperialist traditions serving great nations. If Russia has not descended into the lows of becoming the prisoner of imperial traditions, what business did it have concocting literary languages and alphabets from the regional vernaculars? If you are alive, perhaps you can personally correct some of these errors. I have but one request: I ask that permission be given to my wife Nefise to meet me in Germany; she cannot accompany me tomorrow on the way to Iran,[34] due to her pregnancy.

Ahmet Zeki Validov

Notes

1. Despite their names, neither was Russian, but both had been baptized. Togan calls Katanov a Sagay-Turk from the Altai region, and Ashmarin, a Chuvash-Turk.

2. See Uli Schamiloglu, "The Formation of a Tatar Historical Consciousness: Shihabeddin Marcani and the Image of the Golden Horde," *Central Asian Survey*, vol. 9, no. 2 (1990), pp. 39–49.

3. For an English translation, see V.V. Barthold, *Four Studies on the History of Central Asia* (Leiden: E.J. Brill, 1963), Volume II, *Ulugh-Beg*.

4. Radloff was a German-born and -trained compiler of Turkish materials.

5. See H.B. Paksoy, "Basmachi," *Modern Encyclopedia of Religions in Russia and the Soviet Union* (Gulf Breeze FL: Academic International Press, 1991), vol. 4, pp. 5–20.

6. See Edward J. Lazzerini, "Ismail Bey Gasprinskii's *Perevodchik/Tercüman*: A Clarion of Modernism," *Central Asian Monuments*, ed. H.B. Paksoy (Istanbul: Isis Press, 1992), and the sources quoted.

7. For the last two, see Audrey L. Altstadt, *The Azerbaijani Turks* (Stanford: Hoover Institution Press, 1992).

8. According to the handlist of his papers, Togan also completed a history of the *Bashkurts and the Bashkurt Army*. This work remains unpublished. In *Hatiralar* there are extended references to the past of the Bashkurt Army and its operations.

9. One member of this organization, and onetime secretary to Togan, was the Özbek poet Abdülhamid Süleyman (pen name: Cholpan), often treated in Soviet historiography as a loyal Bolshevik. See Naim Karimov, *Cholpan* (Tashkent: Fan, 1991). Cf. Naim Karimov, "Exposing the Murderer of *Alpamysh*," in this volume.

10. In Russian-language sources, Sultan Galiev. For more on Sultangaliev and other Central Asians referenced by Togan, see Alexandre Bennigsen and Enders Wimbush, *Muslim National Communism in the Soviet Union: A Revolutionary Strategy for the Third World* (Chicago: University of Chicago Press, 1979). For a more recent treatment, see Masayuki Yamauchi, *The Dream of Sultangaliev* (Tokyo, 1986), in Japanese; and the sources cited by Yamauchi in his "One Aspect of Democratization in Tatarstan: The Dream of Sultangaliev Revisited," presented to the Conference on Islam and Democratization in Central Asia, held at the University of Massachusetts–Amherst, September 26–27, 1992.

11. On Jemal Pasha and Halil Pasha and the organization, see S. Shaw and E. Shaw, *History of the Ottoman Empire and Modern Turkey* (Cambridge, 1977).

12. This structure had been provided to the Bashkurt Revolutionary Committee by the Bolsheviks, along with several automobiles confiscated from foreign missions.

13. Togan notes that a copy of this letter was later brought to Berlin in 1923.

14. As a postscript, Togan adds that Krestinskii and Preobrazhenskii were tortured and, after making "confessions," executed in 1937.

15. Togan notes that up to a certain location in Karakorum, he was reading the memoirs of Babür and Marx's *Das Kapital*, which he carried along with his field glasses, but prior to his arrival in Kongrat, he finally had to give up those items in order not to attract attention.

16. On Bukhara in the Russian/Bolshevik period, see Seymour Becker, *Russia's Protectorates in Central Asia: Bukhara and Khiva, 1865–1924* (Cambridge, MA, 1968). For the earlier period, see R.N. Frye, *The History of Bukhara* (Cambridge, MA, 1954).

17. Abdulhamid Arif, the first Minister of Interior and later of Defense, had been Togan's military aide in the Bashkurt movement.

18. Togan provides the details of intellectual currents "that might have affected the thoughts of the individuals preparing this program" in *Türkili Türkistan*, pp. 415–16.

19. According to Togan, this program was expanded and republished in Prague during 1926 in a bilingual edition. See ibid., pp. 411–14. The Jadid program, below, is from ibid., pp. 416–18.

20. See Uli Schamiloglu, "The Formation of a Tatar Historical Consciousness: Shihabeddin Marcani and the Image of the Golden Horde," *Central Asian Survey* (London), vol. 9, no. 2 (1990).

21. See Chantal Lemercier-Quelquejay, "Abdul Kayum Al-Nasyri: A Tatar Reformer of the 19th Century," *Central Asian Survey* (Oxford), vol. 1, no. 4 (1983).

22. Gaspirali supported and spread the movement through the newspaper he published, and the schools he had established. See Lazzerini, "Ismail Bey Gasprinskii's *Perevodchik/Tercüman*," and the sources cited therein.

23. See the introduction to *Central Asian Monuments* for a bibliography of readily

accessible versions. According to Ottoman archival material (in Bashbakanlik Arshivi), it appears that Köroglu was a real person living in the sixteenth century, around Bolu province in Asia Minor.

24. See the short biography of Akchura by David S. Thomas in the introduction to "Three Types of Policies," in this collection.

25. Given the date when this was written, the references are to the respective liberation movements.

26. Glenda Fraser, in her "Haci Sami and the Turkestan Federation 1922–3," *Asian Affairs* (London), vol. 17 (Old Series vol. 74), part I (February 1987), follows Haji Sami tied to Enver's path.

27. *Mürteci*—recidivist, has a much stronger meaning than just "reactionary." Togan is remarkably restrained in his reference.

28. See S.S. Aydemir for a biography of Enver, *Makedonya'dan Orta Asya'ya Enver Pasha* (Istanbul, 1972), 3 vols. Aydemir himself was one of the early students at KUTVA, in Moscow. He met Enver in the Caucasus during World War I, and later in Moscow. Aydemir subsequently worked to propagate Bolshevism in the newly established Turkish Republic (which had waged a similar and successful war of independence, 1919–1924, in Asia Minor), and was jailed. After his release, Aydemir entered the Turkish Republic government service. See also Azade-Ayse Rorlich, "Fellow Travelers: Enver Pasha and the Bolshevik Government 1918–1920," *Asian Affairs* (London), vol. 13 (Old Series vol. 69), part III (October 1982).

29. Togan knew this individual well, having met him some years earlier during a trip sponsored by the Imperial Academy of Sciences.

30. It appears that the referenced memoirs were kept very much in the tradition of the *bitikchi* of earlier eras. It is well known that military units of the Turks always employed such recorders on the battlefields for the purpose of keeping tabs on the performance of individual troops. After the termination of fighting, rewards and promotions or punishments and demotions were dispensed accordingly.

31. See Kevin Krisciunas, "Legacy of Ulugh Beg," in *Central Asian Monuments*.

32. The text in the rest of this paragraph was garbled in the typesetting of *Hatiralar*, p. 461.

33. See Altstadt, *Azerbaijani Turks,* for the alphabet issues in Azerbaijan.

34. Togan returned to full-time academic life in 1925. Invited to the Turkish Republic by the Ministry of Education, he was given citizenship in six weeks and began teaching at Istanbul University the same year. After a disagreement on historiography at the First Turkish History Conference, he resigned and went to the University of Vienna (1932), where he earned his doctorate (1935). Togan taught at Bonn and Göttingen universities (1935–1939) before returning to his earlier post at Istanbul University (1939). Togan was jailed for 17 months 10 days (1944) by the Turkish government "for acts against the Soviets," released, and later returned (1948) to his post; organized and convened the Twenty-first International Congress of Orientalists (1951); was appointed Director of the Islamic Institute at Istanbul University (1953); became a visiting professor at Columbia University (1958); was awarded an honorary doctorate from Manchester University (1967); and remained a historian until his death in 1970 in Istanbul. His lifetime publications, in various languages, approach 400 in number. See *Fen-Edebiyat Fakültesi Arashtirma Dergisi* (Erzurum: Atatürk Üniversitesi, Sayi 13, 1985). This source contains some biographical material, especially on the post-1925 period, not found in *Türkili* or *Hatiralar*.

Sheik-ul-Islam al-Haj Allahsükür Pashazade

Address to the Fourth International Conference on Central Asia

The tradition of Islam was already thirteen centuries old by the year 1920, a turning point for my land, when the invasion of the Red Army resulted in the overthrow of the legitimate government of the Azerbaijani Democratic Republic and the proclamation of Soviet power.

. . . We have to recognize that the idea of socialism, its promising slogans and declarations proved attractive for the masses of Azerbaijan, primarily because they responded to their aspirations for social justice, a free and dignified life. Naturally, their hearts could not but respond to such declarations in the first postrevolutionary years as, for instance, the Soviet government's Appeal "To All Toilers of Russia and the East." It stated, among other things:

> Henceforth, your beliefs and customs, your national and cultural traditions shall be declared free and inviolate. Arrange your national life freely and without hindrance. You have a right to this. Know that your rights, just like the rights of all peoples of Russia are protected by the entire might of the revolution and its organs.

What could be more convincing than those words signed by Lenin himself? A religion free of supervision, pressure, and suspicion of power, and government

Sheik-ul-Islam al-Haj Allahsükür Pashazade read the text of this address to the Fourth International Conference on Central Asia, held at the University of Wisconsin at Madison, September 27–30, 1990.

Excerpts from the address were published in the *AACAR Bulletin*, vol. 4, no. 1 (spring 1992). The English translation was provided by Mr. Pashazade.

At the time of the address, Sheik-ul-Islam al-Haj Allahsükür Pashazade was a USSR people's deputy as well as the Muslim Spiritual Board Chairman for the Caucasus Region, based in Baku, Azerbaijan.

free of antireligious sanctions whose tolerance of religion promoted the unity of citizens of a multinational state. This could have been the ideal of society, the aim of its future development.

But the tragedy of historical reality was that neither during that turning point nor in subsequent years could Communist power shed its ideological dogmas and thus assess objectively the sentiments of believers, their aspirations for a new life, the ideals of equality and justice.

In noting this, however, we should not fall into the trap of onesidedness or lose sight of ambivalent positions of religious authorities. True, there were cases of open resistance of the clergy, including Moslems in Azerbaijan, to Soviet power and its principles of organizing a new society. But obviously, it was primarily ideological, political and practical considerations rather than the above-mentioned factors that determined the state's negative attitude toward religion and believers. Let us recall that in 1922 Lenin invoked economic need to justify appropriation of multimillions of rubles' worth of valuables that belonged to churches and monasteries, demanding the harshest penalty for resisting clerics.

So, on the one hand, there were declarations of religious tolerance, freedom of conscience, allegedly protected by law; and on the other, the rights of believers and the clergy were cynically trampled upon: they were subjected to violence and became outcasts in society.

Looking back at the events in those years we see: the more the government consolidated its position, the more obvious its attitude toward religion became, inexorably bringing closer an open confrontation aimed at totally annihilating religion.

A specific feature of Azerbaijan was that there, unlike in the country's central regions, the Islamic clergy retained their solid positions in the 1920s and continued to exert a substantial influence on the population. Any underestimation of that reality could not but aggravate the difficult situation of Soviet power, which determined its tactic of a temporary compromise. The influence of some local figures brought up in the spirit and traditions of the Moslem environment, such as Nariman Narimanov, had also a certain role to play.

But the process of destruction could not bypass Azerbaijan. Moreover, it was particularly devastating there, as if it sought to make up for the time lost. The waqf lands whose income was used for religious needs were confiscated, sheriat courts were prohibited and religious educational establishments were shut down.

In addition to "standard" accusations leveled against all Soviet people, Azerbaijan Moslems were charged with Pan-Turkism and Pan-Islamism. The charges were made even against those who resisted the transition from Arabic characters, used for more than a millennium, to Latin.

The cruel repressions against the clergy and believers were determined by the very slogan of the antireligion movement: "The struggle against religion is the struggle for socialism!"

The blind fanaticism knew no limits: clerics and ordinary believers were repressed or shot, prayer buildings of the Moslem and other confessions were barbarically destroyed. Aside from the famous Bibi-Heibat mosque, a grandiose Russian Orthodox church, a Polish Roman Catholic church, and other religious buildings in Baku that were valuable cultural monuments were torn down. The number of mosques in Azerbaijan declined sharply.

The religious structures lay in ruins before World War II. The space cleared of the annihilated religions was to be filled with the cult of Stalin, his deification. It was only the war that made the dictator change his religious policy. This was no reverence of repentance, but a forced necessity prompted, among other reasons, by the desire to please the war allies—the United States and Great Britain. Thus 1943–44 saw the appearance of four Moslem Religious Boards which covered the entire territory of the Soviet Union. Among them is the Board for the Transcaucasus, of which I have been the head for the last decade.

Certainly, religion was totally dependent on the government, which exercised unremitting control over activities of communities. It is an eloquent fact that heads of the Council for Religious Affairs were appointed from among the members of the NKVD, a punitive organization whose very name causes older people to shudder.

Khrushchev's thaw, which had a beneficial effect on society's life, did not, however, put an end to the old attitude toward religion and believers. Little was changed in subsequent years, albeit the wave of violence was abated.

Until recently Moslems were excluded from social life, restricted by the walls of mosques that were in fact turned into reservations. Links to the external world and contacts with coreligionists abroad were allowed only within the framework of "the struggle against imperialism, for the triumph of peace throughout the world."

We fought for years to have a medrese opened in Baku to train clerics. But to no avail. It was only the holding of the representative international Islamic conference "Moslems in the Struggle for Peace" in Azerbaijan that helped to get things moving. For something had to be shown to the foreign guests to prevent any doubts they might have about the freedom of conscience in the USSR.

Yes, we should be grateful to the world public for even today much is being done with an eye on the external effect.

Yes, major changes have taken place in the life of believers in recent years. Slowly and with difficulty new shoots sprout in relations between the state and religion. But it seems to me that the most important thing is the understanding and recognition of the fact that unscrupulous atheization has had the most pernicious effect on society's morality.

The Islamic clergy has warmly welcomed the policy of perestroika, calling upon believers to use all means at their disposal to support the renewal of society and the efforts aimed at its democratization. For their part, Moslems are entitled to expect that the state will shed its suspicion of them and their faith and will see them as loyal citizens. For those who think that the Moslem religion prescribes enmity of Christians are mistaken, since the Holy Quran states: "And nearest among them in Love to the Believers are those who say 'we are Christians' " (Quran, 5–82).

The recently heightened interest in religion, primarily from the cognitive perspective, is characteristic of the entire Soviet Union, all confessions; and Azerbaijan and Islam are no exception. This is also true of the opening of prayer houses, spiritual educational establishments, the expansion of publishing activity (though Azerbaijan lags considerably behind other republics in this respect).

Naturally, these beneficial changes are perceived by our Moslems as a result of democratization of Soviet society, legitimate realization of the freedom of conscience recorded in the Constitution.

It is regretted that the revival of religious life, which is natural for the entire country, is seen as a threat of "Islamic fundamentalism" in our case. I see no root cause of this in the persistence of anti-Moslem stereotypes which artificially model a phenomenon out of individual facts, for certain political purposes.

By calling for reason, peace, and good neighborliness in the midst of hard interethnic conflict, . . . Moslems proved their unfailing commitment to the sacred ideals of Islam. We acted on the conviction that both Moslems and Christians believed in one Creator. And they must realize that the commitment to religious ideals admits no veneration or the fanning up of interethnic enmity; that it is the duty of preachers of all religions to prevent and overcome ethnic strife. But, to our profound regret, the calls of Moslems to unite the efforts of the two religions were unheeded. Yet, in spite of the very difficult situation, in our region and the country as a whole, we still hope for the better. We believe that what unites and bids us together as members of one human family is immeasurably more profound, solid, and strong than that which separates us.

Let us not spare our efforts in the name of sacred ideals of Good, Justice, and Brotherhood. May the Most High help us in our endeavors.

4

REDISCOVERY OF POLITICAL IDENTITY

Turkestan

On April 4, 1990, both *Kazakhstanskaia pravda* (in Russian) and *Sotsialistik Qazaqstan* (in Kazakh) published a strongly worded protest from the head of the republican veterans' council about the content of an eight-page newspaper titled *Turkestan*. Compiled by Almaz Estekov, a Kazakh, *Turkestan* had been printed in Estonia in the early part of the year (in Russian) and circulated in Alma-Ata. The newspaper contained documents and reports, with accompanying photographs, on events in Central Asia (as well as in the Baltic region) that the Soviet government was expending considerable efforts to cover up.

The main grievance of the republican veterans' council was apparently Estekov's coverage of the events that occurred in Alma-Ata in December 1986. *Turkestan* included stories of attacks on demonstrators by troops armed with shovels and of victims being dumped in the steppe. Estekov was criticized for portraying these events as an organized assault by "the state, the party, and a brazenly chauvinistic part of the core population." The letter from the veterans' council specifically attacks Estekov's statement that at least 185 people were killed in the disturbances (the official claim was that only three had died) and demands that legal action be taken against him.

The reports that follow—on Alma-Ata, ethnic conflicts, the Crimean Tatars, the Nevada-Semipalatinsk antinuclear movement, and events in Baku—are all from *Turkestan*. The translations are by Joseph Nissman.

The section closes with an interview with Etibar Memmedov, Rehim Gaziyev, and Nemet Penahov, early members and leaders of the Azerbaijan People's Front. This piece was published in Azerbaijan in August 1991, and translated by A.L. Altstadt.

H.B. Paksoy

Alma-Ata, December 1986

An Echo of the Events of December 1986

Attention readers! On this paper are the hope and pain of a people! To peoples and governments and humanitarian meetings! To all to whom the ideals of progress are dear!

On December 17–18, 1986, events unprecedented in their antihumanity took place, portrayed by TASS as riots organized by alcoholics and drug addicts. What in fact occurred was the organized liquidation of the core population. It was provoked by the authorities who were attempting to suppress a peaceful demonstration that was not making the slightest commotion, and then donned a mask of decency. The orders of the commanders and the actions of those who executed them were magnificently coordinated, as if they were expecting an event and had been prepared in advance. And it is no less amazing that the state, the party, and a brazenly chauvinistic part of the population turned out to be on one side.

The appointment of [Gennadii] Kolbin as leader of Kazakhstan served as the cause. At 5 P.M., thirty thousand people, 60 percent of them workers and the rest students, assembled on Brezhnev Square.

The intent of the crowd was democratic. They heard the complete incompetence of the leadership revealed. It appeared that it was easier to destroy than to reform earlier ways. As far as the formal sovereignty and honor of the nation were concerned, these concepts were not even considered.

Placards demanded "We Demand Self-determination!" "To Each People Its Own Leader!" "Never Again 1937!" "Put An End To Great Power Madness!"

From the very beginning, in order to legitimize countermeasures, the authorities attempted to stimulate fights among the demonstrators. Trucks came through the military cordons distributing free vodka, snacks, and cigarettes filled with narcotics. The youth did not know that the authorities had planned reprisals. As was assumed, the conduct of some among the masses became aggressive and disorders broke out in places.

And then the beating of the peaceful crowd began, with shovels, clubs, steel bars, and cables, which had been specially prepared by order of the party committee. Soldiers struck defenseless people on the head, knocked them to the ground, and kicked them in the genitals. This is why there were so many casualties among the demonstrators. They died after their skulls were cracked, or suffered traumas of the kidney, womb, or glands; there were some struck by bullets. Many are destined to be cripples for the rest of their lives, and the women infertile.

Fire trucks standing in the front hit rows of people with powerful jets of water. People fell down. After every attack by the soldiers on the demonstrators, seriously wounded or stunned bodies remained in open areas. Then an "ambulance" collected them, drove the casualties into the steppe or mountains, abandoned them there or buried them; doctors gave the wounded injections, little children were trampled down by dogs, and the cries and moans of the wounded were drowned in the war cry of the commanders and the howling of dogs.

December 18 was especially bad because the people were kept out of the square by force. But thirty thousand people were out in the streets of the city. Now the people expressed their anger and indignation about the events that took place that night.

The hospitality of the Kazakhs is well known. They truly and correctly served Russian and Soviet power despite all the burdens and trials connected with this trust in the Russian people, especially with the changes of recent times. No one could have assumed that Moscow would have answered their peaceful request in this manner.

The people at the meeting demanded that the bodies of the victims be turned over. Without answering, the soldiers started a battle without any provocation. Whenever the scene of those days is revived in memory, reason fades. It can never be forgotten. Human blood was being washed from the square the entire next day. The customary taste of Kazakh women for jewelry cost them their lives. Soldiers hacked off fingers because stones were glistening on them, and ears because of the gold.

The democratically inclined Russian people were on the side of the defenseless. They refused to obey the orders of the commanders, denounced the actions of the authorities, called off the soldiers and their bloodhounds. One Russian woman saved the lives of twenty-four Kazakh youths.

Now the peaceful affair wound down to its bloody finale. The ministers—Miroshkin, Kolbin, Meshcheriakov, Kniazev, and Shuliko as well as Kamalidenov, Mukashev, and Elemisov—led the mass slaughter. Instead of making the executioners and their patrons responsible, the authorities today are accusing the Kazakh people and their patriotically inclined part for all the losses, but of their own chauvinism, not a word. A people without rights bears all, and its fawning leaders are silent and in fear. The real reasons for the uprising: the chauvinism of the sycophants holding all the key positions, the forceful assimilation and russification, the elimination of the language and culture under the guise of internationalism, the growth in disease and infant mortality, the denigration of the honor and values of the nation, the poor way of life of the core population.

Representatives of the Kazakh people appeal to all Russians and non-Russians, communists and noncommunists, believers and nonbelievers on the planet. Support us! We who are engaged in an unequal battle against a centuries-old yoke. Our entire tragedy is connected with this yoke. Now genocide is being moved from the streets to the quiet offices of the executioners. But our spirits will not be broken. We will continue the struggle until full independence is obtained. This annihilation is taken by us to be gratitude for the blood of our fathers, shed in the defense of Russian lands, for the valor of our daughters—heroines of the USSR, younger sisters, who today are jeered for their honor.

Events show that the existing system cannot guarantee smaller peoples not only sovereignty but even the right to live. Demand an open trial, accessible to all, of the executioners, and it will become clear to you with whom you sit down at the negotiation table, what a blessing your partner will promise you. We are deprived of rights.

People of the world! Fight the violence of red fascism! Declare the twenty-first century the century of the self-determination of the peoples of the USSR. This must be the first condition for good relations with the USSR. And there should be no talk of peace while there are hundreds of peoples of the USSR under colonialist tyranny. Demand an international trial on the Alma-Ata events.

The dead will not return. Not only we must be aware of the lessons of these events, but primarily the Russian people, its progressive strata, must know them also. We are grateful for this people's help; we consider that whoever knows the value of national liberty also respects the will of others.

Comrade Gorbachev, we value your ideas. Deliver us and protect us from arbitrary action and lawlessness! Freedom for Kazakh fighters and prisoners of conscience!

General Secretary of the UN! Turn the attention of the international community of nations to our tragedy, provide our fighters with representation in the UN!

Readers! Do us, the suffering, a good turn of conscience. Translate this into your language, copy it, hand it out, send it to international organizations. And may the unmourning spirit of our fighters preserve you and yours!

From Pamphlets on the December [1986] Events

Evidence of the true scale of the tragedy on the consciences of the Central Committee, the KGB, and the MVD has been carefully concealed. We will give certain facts gathered under difficult circumstances. According to an approximate count, more than 185 died, 2,000 were seriously wounded (400 soldiers), and 3,000 were arrested, the majority of them women. All of this was done in such a way that it would go unnoticed by anyone in the world.

Trials are being held in secret. People are invited to the court, heard, and released. The truth about the deeds frightens the authorities because they are afraid of the voice of the world community. More than 2,000 were sentenced as criminals, of whom two were sentenced to the firing squad, and three women from the Poshen factory were sentenced to 10–15 years of hard labor.

More than 700 have disappeared without a trace. The disappearance of people today is a normal occurrence in Kazakhstan: 212 are missing from KazSU, 6 from ZhenPI, 30 from SKhI, 23 from AZBI, 26 from AKhBK, 6 from Poshen, and 10 from the meatpacking plant.... The Kazakhs in Suzak Raion demanded from Kolbin that the bodies of their children be found and turned over. Ninety-two bodies were turned over that had been secretly buried under the supervision of the KGB.

According to incomplete sources, there were seventeen victims from Panfilov Raion, two from Tyulkibass (of which one was German), two from Lenger, three from Saryagach, two from Yany-Kurgan, two from Dzhalagach, three from Kazalin, and six from Moyynkum.

More than 500 workers and students were discharged or expelled; 139 communists were expelled from the CPSU. More than 100 were discharged from the ranks of the KGB and MVD, including eight ranking officers, allegedly for sympathizing with the rebels. More than 1,000 demonstrators are in holding cells, including some who were not involved. The seriously wounded are in need of medical aid, but it is refused them as enemies of the people.

The arrests are continuing; they are torturing and beating prisoners, and women are being attacked and raped. On the whole, those suffering for the cause are labor leaders, Komsomol activists, veterans of Afghanistan, and honored scholars. The chauvinists mock the graves of the Kazakhs, and the demonstrations have continued throughout Kazakhstan and most military units. Many Kazakh soldiers have committed suicide as a mark of protest.

The Kayrat Society

P.S. Today the people of Kazakhstan are demanding a public trial of those guilty of violence against the demonstrators: Procurator-General Elemesov, judge of the Supreme Court of the Kazakh SSR Aytmukhambetov, and chairman of the Kazakh SSR KGB Miroshnik.

**From the Kazakh Public Committee
for the Rights of Man**

In spite of the opinion of members of the commission, the Supreme Soviet of the Kazakh SSR dissolved the Commission for the Study of the December 1986

Events in Alma-Ata at the request of the party leadership of the republic, even though it had not completed its work. It is good that the Supreme Soviet, in the second point of its decree, decided to turn to the Central Committee of the CPSU with a request for the removal of the formulation "manifestation of Kazakh nationalism" in the evaluation of the events. Consequently, the question raised about the December events from the very beginning was not for nothing. There is no such thing as taking glasnost halfway—it must be taken right to the end! But as we see, the Supreme Soviet of the Kazakh SSR in the fourth point of its decree entrusted the examination of the complaints and declarations of the citizens to the Procurator of the Kazakh SSR, the Supreme Court, the MVD, the KGB, the Ministry of Education of the Kazakh SSR, and the leaders of the Alma-Ata operation—that is, the same people who were guilty of the violence against the demonstrators in December 1986. As they say, they have punished the fish by throwing it into the river. In order to preserve the appearance of objectivity and justice, they created a working group of seven to supervise the fulfillment of the given decree and exercise all the authority of the former commission; it is headed by USSR People's Deputy M. Shakhanov. Why? Because the commission almost revealed the perpetrators of the crime. Because a certain circle of people in the high echelons of authority in the republic did not want to allow the work of the commission to proceed to its logical end—the recognition of the use of force against the people themselves. The reasons behind this are clear: the majority of the leadership of those days are still sitting comfortably in their chairs or have even been promoted higher. And the people know this. A true, just, clear evaluation of the events of December 1986 and their consequences might have surfaced. The lies and half-truths in the republic press today only excite the people. Of the ninety-nine people tried for taking part in the December events, eighty-eight have been pardoned and eleven are still being detained in prison. Thus, on the basis of what we have said, we ask that the question on the creation of an independent commission composed of people's deputies of the USSR—representatives of Kazakhstan and other republics—to study the December 1986 events in Alma-Ata be put before the Third Session of People's Deputies of the USSR.

M. Imanbayev
Responsible Secretary,
Kazakhstan Public Committee for the Rights of Man

Ethnic Conflict in Central Asia, Summer 1989

Ferghana—The Events and the Facts:
Prologue

"The good grand master always forces his game on his partner!". . . In life, this looks like this:

When in one region or another of the USSR the development of events becomes dangerous for the authorities, the malicious forces of the partocracy organize artificial conflicts of peoples there.

Misery, a 20 percent unemployment rate, economic crisis, popular lack of faith in the party leadership, plus provocation by criminal extremists—these are the real reasons motivating people to commit acts of reciprocal violence such as took place between Meskhetian Turks and Uzbeks in the Ferghana Valley.

Here the "grand master" gained the upper hand over the neophyte. The "guilty" are the "extremists"—the "informals"—but not the party elite of Moscow and the Nishanov clique, which contributed to the despair of people terrified by poverty.

Almaz Estekov

Tashlak: Some Details on Past Events

As is known, a clash started between Uzbeks and Meskhetian Turks in Kuvasay, apparently on trivial grounds. But in Tashlak Raion, especially in the raion party committee, they had interpreted this, as soon as it was confirmed, with special anxiety. Even before the event began, signals from the raion party committee were passed on to higher organs, including the oblast party committee, on the possibility of a repetition of the Kuvasay incident. Without waiting for this, apparatus workers went to organizations and precincts explaining the truth about what happened in Kuvasay and debunking rumors and conjectures. How? By saying that women and children had been murdered, and houses burnt down. This did not occur.

But the anxiety remained. On June 2, facts reached the raion committee that extremists would commit illegal actions on June 3. Organs of the raion administration of internal affairs and the raion party committee had been made aware of this. A. Khodzhimuratov, chairman of the Tashlak Raion Executive Committee, had reported on this at the bureau of the oblast party committee.

On June 2 a broad session of the bureau of the raion party committee was convened. Taking part in it were A. Mamatkazin, secretary of the oblast party committee, A. Shermatov, chief of the ideological department of the oblast committee, and other responsible workers. They were informed in detail about what happened in Kuvasay, and made recommendations for the prevention of possible disorders. On the same day, a workers' committee was created to conduct explanatory work among the population.

Nothing seemed to foreshadow a threat: the next morning, calm ruled in Tashlak. However, around ten o'clock a crowd of excited people began to gather at the Avrora film theater. In order to calm them, workers from the raion party committee hurried to the spot. This did not help!

It was amazing that among the hostilely disposed elements, none were from the local population; that is, the people of Tashlak. They called for reprisals on the Meskhetian Turks and soon burst into International Street, destroying everything in their path. People were killed, houses were burned.

Workers from the Ferghana organs of the MVD attempted to halt this first onslaught by enraged youths, and drove the thugs back along Navoi Street. It appeared that it was all over and the situation stabilized. But, as became clear, this was not in the plans of the extremists. About three thousand of them assembled. Trying to secure the freedom of prisoners and promising that they would end the violence, they rushed into Yalta, International, and Gagarin streets. The rioters completely ignored all appeals to reason and for an end to violence, and continued their dark deed.

Leaving bloody traces behind them, the bandits moved in the direction of the Komsomol settlement. But a significant part of them later returned to Tashlak. It was already half past five, just before evening. The sun was still rather high, and more and more houses of the Meskhetian Turks were set aflame. First they would rob the house and then, taunting the people, they threw burning torches in the window. Not even the voice of the mullah was heard; the marauders threatened him with violence. Not hearing the remonstrations, they burned down two houses at the raion car park. While the senseless band wreaked havoc on the streets, Meskhetian Turkish families were evacuated, under the leadership of the first secretary of the raion party committee, O. Sabirov, to a safe place—the raion committee building, which was guarded by its employees.

On the morning of June 4, militia workers from the Buvaidin and Baghdad raions arrested three hooligans and stood in defense of the raion party committee building. A mob of thousands of riffraff tried to take the raion committee by storm, but were driven back by the power of the militia.

The measures halted the mob of attackers only for a moment. Demanding release of the prisoners, they took the raion committee secretary and the executive committee chairman as hostages. The bandits suggested that the First Secretary Sabirov should go to the raion administration of internal affairs, where the criminals were imprisoned, and, at this, the conflict would be settled.

What should he have done in this situation? He went; but, on the way, the driver of the car, as now appears evident, deliberately stopped in the midst of a group of bandits, who pulled the first secretary out of the car and began to beat him up. Only after a warning salvo was fired into the air did the unrestrained youths retreat. Sabirov hastened to take shelter in the raion internal affairs building, where A. Khodzhimuraev, the chairman of the raion executive committee, who had miraculously escaped from mortal danger, and V. Danilov, second secretary of the raion party committee, were to be found. Two raion committee officials, R. Tuychiev and T. Kurbanov, were seriously wounded in the hoodlums' attack. It remains to add that the bandits had seriously threatened Danilov: if he did not speak out in support of releasing the imprisoned thugs, they would burn the raion executive committee chairman alive.

Not succeeding in freeing the hostages, the extremists opened fire with rifles, sawed-off shotguns, and pistols, and threw explosives and bottles with a flammable mixture. This lasted for four hours. At the same time, the siege of the raion party committee building was not lifted. Fifteen raion MVD workers were wounded, one of whom died soon after.

The bacchanalia, which exceeded all bounds of savagery, led to unforeseen serious consequences. Forty-three houses were burned down and 170 were damaged and broken into. Ten automobiles were consumed in the flames of the fire as well as twelve motorcycles and mopeds and one bus. Murder, rape, arson. . . .

The amount of material damages was about 430 thousand rubles. But one cannot calculate the moral losses. I will be absolutely frank: if the leading workers of the party had demonstrated any courage or support, they would have been able to overcome their fear of the malicious extremists, but that does not mean that they would have done everything required of them. Outside the events, the communists essentially constituted a majority. They could have come to the aid of the raion committee, their colleagues, but they did not. Why? Because the people did not come to the rescue of the raion committee offices.

But even under these, let us say, unpleasant conditions, the raion committee workers could have moved the Meskhetian Turkish families into refugee camps.

The lesson for the party organization of Tashlak Raion, for deep thought about what occurred, and the practical conclusions to be drawn were unforgettable. It was as if the feeling of responsibility for revolutionary reform, the need for which is dictated by perestroika, had been deadened. How is it that the raion committee knew or guessed about the events coming to a head and still they took place anyway. Why?

N.I. Ryzhkov, Politburo member and chairman of the USSR Council of Ministers, answered this question in his speech at a meeting of republic party and economic activists in Tashkent: "Under the high tempo of population growth in Uzbekistan," he said, "every fifth adult who is capable of working is not working in social production. . . . In a number of places—for example, the Ferghana Valley—the situation is even more critical. . . . We have to address the fact, comrades, that there has been an obvious underestimation of the urgency of the problem of employment by the executive committees of local soviets and the leaders of enterprises and organizations. In a complicated situation, this verges on political shortsightedness. . . . Inertia and an intolerable policy of temporizing have manifested themselves."

If in fact a workers' volunteer squad was organized on June 2, it never made an appearance. Perhaps it was only created in a formal manner. It may have been a mistake to weaken vigilance, but delays in resolving social and economic questions and the conduct of ideological work were simply intolerable. Sharing the difficulties with the people, raising the personal responsibility of communists for the work with which they are entrusted, adding a steady advancement toward socioeconomic development and the influence of educational measures on the consciousness of the people—this is needed today, now.

I. Korolev
Ferganskaia pravda, June 19, 1989

From the Inquiry of the Ferghana Oblast
Bureau of Forensic Medicine

For the period June 23–27, 1989, the coroner's department examined the bodies of one hundred people. No narcotic substances were found. Alcohol appeared in fourteen cases.

For this period blood and urine of injured people in stationary care in the Tashlak, Rishtan, and Baghdad raion hospitals and the Margilan city hospital were examined, a total of sixty-one people. Alcohol appeared in three cases—a light degree of intoxication. Narcotic substances were not found.

On June 22, 1989, a list of the number of victims of various nationalities was published in the oblast newspaper *Ferganskaia pravda* by the press center of the staff of the MVD USSR: there were ninety-nine victims in all, of whom twenty were Uzbek, sixty-nine Meskhetian Turks, and ten of other nationalities.

According to data from the oblast bureau of forensic medicine, one hundred people were, in fact, victims: thirty-five Uzbeks, fifty-three Meskhetian Turks, and twelve of other nationalities.

This is to say that the press center of the USSR MVD is engaged in disinformation; that is, the number of Uzbeks was reduced and the number of Meskhetian Turks was increased.

> Information received from Kh. Khaidarov, chief
> of the Fergana Oblast Bureau of Forensic Medicine,
> and F. Akhmedov, deputy coroner

Conflict on the Border of Kyrgyzstan and Tajikistan

In the summer of 1989 the wave of interethnic conflicts in Central Asia also embraced part of the Kyrgyz population.

According to official information from TASS, a long-standing dispute over land and water rights in a number of areas on the border between Tajikistan and Kyrgyzstan led to the conflict.

The situation first became tense in April [1989] when Kyrgyz irrigation specialists voluntarily began the reconstruction of the Matchoy Canal, which supplies water to agricultural raions of both republics. At the end of May inhabitants of the Tajik kishlak "October" threw rocks into the part of the canal in which water from Tajikistan flows into Kyrgyzstan, in order to impede its reconstruction. In Isfara, a raion center in the Tajik SSR, a large contingent of the militia was brought in to head off possible clashes. For the next few days crowds of Kyrgyz armed with hoes moved on the "October" kishlak in an effort to continue the reconstruction of the canal. Through coordinated actions by units of the militia, the conflict between the two republics was successfully averted.

A rumor circulated that disputed issues would be worked out in two days. In reality, however, local authorities were not ready for a just resolution of the conflict. It soon became known that allotments of land in various areas had been rapidly distributed to the Kyrgyz, some of whom did not even live in the raion. Under conditions of a deficit in the resources of agricultural production (land and water) in Central Asia, such actions could only involve new conflicts.

In the evening of June 13, residents of the Kyrgyz settlement of Samarkandyk (Osh Oblast) once again went to the "October" kishlak in order finally to clean out the canal. They were met by the population of not only October but also Vorukh and Chorku. Thousands of people took part in the conflict. Skirmishes broke out and attempts were made to burn down homes in Kyrgyz kishlaks. In response, shots were fired.

The militia and internal troops fired warning shots into the air and, with the help of bludgeons and water hoses, dispersed the crowd. As a result of the clash nineteen people were wounded, one of whom died later as a consequence.

At 22 hours on June 13, a curfew was imposed in the kishlaks of Vorukh, Chornu, and Surkh in Isfara Raion, Tajik SSR. Units of MVD security forces were transferred into the republic. Despite this, a fight between Tajiks and

Kyrgyz in Chornu, a part of the May Kishlak Soviet, flared up again in the latter part of the next day. The militia and internal troops, attempting to suppress the disorders, began to throw rocks. After some answering gunfire, the soldiers used weapons. As a result, two people received gunshot wounds, three suffered from being beaten with bludgeons, and seventy were detained.

That night, unknown persons fired at a militia patrol, seriously wounding one militiaman. Efforts by the militia to clean out the canal that night did not meet with success due to the complicated landscape of the area.

First secretaries of the Central Committee of the Communist Party, representatives of the republic's Council of Ministers, and a group of deputies from the Supreme Soviet of the USSR were flown to the site of the events.

On Saturday and Sunday (June 15–16), joint meetings of the republic leadership and other officials took place. It was decided to establish a party commission to define the border and to begin to clean out the Matchoy Canal in order to supply water to the "100th Anniversary of V.I. Lenin" Sovkhoz in the Batken Raion of Kyrgyzstan. On July 18 the canal began to provide water once again.

The conflict was brought under control. But for how long?

V.P.

Mustafa Jemilev

The Crimean Tatars' Thorny Path to Their Homeland

The Crimean Tatar national question has continued to be one of the most urgent and immediate of the national questions in the USSR up to the present day. The discussion is about the return to their historical homeland and restoration of the autonomy of a people, every one of whom has been subjected to deportation and genocide. The majority of the Crimean Tatars—an ancient Turkic-language people that took form on the territory of the Crimea—now consist of people who were born in places of exile. To a significant degree, many lost their native tongue and their national and religious traditions. Yet the desire of the people to return to their land and found their national state anew was neither lost nor dampened; it was completely clear to all the Crimean Tatars that they had the prospects to revive their national culture in their own Homeland, and that only there could the people survive as a distinct people.

The national movement of the Crimean Tatars for return to the Homeland of which they were deprived began in the mid-1950s, that is, after the death of Stalin, and has always carried and carries to the present day a nonaggressive character. Initiative groups of Crimean Tatars were organized everywhere. They collected signatures for various petitions addressed to the relevant state authorities; they sent representatives to Moscow; and they collected money to finance these trips, assistance to the families of those subjected to repressions, and the expenses of the national movement. In the three and a half decades of the existence of the national movement its members did not commit one murder, act of arson, outburst, or any other aggressive action. The organs of authority beat our compatriots, killed them, put them in prisons and psychiatric clinics, and

Speech at the Session of the Coordinating Council of National-Patriotic Democratic Movements, October 7, 1989, in Crimea.

subjected them to other forms of persecution for signing appeals and petitions or for taking part in peaceful demonstrations.

All those years, the Soviet organs of power completely denied the existence of the Crimean Tatar national question. It was considered that under the so-called cult of personality of Stalin a certain "mistake" was committed in connection with this people, but that this "mistake" has been completely corrected and that the Crimean Tatars in their new location enjoy all civil and political rights and are equal with all other citizens of the USSR. Anyone who contradicts this belief is viewed as a nationalist and a slanderer of the Leninist nationality policy of the Soviet government, which is the wisest in the world. But, as a matter of fact, it was a false claim that the Crimean Tatars in their new location were enjoying all the rights of citizens of the USSR. In reality, a number of secret ukases, decrees, and bureaucratic instructions were issued that effectively limited their rights in a number of spheres of life only because of their national affiliation. In a period of significant growth of the Crimean Tatar National Movement, in September 1967, a decree of the Presidium of the Supreme Soviet was issued which was called "On citizens of Tatar nationality, living in Crimea." In the naming of this decree was an attempt to deny the very existence of the unique Crimean Tatar nation and to represent the matter as if it was about a small part of the Tatar people from the republic on the Volga who had lived at one time on the territory of Crimea. In this same decree, a change of the legal limitations in connection with "Tatars, residing earlier in Crimea" was mentioned: that as of today they have the right to live in all territories of the country in accordance with their existing passport rights. However, even this part of the decree is false. Secret decrees on the legal limitations were not only not changed, but were repeated. In connection with these secret decrees and ukases thousands of Crimean Tatars who had believed in the main decree of September 5, 1967, and had returned to their Homeland were expelled outside the borders of the Crimea through the application of inhuman and cruel methods. At the same time, in Uzbekistan, where the basic core of the Crimean Tatars live at the present time, adventuristic attempts were launched by the authorities to establish for them some autonomous raions within a few arid and sparsely populated oblasts of this republic. In fact, this plan soon faded away ignominiously, because for the Crimean Tatars there was no Homeland other than the Crimea.

With the beginning of the process of democratization in the USSR, the Crimean Tatar National Movement also became more active. Once again, representative sessions of the national movement became possible. The first such meeting, after an interruption of several years, was convened in April 1967. In view of the fact that there were more representatives at this meeting than there had been throughout the entire existence of the national movement and that it included representatives from practically everywhere that Crimean Tatars lived in the USSR, it was called the First All-Union Meeting of Representative Groups of the National Movement. At this meeting an appeal from all the people was worked out, addressed to M. Gorbachev, in which the basic demands of the Crimean Tatars were formulated, measures for the coming months were elaborated, and sixteen representatives were even selected for a possible meeting with the country's high leadership. The lack of a positive response to the appeal of the Crimean Tatars, among whom thirty thousand signatures were collected in a very short time, from the Soviet leadership, brought forth the need to send a large people's delegation to Moscow. After stormy and, for the USSR, unprecedented demonstrations by thousands of Crimean Tatar delegates in Red Square in the summer of 1967, the Soviet mass media published the well known "TASS Report" on the Crimean Tatar question. It elicited a violent protest from the entire Crimean Tatar people because, although the people were acquitted of the charges brought against them in 1944, the popular demands were viewed, by a special state commission that had been established for examining them under the chairmanship of the head of state, A. Gromyko, as being of dubious validity and reflecting the pretensions of certain citizens of Crimean Tatar nationality. A mass campaign began for the discrediting of activists of the national movement, who were once again, as in the past, referred to as "agents of the West," "anti-Soviet," and "extremists" in the official press, especially in the local press in regions where the Crimean Tatars resided. As a counterbalance to the initiative groups of the national movement, puppet "working commissions" and "action groups" were staffed everywhere, the formal tasks of which were to elicit the opinions of their compatriots on ways to resolve the problem and bring these to the attention of the state commission.

Eleven months after the establishment of the state commission, its conclusions were published, according to which an organized resettlement of the entire people to their homeland would not be possible in view of the postwar demographic changes in the Crimea; for this reason, the Crimean ASSR would not be reestablished, but measures would be taken "for the complete satisfaction of the social and cultural requirements" of the Crimean Tatars in the places where they currently reside. In the course of these eleven months, new anticonstitutional decrees were passed directed at keeping the Crimean Tatars outside the boundaries of their Homeland, including the decree of the Council of Ministers of the USSR No. 1476 of December 24, 1987, "On measures for the further stabilization of the situation among the Crimean Tatars," which stands to this day. The cynical conclusions of the "Gromyko commission" brought forth a new wave of protest meetings and demonstrations, and even strikes by the Crimean Tatars in some places. The demonstrations were broken up by the militia and MVD troops with the application of especially cruel methods, especially in Tashkent, Simferopol, and some other places. The authorities were also rather unceremonious about the participation of the Crimean Tatars in protest strikes. In reprisals on strikers the authorities completely exploited the fact that, because of the dispersion of the Crimean Tatars over a vast territory in the country, they did not constitute an absolute majority anywhere, or even a significant part of the workers and office personnel in administrations and institutions; thus, if they were dismissed, they were easily replaced by citizens of other nationalities. Unfortunately, it was also not worth counting on a broad campaign of solidarity and high civic values among the citizens of other nationalities who surrounded the Crimean Tatars.

Along with this, restrictions on the return of Crimean Tatars to their Homeland were loosened by the authorities beginning in the summer of 1987. Consequently, around forty thousand Crimean Tatars were able to relocate to the Crimea over the next two years; their number today is roughly fifty-five thousand, which is some 2 percent of the population of the peninsula and roughly 10 percent of the whole Crimean Tatar population in the USSR.

At the present time Crimean Tatars can, in practice, only resettle in their Homeland in the event that they are permitted to buy a private home and find a job; but if they are refused employment, then they cannot register for the purchase of a home. But in order to receive employment, under new rules that were hastily introduced in many cities and raions of the Crimea, employers and enterprises have to pay a substantial sum into the state budget. In only the last two years the values of private homes in the Crimea have almost tripled. Crimean Tatars are obliged to lay out their entire fortune just to be able to buy back the same little house which was seized from them by the state forty-five years earlier and sold for a symbolic sum to colonist-settlers from Russia and Ukraine. All this has led to the fact that the number of homeless and unsettled among our compatriots in the Crimea is growing. Many of them have appealed to the authorities with a request to grant them parcels of land so that they could hastily build something for themselves before the onset of winter. In most cases, however, the authorities respond with a coarse refusal. At the same time, empty and even arable lands are being distributed feverishly to citizens of other nationalities for the construction of dachas and private residences all over the Crimea. In the last few months alone approximately six thousand parcels for dachas and other individual structures have been given out to citizens of other nationalities in the vicinity of Simferopol, and tens of thousands of parcels in other raions of the Crimea. In some places the authorities are simply persuading people to occupy land parcels because if they do not, Crimean Tatars could come flooding in. Dozens of contracts are being concluded with various leaderships and trusts, including some in Tiumen, Bratsk, and Yakutia, for the construction of thousands of homes for new settlers from oblasts of Russia. Under these circumstances, no other choice is left to the Crimean Tatars but to voluntarily occupy vacant land and start to build housing. But for this completely justified action, the authorities are responding with cruel measures and attempts to mobilize public opinion against the Crimean Tatars.

The official point of view of the higher party leadership on the Crimean Tatar question at the present time comes down to the need to satisfy all the demands of the people to return to their Homeland and to resolve their other problems. But now there are various reservations about this, namely, that the questions lead to a solution within the framework of "established reality"—that is, within the frame-work of the changed demography and national composition of Crimea. It is in this context that the problems of the deported peoples, including the Crimean Tatars, were stated in the party platform on the nationality question passed at the recent Plenum of the Central Committee of the CPSU. The question of the administrative-territorial status of the Crimea is being viewed by the authorities from the position of this so-called "established reality." If the possibility of establishing a Crimean Republic or a Soviet Republic of Tauridea is being con-sidered, it is only from the viewpoint of a proposed status of an "all-Union resort" or the financial and economic development of the peninsula. The ques-tion of the state language of the possible republic is being discussed in an animated manner, but basically only in the context of whether the state language should be Russian, Ukrainian, or both of them simultaneously. There is no talk of this land's native population, to whom priority rights for the determination of the status, structure, and state language of the republic should be given. The opinion is spread around in the press by agitators from the party and bureaucratic apparatus, banal historians, and publicists to the effect that the Crimean Republic was established in 1921 not along national lines, but territorial, and that the Crimean Tatars had only a very distant relationship to this republic. In publica-tions from the beginning of the 1920s in connection with the establishment of the Crimean SSR, it is clearly indicated that the republic was established in the interests of and in order to satisfy the rights of the core population—the Crimean Tatars. In the constitution of the Crimean SSR it was emphasized that the state languages of the republic were Crimean Tatar and Russian, and that the state seal of the republic would have an inscription in these languages. Nor did the Bolshe-viks conceal their propagandistic goals, which might be achieved through the establishment of the republic. They wrote that the Crimean SSR might become a torch that would enlighten the peoples of the Muslim East, and that the problems of Muslim peoples, formerly oppressed by tsarism, were now being justly re-solved in the new Russia. Finally, the decree of the Presidium of the Supreme Soviet of the RSFSR of June 25, 1946, "On the abolition of the Chechen-Ingush ASSR and the reorganization of the Crimean ASSR into the Oblast of Crimea" was motivated by the fact that the Chechens, the Ingush, and the Crimean Tatars had been resettled outside their republics. Until 1783 our independent state was on this land and the Crimean Tatars constituted 90 percent of the population of Crimea. And if the Crimean Tatars would now constitute a minority of the population of the peninsula even after their full return to their Homeland, this is the result of the crimes of the pre-Bolshevik administrations of Russia and Soviet power against the Crimean Tatar people.

There are no circumstances, either in Soviet or in international law, according to which a people may be deprived of the right to their land and their govern-ment on the basis of the fact that these people are a minority. In the last decade and a half the core population of ten of the twenty autonomous republics of the

USSR became national minorities on their own lands. It may be that plans have been prepared for them to be reorganized into oblasts or raions of Russia. Such plans are already being drawn up for several union republics. When the issue is stated in this way, the efforts of core populations of republics of the USSR to oust the Russian-speaking population are fully justified for the defense of their own national rights. This is why the question of the restoration of the legal rights of the Crimean Tatars for their national statehood in the Crimea would be a precedent of primary importance for all peoples, not only by virtue of the fact that all honorable people are devoted to justice, but also due to considerations of the security of their own national territories from encroachment by chauvinistic forces. The Crimean Tatars are hoping for the solidarity and support of all progressive forces in the world, including the national-patriotic movements of peoples that have formed and are still forming within the USSR.

The Nevada-Semipalatinsk Antinuclear Movement in Kazakhstan

Data on the Health of the Population

The testing of nuclear weapons has been taking place on the territory of Kazakhstan since 1949. Comprehensive scientific expeditions of the Ministry of Health and the Academy of Sciences of the Kazakh SSR, with the participation of specialists from Moscow, having studied the population and environment of raions bordering on the area of the nuclear explosions, concluded that part of the territory of central Kazakhstan was exposed to radioactive contamination. Sources of radiation were found in the soil, foodstuffs, water, people's clothing, and animals as well as in homes.

Underground nuclear testing grounds began operating in the 1970s, and these continued to have a definite effect on the health of the population.

Apart from this, the presence of atomic energy power stations in Kazakhstan as well as large mines and industrial establishments connected with the production and processing of materials are also sources of ionized radiation.

Medical studies of the population exposed to the effects of nuclear atmospheric explosions in the past and also of the populations adjoining the nuclear testing ground at present have shown that the basic indicators of the health of a population are worsening. They are characterized by a high incidence of malignant tumors and a high general mortality rate in comparison to the corresponding average figures for the republic. The high level of infant, child, and maternal mortality and the increase in birth anomalies arouse special concern. This negative trend in the data on the health of the population began in the 1960s at the time of the anticipated appearance of radiation effects and has been maintained to this day.

An especially high rate of cancer is characteristic for the population of Abaev,

Zhana-Semi, and Beskaragai raions, which directly adjoin the testing ground. Here the number of those suffering from malignant tumors is 3.4 times greater than in Chubartau raion.

The incidence of hemoplastosis and leucosis is growing in the oblast. The number of those suffering from leucosis grew from 51 in 1980 to 118 (per 100 thousand) in 1988—that is, by 2.3 times. This increase in the number of the sick takes into account only those afflicted with leucosis; thus, in 1980–84, 8–12 patients were registered per day, but between 1985 and 1988, 20–30 patients were registered per day.

Aside from this, leukopenia is characteristic for the population of this region between the ages of 18 and 55: the number of people with leucocyte counts lower than the permissible norm has reached 86 percent.

The level of child mortality in the oblast in 1988 was 34.4 percent (the republic average is 29.2 percent). A tendency for a growth in the number of stillborn children (from 6.1 percent to 12.5 for every 100 births) has been observed. The growth of birth anomalies (within the structure of infant mortality) in 1980 was 11.8 of every ten thousand born; in 1985, 29.2; and there has been a threefold increase in perinatal mortality (from 28.6 in 1970 to 93.6 in 1980 per ten thousand births).

The general sickness rate of newborns in Zhana-Semi Raion grew by 13 percent between 1980 and 1987 and in Semipalatinsk by 2 percent; within the structure of the sickness rate birth anomalies constituted 7.4 percent.

Anemia among children grew from 6.1 percent in 1970 to 7.2 in 1988 (for every ten thousand children).

Information from the special dispensary that underground explosions do not impact on people's health does not correspond to the facts. Thus, it has been concluded by physicians from the Zhana-Semi Central Raion Hospital that the number of sick people coming for aid in the ten days immediately following the test (2,301) conducted on October 16, 1987, was 20 percent higher than for the ten days prior to this test (1,682). Analogous patterns were observed after the tests of May 15, 1988, and January 21, 1989.

The incomplete enumeration of factors that negatively influence the population's health and the data on public health which have been presented here pose to the medical scientists of the republic the problem of the thorough study and evaluation of radiation and the development of methods for the prevention of radiation disease and for treatment of the consequences of radiation.

History of the Creation and Activities of the Nevada-Semipalatinsk Antinuclear Movement

Prehistory

August 29, 1949: First trial of a nuclear weapon at the Semipalatinsk testing ground. Then forty years of uncontrolled trials—above ground, until 1963; underground, until the present day.

Crisis Point

February 12 and 17, 1989: Regular testing, with a fallout of "rare" gases that increased the radiation level.

February 26: Speech of Oljas Suleimenov on Kazakh television with an open appeal to the people.

February 28: Public meeting in Kazakhstan and the establishment of the Nevada-Semipalatinsk antinuclear movement. Oljas Suleimenov was elected chairman.

February 28 through March: Spontaneous collecting of signatures in support of the movement (more than a million signatures) and the collection of charitable contributions. Thousands of letters and telegrams of solidarity were received.

March: First reports in the foreign press (France, USA) on the establishment of the first Soviet antinuclear movement, with information on its goals and duties, and an expression of solidarity.

April–May: Mr. Matlock, U.S. ambassador to the USSR, visited Alma Ata. The reason for his visit—interest in the movement. The first documents on the movement were turned over to the ambassador. Moser, representative of the antinuclear movement of the USA (Las Vegas, Nevada) is the unofficial guest of the movement; establishment of the movement's coordinating council; the program and statutes of the movement are worked out. Distribution of the movement's first documents. Establishment of support groups for the movement and committees throughout Kazakhstan.

June–July: speech by Oljas Suleimenov, people's deputy of the USSR, at the First Session of USSR People's Deputies; he reports on goals and efforts of the movement. Visit of the movement activist Murat Auezov to the USA. First personal contacts with activists of the American antinuclear movements. The elaboration of a joint program of action. First visit by Suleimenov with representatives of the press to the testing ground and to the closed city of Kurchatov; the publication of materials in *Ogonëk*. Convening of a scientific-practical conference in Semipalatinsk with the participation of representatives of the public, physicians, and specialists in the efforts of the movement. The scientific-practical conference unanimously comes to the conclusion that the Semipalatinsk testing ground must be closed down.

July 8: After an interruption of nearly five months, regular testing is resumed. Representatives of the press and the movement are present.

August 5: The beginning of an international solidarity action with victims of the atomic bombing of the Japanese cities of Hiroshima and Nagasaki. The visit of a group of representatives of the public in Kazakhstan together with the Soviet Committee for the Defense of Peace and the press to the city of Kurchatov; discussions with the soldiers.

August 6: Public protest meeting at Mt. Karaul, near the Semipalatinsk testing grounds; adoption of the movement's appeal to the peoples of the world; the birth of the movement's symbol (an open palm—a new peaceful symbol of protest); the birth of the movement's hymn "Zamanai" ("Oh, Time"). Meeting

participants, passing between two bonfires as a mark of purification from preju-
dice, and the opening of the Road to Peace. At the place where the meeting is
held, a stone kurgan is erected. White ribbons of hope are hung on the tree of life.

August 7: A public protest meeting at Semipalatinsk. On the same day, the
"Wave of Peace" (actions and protest demonstrations against nuclear testing
at the Nevada testing ground in front of the departments of Energy and Defense in the USA) took place in the USA, Japan, and other countries.

August 29: The fortieth anniversary of nuclear testing on Kazakhstan's soil,
[marked by] meetings in Semipalatinsk and other cities; internal support and
memorial actions in the USA.

September 1: The movement conducts a peace lesson in Kazakhstan's schools.

September 2: A regular explosion in the Semipalatinsk testing ground.

September 9: First republic conference of the movement, with the participation of
local departments and committees. Adoption of a resolution as a response to the
continuation of testing. The movement's organizational structure is developed.

September: Establishment of branches of the movement in Yakutia and
Chukotka; the arrival of a delegation of Yakut scholars headed by People's
Deputy of the USSR M.M. Yakovlev.

October 4: Regular test of nuclear weapons in the magnitude of 60 kilotons
(according to unofficial information).

The holding of a meeting at the USSR Ministry of Defense by Kazakh countrymen;
the first press conference with foreign journalists in Moscow; appeal to Chairman
of the Supreme Soviet M. Gorbachev and USSR Minister of Defense D.T. Yazov
recommending a unilateral moratorium on nuclear testing; appeal to U.S. President G. Bush and the U.S. Department of Defense. Participation by representatives of the movement at the Ninth International Congress of Doctors for a
Non-nuclear World. Congress participants protest against nuclear testing, and
Hiroshima workers support them at a sit-down strike. Karaganda miners appeal to
the governments of the Kazakh SSR and USSR with a demand to halt testing and
proclaim their readiness for a preventive strike.

October 19: A regular nuclear explosion at the Semipalatinsk testing ground of a
magnitude between 20 and 75 kilotons.

October 21: Mass protest meetings in Moscow, Alma Ata, Semipalatinsk, Sarani,
Abai, and Karaul.

October 22: Meetings in Karaganda and Pavlodar. Appeal to the government of
the Kazakh SSR with the demand that the question of closing the nuclear
testing ground be raised at the USSR Supreme Soviet.

October 23: Speech by Oljas Suleimenov at the session of the USSR Supreme
Soviet with a statement on the efforts of the movement, supported by USSR
Minister of Foreign Affairs E. Shevardnadze. Creation of a commission of
representatives of the country's miners' committees.

October 24: In Moscow, a founding conference of the Moscow chapter of the
Nevada-Semipalatinsk Movement was held. A program and statutes were

accepted and a committee of fifteen members from the Moscow chapter was elected.

October 25: A publication in the Semipalatinsk newspaper *Irtysh:* "For the attention of the population. The staff of the GO informs you that work connected with the application of methods for extinguishing fires in large industrial enterprises [will be conducted] between October 25 and 30. The work will be accompanied by noise and seismic effects as well as clouds and smoke which are not connected with nuclear testing."

October 28–31: A meeting of representatives of the movement with miners' committees, physicians, and specialists on the problems of the testing ground, with the participation of journalists from the television program "Vzgliad."

November 24: An action at the Hotel Moskva in the center of the USSR's capital. Signatures were collected under the proclamation "Shut down nuclear testing." One thousand seven hundred signatures were collected, including two hundred from members of the USSR Supreme Soviet.

December 9–10: In Alma Ata, the second conference of the Nevada-Semipalatinsk Antinuclear Movement was held. A unanimous decision was taken to write a letter asking for recall of the deputy from the armed forces—Petrushenko. A decision was accepted to hold a universal congress of voters in May 1990 with the goal of imposing a veto on the building of nuclear weapons.

December 19–20: A public tribunal was held in Semipalatinsk at the initiative of the Oblast Committee for the Defense of Peace, headed by Professor of Medical Sciences M.B. Zhangelova. The public tribunal, which was attended by delegates from all oblasts of Kazakhstan as well as guests from other union republics, passed judgment on the military-industrial complex of the USSR and decided to demand the rapid closing of all testing grounds in the world, and demanded of the Soviet government and the Session of USSR People's Deputies that they declare a unilateral moratorium.

December 30: According to a decision of the chairman of the presidium of the Council of Ministers of the Kazakh SSR under the Council of Ministers of the USSR S.A. Abdalin, as well as bureaucrats I.A. Aliev, A.B. Baiduanov, E. Prantsuzov, K. Irgaliev, and A. Mikhailov, members of the Moscow chapter of the Nevada-Semipalatinsk Movement have moved out of their hotel. Since the Moscow chapter of Nevada-Semipalatinsk lacks a headquarters, it does not have an exact address; representation of the interests of its people at the mercy of Kazakh bureaucrats is now in the situation of lacking a fixed residence.

Letter from the Inhabitants of Egindybulak Raion, Karaganda Oblast, Kazakh SSR

To the Nevada-Semipalatinsk Movement:

We, like the residents of Semipalatinsk Oblast, are among the first to become the objects of study of the effects of an atomic bomb and radiation, a cruelty for which we are paying to this day. Dozens of villages of our raion are between 30 and 70 kilometers from the epicenter of nuclear explosions. But no one ever thought of evacuating the inhabitants of these villages or of [conducting] medical examinations of all the inhabitants of the raion.

It is impossible to convey the horror and sorrow of parents who, instead of the impatiently awaited healthy child, see a two-headed, armless, disfigured creature. Most of our people do not live beyond the ages of fifty or sixty. Anxiety about future children, heirs, tortures us. And not without basis. Here are some facts.

If [the incidence of] illnesses of the blood and blood-producing organs was 32.2 (per ten thousand) in 1983, it was 155.7 in 1988 or 4.8 times greater, and illnesses of the heart and circulatory system increased from 400 to 916.2—by 2.4 times, and almost twice the oblast figures.

Child mortality for 1976–86 (per ten thousand of population) was 728.8, or 2.3 times greater than the oblast figures for the same period. And one cannot neglect to mention the people's fear of being struck by cancer. It is difficult to find a family today that has not suffered losses from this terrible disease. There are families who have lost up to eighteen members of the immediate family or close relatives to cancer. The trends in general mortality are increasing. It remains to mention also the negative effects of radiation on people's minds. In the last five years alone, twenty-four people committed suicide in our raion, all of whom hanged themselves.

We, the inhabitants of Egindybulak Raion, join our voices to the efforts of the participants in the Nevada-Semipalatinsk Movement. We appeal for full support of all the noble undertakings of activists of the movement, which is headed by the people's deputy of the USSR and beloved poet of our Kazakh land Oljas Suleimenov.

We need and ask you to support us in the following:

1. To quickly close the testing ground located in the territory of Semi-palatinsk Oblast. To begin work toward the removal of plants producing nuclear materials for military goals. To conduct a public inventory of places where nuclear wastes are buried.

2. To draw up an ecological map of Kazakhstan with the goal of identifying "dead" territories and excluding them from public use so that work on their restoration may begin. To immediately forbid the cultivation of grain and the grazing of cattle on such lands.

3. To improve work with the population in a comprehensive manner in order to raise their awareness of the danger of radiation. To use all channels of mass information for this. To place dosimeters for collective usage (DKP–1) in the raion center—the Egindybulak settlement—and in central locations in the Ayryk, Abai, and Dogalan sovkhozes.

4. To conduct a study of the health of the population of our raion. To estab-

lish a commission for this purpose and to attract the best scientific talent and medical experts in the country to work with it.

5. To resolve the question of equipping the medical facilities of the raion with the most modern medical equipment and instruments. To expedite construction of the 150-bed raion hospital and the polyclinic in the Egindybulak settlement which was begun in 1984.

6. We consider it essential for the study of the consequences of the forty-year activity of the nuclear testing ground to bring in the combined commission which has been working in Semipalatinsk Oblast under the leadership of the director of Scientific Research Institute of Medical Radiology of the USSR Academy of Medical Sciences, corresponding member of the USSR Academy of Medical Sciences Professor A.F. Tsyb, to work in our raion.

7. Calling attention to the fact that the aggravation of endocrine illnesses through exposure to radiation has already been proven, we propose strengthening prophylactic measures in anticipation of endemic goiters. We consider it necessary to expand deliveries of products containing iodine to our raion: meat, fish, and green vegetables; and to establish a system of safeguards against endemic goiter and diagnostic laboratories equipped with the latest equipment.

8. It is necessary to supply the raion's population with foodstuffs and commercial goods; the material incentive for workers should be arranged by special rates at the cost of Union funds—that is, the way soldiers and civilians in Kurchatov are provisioned. In this context we especially ask for an increase in deliveries of citrus fruits: oranges, tangerines, lemons.

9. To permit inhabitants of our raion and other raions adjoining the nuclear testing ground to have a medical examination at the best clinics in the country, especially in Moscow and Leningrad.

10. Taking into consideration the fact that young people of the present generation, aware of the raion's dangerous proximity to the testing ground, are leaving their native villages, to increase the coefficient of supplement to salaries, the so-called "Kazakhstan coefficient," up to 60 percent (i.e., establish a coefficient of 1.6 for the raion) and review the duration of regular leaves and the average pensionable age of the raion's inhabitants.

[Signed]
The Inhabitants of Egindybulak Raion,
Karaganda Oblast, Kazakh SSR
(10 thousand signatures)
December 2, 1989

Events in Baku, January 1990

Decree of the Presidium of the USSR
Supreme Soviet "On the Introduction
of a Special Situation in the City of Baku"

In connection with the sharp intensification of the situation in the city of Baku, due to attempts by criminal extremist forces which have organized mass disorders to remove from power by means of force the legally acting state organs, and in the interests of the defense and security of citizens, the Presidium of the Supreme Soviet of the USSR, guided by point 14 of Article 119 of the Constitution of the USSR, resolves that:

Dating from January 20, 1990, a special situation is declared in the city of Baku, the action of the Decree of the Presidium of the Supreme Soviet of the USSR of January 15, 1990, to take effect in its territory.

Chairman of the Presidium of the USSR Supreme Soviet
M. Gorbachev
Moscow, the Kremlin, January 19, 1990

Appeal to the General Secretary of
the Central Committee of the CPSU and
Chairman of the USSR Supreme Soviet,
Mikhail Gorbachev

My words cannot express the sorrow of the people of Azerbaijan, their endless grief which has been instilled in millions of hearts.

I speak about this not with the goal that you share our grief or that you respond compassionately. This would be an insult to my entire people. This would be a cynical mockery to the remembrance of fallen compatriots.

The evil deed, committed in Baku on January 19–20, is not supported by reason. The streets of the city flowed with the blood of hundreds of innocent souls, among whom were women, children and old people. The mutilated corpses arouse shudders: crushed beneath tank treads, shot point-blank by machine guns and automatic weapons.

No, there was no justification for this bloody battle, this monstrous crime sanctioned by You, as head of state.

The people of Azerbaijan reject with indignation and contempt the provocative charges which served as the excuse for the entrance of the army, one of which—the so-called "Islam factor"—is presented as a threat to the existence of the Soviet state.

On this matter I would like to say the following. Adherence to a religion, including Islam, rejects the call to chauvinism and national exclusivism, which are considered to be sins. You are well acquainted with my words, that the Islamic clergy of the Transcaucasus have considered and do consider the use of religious ideas in political struggle and interethnic conflicts to be intolerable. You know well that even in the tensest times in the region Islam has called for reason, peace, good neighborliness rather than the intolerable assertion of an "Islam factor," which has been presented as a destabilizing factor. It is completely evident that a fully defined objective is being pursued by this, to set Muslims against Christians, and that this might result in an interethnic conflict of an even crueler character.

I make bold to assure you that we will do everything the international community has recognized as right. It is a disgrace when the leadership of a country inflames rather than pacifies interethnic tensions for its own imperial goals: a country whose army has turned to the murder of its own compatriots, where a man has a greater right to death than to a worthy life.

The shots in Baku, these shots into human living hearts, these shots killing in millions of people the last hopes for perestroika. A punitive army entered Baku, where they conducted themselves like occupiers. You have discredited Soviet authority which has confirmed that such concepts as sovereignty and the dignity of peoples are not understood and alien to it. You have completely discredited yourself as a politician, and have proven your unfitness as a head of state. You have destroyed the myth about you as a "fighter for peace," as it would be blasphemous to give such a name to a person who concludes peace with foreign powers with one hand, and with the other sanctions punitive actions against citizens of his own country. Physicians and nurses were not killed in one bloody war. But you sanctioned the killing of a people, including two doctors who were hurrying to help the dying.

Expressing the will of the entire people of Azerbaijan, I demand the rapid withdrawal of the army from Baku. With no people, including the Azerbaijanis, can one speak the language of weapons. This might last ten days or ten years as in Afghanistan, but sooner or later, justice will prevail. With the help of Allah

Almighty, justice will prevail even in Azerbaijan in the name of those who gave their lives, sons and daughters of my people, who perished through the bullets of Soviet soldiers.

With deep faith I direct my prayers to the Almighty Creator, asking for his eternal beneficence for the souls of the innocent victims, and stern punishment for their murderers, their organizers and inspirers.

May the mercy of Almighty Allah be upon us! Amen!

Sheikh-ul-Islam al-Haj Allahsükür Pashazade
Chairman of the Spiritual Administration
of Muslims of the Transcaucasus
Baku, January 21, 1990

Decree of the Supreme Soviet of the Azerbaijan SSR "On Changing the Special Situation in the City of Baku"

The Supreme Soviet of the Azerbaijan SSR, noting that according to Article 81 of the Constitution of the USSR the only goal for the introduction of military units into the republic is the normalization of the situation of the Nagorno-Karabakh Autonomous Oblast and the restoration of the sovereign rights of the Azerbaijan SSR, and expressing the anger and indignation of the Azerbaijan people in connection with the bloody reprisals on the peaceful population of the capital of the republic, the city of Baku, committed by the armies of the USSR Ministry of Defense, which led to the deaths and injuring of hundreds of people, and noting that the conditions of the Treaty on the Organization of the USSR and the Constitution of the USSR were grossly violated by higher organs of authority and without the agreement of the sovereign Azerbaijan Soviet Socialist Republic, a resolution was passed on the declaration of a special situation in the city of Baku and the army was introduced which resulted in the open violation of the sovereign rights of the Azerbaijan SSR, decrees:

1. The decree of the Presidium of the Supreme Soviet of the USSR of January 19, 1990, on the introduction into Baku of a special situation is to be considered aggression against the sovereignty of the Azerbaijan SSR, and that the actions of the higher organs of the USSR and high responsible people who were seeing to the realization of this decree, which led to the deaths and injury of hundreds of people in the city of Baku and environs—is a crime against the Azerbaijan people.

2. In view of the fact that the Decree of the Presidium of the USSR Supreme Soviet of January 19, 1990, on the introduction into the city and other regions of the Azerbaijan SSR of a special situation was passed in violation of point 14 of Article 119 of the Constitution of the USSR and without agreement with higher organs of power of the Azerbaijan SSR, on the basis of Article 8 of the Constitu-

tional Law of the Azerbaijan SSR on sovereignty, it is demanded that the fulfillment of this Decree be suspended everywhere, with the exception of the
Nagorno-Karabakh Autonomous Oblast and areas in raions bordering Armenia.

3. To demand the rapid change of the Decree of the Presidium of the USSR
Supreme Soviet of January 19, 1990, on the introduction of a special situation in
the city of Baku and raions of the republic with the exceptions indicated in point
2 of this decree, and the departure in the shortest period of all military divisions
and units from the city of Baku and raions of the republic.

4. To create a deputy commission with the participation of representatives of
public organizations for the exposure of the immediate organizers, guilty of the
bloody reprisals on the citizens of the Azerbaijan SSR in the city of Baku and
other regions of Azerbaijan.

5. To make an appeal to the supreme soviets of union republics and the
governments of all democratic countries of the world with a request to condemn
this act of vandalism and aggression, which is counter to international law and
which led to the death and injury of many hundreds of people.

6. In the event that the union republics do not return a positive answer, to
continue the work of the special session and enter on a discussion of the question
of the advisability of preserving union relations between the USSR and the
Azerbaijan SSR.

Chairman of the Presidium of the
Supreme Soviet of the Azerbaijan SSR
E. Kafarova

Secretary of the Presidium of the
Supreme Soviet of the Azerbaijan SSR
R. Kazyyeva

City of Baku, January 22, 1990

We Are Ready to Help

Armed forces were brought into the republic by a decree of the Supreme Soviet
of the USSR in disregard of the sovereign rights of the Azerbaijan SSR and
without any basis whatsoever. The blood of innocent people was shed. Our
hearts overflowed with sorrow. But certain irresponsible people permitted gross
attacks on representatives of the Russian population.

We categorically and with full responsibility declare that Azerbaijanis will
not tolerate the sowing of discord and enmity between them and the Russians.

We are convinced that all honorable Russian people of the city, the republic,
and even the whole country, knowing our problem well, have been and will be
on the side of the just cause of the people of Azerbaijan.

In these serious and sorrowful days for Azerbaijan, we appeal to the entire population of the raion and of the city of Baku to join together, to display calm and restraint, and not to support provocations or heed unconfirmed rumors.

We are prepared to come to the aid of all who need it.

Board of the Narimanov Raion Department
of the Azerbaijan People's Front

An Appeal

A danger has been looming over the Azerbaijan people, the threat of their complete liquidation. Our land has been stained with the blood of innocent people—women, the old, children. They are shooting Azeris who fought for freedom and democracy, without a trial and without a judge. In the last two days alone the number of those who have died from the bloody terror of the Armenian cutthroats has reached two thousand.

This monstrous genocide against the people of Azerbaijan stirred up our people. All the people of Azerbaijan rose up against the Armenian units, who were armed to the teeth and attempting to cross the borders from the sovereign Azerbaijan Republic. And the occupiers are stopping at nothing; for the sake of their imperial ambitions they are ready to liquidate the seven million people of northern Azerbaijan.

Incredible, monstrous events are taking place. In order to conceal the traces of the military brutalities that have been committed, corpses are being disfigured beyond recognition, or thrown under tanks and in the sea. The army is opening fire on doctors attempting to aid the wounded.

In order to conceal the traces of the bloody crime from the world community, Moscow has isolated Azerbaijan from the outside world. Post, telegraph, radio, and television are not operating.

Today the major line of the front of the struggle for freedom and democracy runs through Azerbaijan, and this is why Moscow has turned this republic into a testing ground for means of suppression of popular uprisings. The experiment acquired in Azerbaijan today will be applied in other regions of the country where there will also be uprisings for freedom and democracy.

After the bloody events in Alma Ata, Tbilisi, and Baku, the national liberation movement in the USSR entered a new phase of its development. We must learn from our past mistakes when everyone conducted the struggle in isolation. Today it is impossible to do this. Lone struggles are easy prey for Moscow's imperialists because to us, fighters against a colonial system, it is necessary to unite common forces in the struggle against the imperial policy of the center. The blood of Azerbaijanis and Soviet soldiers is not flowing somewhere in Afganistan, but in Azerbaijan. Gorbachev and his clique have set the Russian soldier against the Azerbaijani people, and have made the soldier take up arms against us.

We appeal to all with a call to support the just cause of the people of Azerbaijan, and to pass judgment on the action of the imperialist circles of Moscow.

The Lachyn Department of the Azerbaijan People's Front

Dispatches from Riga and Tallinn, on the Shores of the Baltic

TALLINN. On January 23, representatives of the Armenians and Azerbaijanis living in Estonia gathered at the building of the Presidium of the Supreme Soviet of the Estonian SSR.

Participants in the joint action, organized by the Azerbaijani and Armenian cultural centers, issued a protest against the application of military force against the people of Azerbaijan, and demanded the recognition of the independence of Azerbaijan and the withdrawal of the army from Baku. A. Ruutel, chairman of the presidium of the Supreme Soviet of the Estonian SSR, met with the demonstrators. In his brief speech the President of Estonia stressed the need for the recognition of the independence of all peoples. Ruutel promised to transmit the protest of the Azerbaijanis and Armenians to M.S. Gorbachev.

RIGA. During February 1–3, consultations between representatives of the Azerbaijan People's Front and the Popular Movement of Armenia, organized by the Baltic Council and joined by the popular fronts of Estonia and Latvia and the Lithuanian people's movement Sajudis, took place in the capital of Latvia.

The possibility of a political settlement of the Transcaucasian crisis was discussed. At the end of the meeting a joint communiqué was signed which stressed that a further escalation of the conflict did not meet the interests of either side and that conflicts had to be eliminated by peaceful means. The initiative by the Baltic Council is the first constructive step toward the solution of the Azerbaijani-Armenian conflict.

Appeal to the Azerbaijan People's Front

Brother Turks! I appeal to all Azeri Turks!
Muslim brothers! I appeal to all believers—Sunni and Shi'i!
Peace be upon you! With my word of greetings, I wish you peace!

In the Name of Allah the Compassionate and Merciful!

The hard times were when our faith and our culture were subject to violent genocide, when earthly demons sought to tie us to an atheistic and false ideology, but we retained our Turkic language and preserved the faith of our fathers—

we did not exchange our past for a vague future! We passed through difficult trials. And now our time has come! Perestroika is a step toward our freedom! The sole possibility to achieve that goal for which Babek and Nizami, Isatay and Saken prayed has arrived. They prayed for the independence of our peoples. The goal is clear! But instead of that, today we are helping those who ruled over us for many centuries. Brothers and sisters! The Armenians are not your enemies, they are your neighbors, and with neighbors you can reach an understanding when you both have a single, powerful enemy, who thirsts for your blood in order to strengthen his rule over you. Today as never before the peoples of the Caucasus need unity in order to withstand Moscow's imperial policy!

Greetings to the Caucasian Assembly of Independent States!

To you, Azeri Turks, the Lord has entrusted a great mission: through His mighty example will come the political self-recognition of the Turkic peoples of Central Asia and Kazakhstan. May they understand my reasoning! *"Not emotion, but reason in politics!"*—this is a slogan for the present day. Brother Azeri Turks! Do not support provocations! In the name of those who have died for their country I call on you to boycott the election of party candidates to be deputies in the local soviets! The people must nominate their own candidates! They must not only be alternatives, but true to their people! Only thus will we turn from the true face of Satan! Only thus do we justify the lives of the fallen! May the will of the Almighty be with you!

Abdulla (Almaz Estekov)

"The Unifying Line Must Be the National Liberation Idea"

An Interview with Etibar Memmedov, Rehim Gaziyev, and Nemet Penahov by Memmed Nazimoghlu and Gulu Kengerli

After the First Congress [Kurultay] *of the Azerbaijan People's Front [APF], the press received many calls and letters and the majority asked: Why did Etibar Memmedov not participate in the Congress? Why did Iskender Hamidov and Rahim Gaziyev abandon the kurultay? What does Nemet Penahov want from the APF?* Aydinlik *asked the three to come for discussion, reporters asked questions readers most often ask:*

Question: Etibar Bey, why did you refuse to participate in the APF Kurultay [Congress]? Rahim Muellim, why did you leave the kurultay and issue your statement? Nemet Bey, you were invited to the kurultay and in your address you sharply criticized the internal structure of the APF. You probably have reasons for all this. In general, what did you expect of the kurultay?

Etibar Memmedov: I did not expect a thing from the kurultay. In the Front, nothing remains but political maneuvering. Every political organization must have political principles and, if the organization itself accepts those principles, it must be respected. Decisions accepted on the basis of those principles must remain unchanged. But the APF has often deviated from the principles which it itself accepted. True, sometimes decisions have been made on the basis of these principles, but their practical execution has been contrary to the decision itself.

"Birleshdiriji khett—milli-azadlig ideyasi olmalidir," *Aydinlig*, August 2, 1991, no. 22 (44), published by the Gaghi [Refugee Aid] Society. Translated and annotated by Audrey L. Altstadt.

This has led to the Front's weakening and losing authority as an organization. This happens repeatedly. At the last Front meeting, matters of principle were so skillfully distorted into personal issues that I was sure it was groundless to expect any changes [from the APF]. The kurultay, too, fundamentally would be dedicated to finding these [personal] relationships and would resolve not one concrete issue. Because I saw the future of the Front in this form, I did not go to the kurultay and left this political organization, or more precisely, announced my leaving. This is my final and resolute decision. In fact, a kurultay that went on for five days did not resolve a single problem and did not adopt a single major decision. In the future also I will not participate in this political organization. But this does not mean I am leaving the movement. When there is a true people's Front, a nation's Front, I will be a member of that Front. But I am not a member of a political organization called the APF.

Rahim Gaziyev: Unlike Etibar Bey, I was able to attend the kurultay. I am a witness that from the founding day of the APF to the present, no creative work has been accomplished. I have indicated that in my statement in *Azadlig* [newspaper of the APF] and in the statement I gave at the APF kurultay.

Instead of doing real work, the Front has engaged in talk and gossip. At the Fourth Conference, a decision was taken that the kurultay would be held on July 13. On the morning of the Conference, the Organizing Committee began its work and Isa Gemberov resigned from that committee. The responsible group did not fulfill its responsibility of preparing the bylaws [nizam-name] and program until the last day, in other words, the members of the Governing Committee Isa Gemberov, Penah Hüseyinov, Hikmet Hajizade, and Vurghun Eyyubov did not soil their hands [did not bother to do the real work] for the kurultay. They thought perhaps the kurultay would not take place. I tried with all my strength to get ready for the kurultay. Therefore, in my conference statement that said I. Gemberov's creating the ShADP [Shimali (Northern) Azerbaijan Demokratik Partisi] was a disaster for the Front, he criticized me during a [conference] recess. I think the same thing today. They expected the [APF] kurultay would not take place and that they would bring ShADP out into the open. Sooner or later all this will be revealed. Whether my idea was right or mistaken will be clear. From the first moment of the kurultay, they busied themselves with soliciting votes from individuals rather than with the business of the kurultay. Because of that the daily agenda of the kurultay was chaotic. The essential issues were set aside and the kurultay was turned into a meaningless uproar. In one of the world's most reactionary systems, [even] if every such organization has a congress [kurultay], from the first moment the entire authority is established and the kurultay's line will be clarified by the positions brought out from the bylaws and program. Unfortunately, only on the last two days were the essential matters illuminated, and this did not produce the desired result. It was proved that today the APF is not a powerful force that stands at the head of the people's movement. I think the entire responsibility for this failure rests with Ebülfez Elchibey

[Aliyev]. Because for the past two years, he did not differentiate between those forces [groups] that worked and those that did not. His basic principle was to see everyone in a good light. This is not always possible.

Since the day APF was created, the result of its lacking a structure and a program of action has been that those who came there to work sincerely and enthusiastically have done nothing and gradually the Front has lost authority. This still does not mean the snuffing out of the popular movement. Probably a more powerful front or party will be created. I do not plan to withdraw from the movement, I have not resigned from the Front.

The kurultay did not give the desired result. The hopes that fed the formation of the APF have remained frustrated. I think the kurultay will not advance to a second stage, and if it does, nothing will come of it.

N. Penahov: It is said that the APF has achieved nothing by its own efforts. Fundamentally, whatever were the goals of those individuals who created it, these have been achieved to the degree desired. Our mistake was that in their achieving their goals, we were tools. They were put in place by the state in order to organize the popular movement.[a] They were the ones who wanted to organize a popular movement with bylaws and a program back in 1988 on the [Lenin] Square. When I got out of prison [summer 1989], I saw that the initiating group had included my name on the list of their members. They told me that these were provisional bylaws and program, and a provisional group. Later a provisional administrative committee was chosen. In October 1989, I felt that it was not possible to work this way. We expected that there would be changes in the Front's bylaws and program, that people serving particular interests would leave the Front. In fact, we became tools in their hands, and as a result we were the ones who were "purged." At the end of 1989, I realized with my whole being that the APF was not a meaningful thing, that its conferences and its kurultay were useless. There remained my going to the kurultay, that was a tactic. On the one hand, they invited me; on the other hand, they said to me, if you come to the kurultay, they [KGB? AzCP?] will kill you. Their goal was that [they could claim] supposedly they invited me but I did not come. At the kurultay, they did not [want to] give me the chance to speak.

What do I expect from the Front? Today, Moscow is more afraid of the disintegration of the APF than of disintegration of the Azerbaijan Communist Party. Because the APF is a brake on the national liberation [*milli-azadlik*] movement. So far, not a single Front decision has been fulfilled. Now the Front's ideologues are saying that strikes and meetings interfere with their work. Actually, the Front stopped after gaining political capital and in the last two years they have done no work, neither theoretical nor practical.

Question: The Front is the hope of the people [*halk*] and after this hope is destroyed . . . what outcome do you see?

E. Memmedov: First, the Front is not the hope of the people; it was the hope of the people. That was [true] until about May 1990. Earlier, too, there were moves that brought harm to the Front's influence and in May 1990, as you know, the group that gave direction to the Front [began serving] completely different aims. Because of that it is impossible to say that the Front is the people's hope [*halk'in ümididir*]. If someone truly has hope that the Front is the former Front, he is deceived; the recent activities of the leadership consist of deceiving the people. To deceive the hopes of the people is the biggest crime.

What do I see as the way out? The Front must be transformed into a party. This necessity arose long ago. But no one wanted to accept this idea. The Front leadership openly came out against it. They want surreptitiously to use the Front's potential, the Front's influence, the Front's forces to create their own parties and groups. But this secret effort from start to finish showed that hope in the Front was destroyed. Why must the Front become "party-ized"? Because the Front from the beginning was created on the wave of general discontent. One person was disgruntled with his housing, another with his job, another with the Armenians' actions, someone else with social injustice. This general discontent united everyone. It was not possible to retain this unity for long. For in the period of unity the basic argument was the Karabagh issue which was related to our national honor. But from the beginning it should have been apparent that this problem was temporary and after it was resolved the Front's disintegration was inevitable. Therefore it was necessary to form various separate groups so that each would have its own clear goal and they should find a broader problem that would unite them. And that shared problem was national independence [*milli istiklaliyet*]. Only this idea would be able to unite all the political organizations, parties, groups. If this sort of formulation had occurred, they would have earned freedom of action and would have assumed full responsibility in the struggle for their own goals. Fundamentally, however, things took a different shape. For example, when social justice is violated in one place, a struggle against it is carried out in the name of the Popular Front, someplace else, a battle against bribery, and in another place, against class bias. This too interferes with the people's uniting around a single goal. Therefore my idea is this: the APF cannot remain in its present form. Today, the existence of the APF is necessary to the government, so it can say to the whole world: we have a big organization that unites all the various forces; it has a parliamentary group, a press organ, and conducts its activities in complete freedom. This, however, is meant to deceive the people and the world. Whoever believes it deceives himself.

R. Gaziyev: I agree with the principles that Etibar Bey has stated. . . . Parties, groups created to work for different goals should unite around a single line, and that must be the issue of Azerbaijan national state sovereignty. Etibar Bey has suggested forming a party. I once made the mistake of becoming a member of the Communist Party for three years and have no intention of joining any other parties. I will be a member of an organization that carries out a struggle for national-state formation.

N. Penahov: When the popular movement started in Azerbaijan it had six currents: (1) the Karabagh issue; (2) social justice; (3) class warfare; (4) the Islamic trend; (5) the struggle for democracy; (6) the national-liberation current. The Communist Party, which exerted hegemony until yesterday, had permitted a multiparty system—in order to save its own empire. In order to destroy the last, the national-liberation current, it created conditions to facilitate the activity of all the other trends. But we were bound to realize sooner or later that as long as we remained inside the empire, none of our goals would be achieved. In other words, I regard the Karabagh issue as Moscow's creation and Moscow will resolve it, and the same is true for bribery, social justice and other problems. I think that our sole path is that of national liberation. The idea that the people's sole hope is in having a Front is, I think, not true. The people [*halk*] understands that the APF is bankrupt. The people itself will take a new line. It will happen sooner or later. All the groups and parties that hold to the national liberation line must create a national liberation organization and should proclaim its structure and its ideas.

Question: According to the things you have said, it would appear that the APF serves the state. If that is so, is it possible for the APF to be bankrupt? And a related question: The "Democratic bloc," when it left the [Supreme Soviet] session, made a statement about creating a national council [*milli shura*]. What are your thoughts on this?

E. Memmedov: Let me start with the second part of the question. At the [Supreme Soviet] session, a declaration was presented about the formation of a National Council, and with that the matter was apparently considered finished. Later we returned and participated in the work of that same session. They were able to say, this is a "Dembloc" matter and has nothing to do with the Front. But the members of that same bloc were also Front members and in elections participated as part of the Front. Therefore, the bloc's decisions were debated in the Front's meetings and usually were approved. After I was released from prison, when Ebulfez Bey was at the head of Front leadership, I suggested the creation of a National Congress or National Council. If the Front had won the elections, this matter would not have been suggested. But after losing the elections (the results were a foregone conclusion), it was decided to raise this issue. Of course, one can announce a National Congress or a National Council. But in announcing any such matter you have to see whether or not the strength ["will"] exists actually to carry it out. Can an organization that could not manage to achieve [desired] results in an election create a National Council or a National Congress? There are ways [to do] this. For example, by collecting signatures. Four million of the population has the right to vote, at least two million signatures should be collected so that [the people] could be made familiar with the National Congress or National Council and they would be subject to its decisions. But at the time of the referendum, the Front's activities showed that even in this serious matter, they could not collect more than 150,000 signatures. But that does not mean, of course, that the people [*halk*] refused to sign. Put simply, it means they [the Front] could not organize it. What I want to say is that they could not organize a National Council either. For this has its own mechanism, forms, techniques and methods. One can announce we are creating a National Council, the deputies that will be chosen from among us will be members of the National Council. Then the communists could rightly say, what is this—we participated in the same election; if our being elected was undemocratic why is your being chosen democratic and legal?

No result can be achieved in this way. "National Council" was put forward like an empty word and nothing came of it. If after all this someone says that we are creating a National Council or National Congress, this is only deceiving people. No campaign has been carried out among the population, nor has it been made clear how this goal is to be achieved.

There remains the matter of the state's protection of the APF; here there is no open protection. As I just said, put simply, the state needs it [the APF] so it can say to the world: there is opposition in Azerbaijan. So they need the APF. No matter how much this group is criticized, because its position is weak, its existence is useful to the state.

R. Gaziyev: Etibar Bey gave an answer to one part of the question and I agree with him. The democratic changes here have essentially a formulaic character. So far, the substance has actually changed very little. Our having a formal democratic organization here is useful to local government and the country's government.

On the second issue: the creation of a National Council remained only a word. Even in the session where it was announced, no one consulted anyone else. Isa Gemberov, who announced it and is considered one of the Front's ideologues, did not take any real steps to facilitate this. If there is no mechanism to create a National Council, we have caused our own fall from influence with empty words. It also shows that the Front is not engaged in any serious programmatic work, that is, it is not interested in resolving concrete issues before it.

E. Memmedov: I would like to add one thing: our opposition is "tame opposition"; that is, it is organized opposition. When I say this, one may think someone is called and given instructions. No one can openly be sold. But all the actions show that this is an organized opposition. This opposition only operates within the framework established for it. Moscow designed this framework with Baku. When we asked Ebulfez Bey why last May did he accept the presidential elections, he said that they [the government] gave permission for our newspaper to be issued, and granted other concessions. It turns out that they are going to squeeze us from every side and then later say, "You make a big concession and we'll make a tiny concession for you." We asked Nejef Bey [Nejef Nejefov, editor of *Azadlig*] why has the newspaper [*Azadlig*] come out in this vein; he said if we keep writing like [before] they will close the newspaper. So the opposition did not depart from the framework laid down for it by the government. They say to them, "However much you want to criticize Gorbachev, Ryzhkov or Pavlov, go ahead, but do not touch Mutalibov or Yazov." They [Front leaders] in turn say "We understand." It turns out that the APF is an organization that does as it's told. If this were an organization that had self respect, they could close its newspaper and it would publish it secretly, if [the state] took other actions against it, it would continue in some other, secret form. But the APF shows no freedom or independence; like it or not it has turned into an instrument of Moscow's game.

N. Penahov: I would like to draw attention to [certain] facts. If you recall, in the summer of 1989, Moscow did whatever it could to set the ethnic groups in Azerbaijan against each other. It was even suggested that the Talysh should have national autonomy. This was greeted angrily in the Lenkoran-Astara zone. Moscow's zeal to fragment the people [*halk*, i.e., *narod*] came to nothing. For all the ethnic groups have united around the idea of Azerbaijan's national liberation. After all this, in the issue of *Azadlig* that included the Front's program and bylaws, the APF lumped together these ethnic groups living in Azerbaijan with the Armenians [and] upset these ethnic groups. Even today, they [officials] try to misrepresent the matter, suggesting that if the national liberation movement is associated with Turkization, that the rights of the ethnic groups will be trampled. Actually Azerbaijan's national liberation is the liberation of Talysh, Tats, Kurds, and all ethnic groups living in Azerbaijan. They are trying to scare us in this way so that the words "national liberation" will not come to our lips. Today the struggle to break up the APF is a very mistaken idea. It will bankrupt itself. The essential issue is how we constitute [manage] our activities.

There is no possibility of organizing any sort of National Council under today's conditions. You will recall that A[bulfez] Aliyev said: Our battle is a Parliamentary battle. Then he withdrew his own candidacy and in order not to lose influence kept out of the game and stood on the sidelines. To create a National Council much greater energy is needed. The APF does not have the potential for this.

Question: Etibar Bey, as you said, the way out is to create a party. Under present circumstances, would such a party be [legally] registered? Before becoming active, how would the parties (registered and unregistered) work out their relations?

E. Memmedov: First, independent of whether they are registered or not, a party can be created and can act secretly, openly, or semilegally. Second, there are already groups that do not wish to join with either the communists or the Popular Front. These groups have great political-intellectual potential. They can show their knowledge and abilities in any organization. For the time being, since they see nothing on the horizon, they remain in their places. Furthermore, every party has its own particular qualities. I have made known my intention to create a party. At the outset, I say that this party will reject class, social or ethnic divisions. Here must be only forces that unite around the idea of the national interest. In the structure of the Popular Front there is a section of religious believers and it unites believers. It is clear that religious freedom will be possible when believers are saved from the slavery of an empire that strangles human freedom. And religious people must never think that they can gain religious freedom within the confines of this empire. Prophet Alleyhuselam said that the best jihad [holy war] is the jihad against tyranny. In other words, religious people must unite with those groups that serve the national interest.[b] Or the democrats say, we are carrying out a fight for democracy. They must understand that Moscow will give democracy only within certain limits. There is also an economic section [in APF]. Those who are struggling to clean up the environment must know that the one who has polluted the environment is neither Mutalibov nor Hasanov.[c] Moscow's interests dictated that as many chemical products and as much oil as needed would be produced here. The workers want increased wages, improved working conditions, that laws should not be broken. But the workers must also understand that in all empires, class tyranny is greater in the outlying regions than at the center. At the center, workers' rights are more or less protected. In the colonies, they exploit [them] as much as they like in order to reap greater [benefits]. Workers must know that all problems can be solved after achieving independence. In the absence of complete independence, any measures [that are taken] are nothing but ornamentation. So they can raise wages 5–10 percent or can temporarily take action against the pollution produced by one factory. But their fundamental resolution can only take place after independence. We have two problems: national independence and state independence.[d] To achieve state independence, two roads are possible—either to take power by the force of arms and proclaim independence, or else for power to be taken by forces that represent national goals,[e] and then to proclaim independence. The goal of the party being created must be to nationalize sovereignty. In other words, those in power will serve the national interest. The next stage is proclaiming state independence and fulfilling that [claim]. To nationalize this sovereignty, it is vital to gather all forces in a tight political organization. The following question may be posed: if the current administration falls from power and APF takes its place, can these conditions be fulfilled? I think not. For it [APF] does not have sufficient talent, or scholarly or intellectual potential.

R. Gaziyev: Etibar Bey has stated the basic principles. Whether the newly created organization is officially registered or not does not interest me at all. The Front did much more work before it was registered than after. And there's a proverb: A son who strikes [acts on his own initiative] does not ask his father [for permission]. I think that the activity of any organization or party must have as one of its basic principles that it will properly analyze the national movement in the USSR, and keeping in mind the fact that the center of gravity is Russia, put into practice their [own] ideas in Azerbaijan. If we were to rise today with enthusiasm, they, with the aid of the reactionary forces, will attempt to strangle us.

I think a party or organization that holds the national liberation line must be a fighter to the maximum degree, it must make intelligent moves, and must not make its appearance without a program for action. In other words, at the moment it appears it must begin its activity toward its goals.

N. Penahov: I am convinced that every organization, party, or society that is registered by the state is nothing but a servant of the state.

Let's take the October Revolution. Did the communists say to the tsar, "Here, approve our program and bylaws, we are going to overthrow you"? Or let's take the Iranian revolution. Did those who made the Islamic revolution say to the shah, "Accept us, we are going to kill you"? So, how can it be that an organization, society, or party that embraces the national liberation movement would be registered by the empire, and that this would be something other than serving the destruction of the national liberation movement?

I have come to the conclusion that we must unite only with enslaved peoples— with the peoples, republics crushed under the heel of the Russian empire. Those parties and organizations must unite which accept the national liberation line and carry out the fight to bring down the imperial structure. From a political, economic, and cultural viewpoint, the fate of the enslaved peoples is the same, and independent of us, there are threads that unite us. What frightens the empire most is precisely this unity. For that reason, the empire tries with all its might to keep the enslaved peoples apart. Toward this end it sows national conflict.

E. Memmedov: I do not agree with Nemet Bey's idea. The results of the revolution made by the illegal Bolsheviks is before our eyes, as is the result of the Iranian Islamic revolution. So the matter of being legal or not does not make a fundamental difference. This does not mean that a registered organization serves the interests of the state. Take Georgia as an example. There, legal forces peacefully came to power by parliamentary means. It was the same in Armenia. In the Baltic, even many parts of the Communist Party assumed a national posture. As for relations among parties, we must distance ourselves from bolshevism; the Front had one period when it was exactly bolshevism that distanced it [APF] from the national forces. We have made clear that we are the enemy of communist ideology, not of individual communists. This ideology is contrary to human interests. We must strive for that part of the people deceived by this ideology to be separated from it and by peaceful means bring them over to the national liberation movement. For a while there was a rich–poor issue in the Front. A battle was carried on in the regional sections against the rich calling them "mafia." But really this was a scuffle for position among different mafia groups. This tended toward division of the nation and resulted in a loss of faith in the Front.

Coming to the ties between parties, one can only speak of cooperation with parties that accept the national liberation idea. Every organization can have its own specific goals. But the general unifying line must be the idea of national liberation. As for parties that do not accept the idea of national liberation, formal relations are possible, but not real cooperation.

R. Gaziyev: I agree with Etibar's idea. But I am against all ties with parties that do not accept the idea of national liberation.

N. Penahov: Every organization, party, and society in Azerbaijan, even the Communist Party, has stated as its goal the sovereignty of Azerbaijan. Is that not so? But it is one thing to talk about it, another to act. In organizations and parties that do not accept the idea of national liberation, I see nothing less than the betrayal of Azerbaijan.

Translator's Notes

a. Penahov is probably right from the viewpoint of the authorities. It is believable that the Azerbaijan Communist Party or state authorities permitted these individuals to lead this movement because they realized the limits of their horizons; they were the least dangerous adversaries. Given the biographies of men like Elchibey, it is doubtful that they were conscious of, much less cooperative with, the authorities' plans.

b. As at the turn of this century, we find a secular intellectual using the language of religion in an effort to draw the religious segment of the community into a national movement.

c. Hasan Hasanov was one of the Azerbaijan Communist Party secretaries under Vezirov and then Mutalibov. His address to the party in early January 1990 criticized the degree to which Moscow acted without consulting Baku in a number of serious issues including policies in the Nagorno-Karabagh Autonomous Oblast and along the Iranian and Turkish borders. When the speech was publicized and these breeches of republican sovereignty made known, Hasanov came to be regarded as something of a popular hero.

d. Here E. Memmedov uses the phrases "milli istiklaliyyet ve dövlet istiklaliyyeti— dövlet müstegilliyi," implying formal and actual independence of people and of the state apparatus.

e. The phrase used here literally means "national forces," but, in context, clearly did not imply armed forces. In order to clarify the implication as well as the literal meaning, this somewhat cumbersome but accurate phrasing has been used.

Index

129850